THE PSEUDO-DEMOCRAT'S DILEMMA

THE PSEUDO-DEMOCRAT'S DILEMMA

WHY ELECTION OBSERVATION BECAME AN INTERNATIONAL NORM

Susan D. Hyde

CORNELL UNIVERSITY PRESS

ITHACA AND LONDON

Cornell University Press gratefully acknowledges receipt of a grant from the Whitney and Betty MacMillan Center for International and Area Studies at Yale University, which helped in the publication of this book. The book was also published with the assistance of the Frederick W. Hilles Publication Fund of Yale University.

First published 2011 by Cornell University Press

Printed in the United States of America

Library of Congress Cataloging-in-Publication Data
Hyde, Susan D.
   The pseudo-democrat's dilemma : why election observation became an international norm / Susan D. Hyde.
      p. cm.
   Includes bibliographical references and index.
   ISBN 978-0-8014-4966-6 (alk. paper)
  1. Election monitoring.   2. Elections—Corrupt practices.
3. Democratization.   4. International relations.   I. Title.
   JF1001.H93   2011
   324.6'5—dc22   2010049865

Cornell University Press strives to use environmentally responsible suppliers and materials to the fullest extent possible in the publishing of its books. Such materials include vegetable-based, low-VOC inks and acid-free papers that are recycled, totally chlorine-free, or partly composed of nonwood fibers. For further information, visit our website at www.cornellpress.cornell.edu.

Cloth printing   10 9 8 7 6 5 4 3 2 1

To
Howard Leichter, Dawn Nowacki,
and Elliot Tenofsky,
who introduced me to this profession,
and David Lake, my mentor

CONTENTS

FIGURES AND TABLES

Figures

Tables

ACKNOWLEDGMENTS

Although I did not know it at the time, this book began its life in the fall of 2001 as my first research paper in graduate school. As a result, nearly everyone with whom I have come in professional contact has helped me write this book, and my debts are immense. I have been fortunate to receive numerous sources of institutional support during the research, writing, and rewriting. My research has been made possible by grants and fellowship from the Brookings Institution's Governance Studies Program, the Institute for Global Conflict and Cooperation (IGCC) of the University of California, and the University of California, San Diego's School of Social Sciences and Department of Political Science, the University of California's Washington Center, George Washington University's Institute for Global and International Studies, Princeton University's Niehaus Center for Globalization and Governance, and the American Political Science Association's Centennial Center. Yale University, including the Department of Political Science, the MacMillan Center, and the Institution for Social and Policy Studies, provided generous research funds, opportunities to present my research, and most important, time to write. The Carter Center's Democracy Program gave me numerous opportunities to serve as an international election observer, invited me to spend a summer in their offices in Atlanta, and gave me the unique opportunity to work with the organization during the 2004 Indonesian elections, which is reflected in this book.

I received extraordinarily helpful advice at a "book bash" in February 2008, sponsored by Ken Scheve and the Leitner Program in International and Comparative Political Economy at Yale. For traveling to New Haven just for the workshop, I thank David Lake, Jon Pevehouse, Ken Schultz, and Duncan Snidal, all of whom read the entire manuscript and gave me extensive and exceptionally helpful comments, as did Sue Stokes, Bruce

Russett, Matt Winters, Nikolay Marinov, Ken Scheve, Karissa Cloward, and Jonathan Monten.

I thank my editor at Cornell University Press, Roger Haydon, for his enthusiastic support and excellent comments throughout the process. The book was published with generous assistance from Yale's MacMillan Center for International and Area Studies and the Frederick W. Hilles Publication Fund of Yale University.

At Yale, my colleague Nikolay Marinov deserves special thanks for many reasons, including working with me for the past five years to produce the NELDA dataset, from which this book draws heavily. The research assistants on that project, particularly Shazan Jiwa, Mary Swartz, and Jerry Wei, deserve special thanks for their excellent work. I also thank my colleagues Chris Blattman, Keith Darden, Alex Debs, Thad Dunning, Don Green, Greg Huber, Stathis Kalyvas, Pierre Landry, Ellen Lust, Jason Lyall, Nuno Monteiro, Susan Rose-Ackerman, Frances Rosenbluth, Bruce Russett, Nicholas Sambanis, Ian Shapiro, Susan Stokes, James Vreeland, and Jessica Weiss. During my year of leave from Yale, my cofellows at Niehaus, Arang Keshavarzian, Heather McKibben, Christina Schneider, Ben Shepherd, Branislav Slantchev, Camber Warren, and Matt Winters were extremely helpful. I also thank Larry Bartels, Sarah Bush, Rafaela Dancygier, Christina Davis, Kosuke Imai, Amaney Jamal, Bob Keohane, Helen Milner, Andy Moravcsik, and Grigore Pop-Eleches for their support and comments on my research.

At UCSD, Gary Cox, Kristian Gleditsch, Clark Gibson, Peter Gourevitch, and Carlos Waisman played a crucial role in helping me start to think about this book. I also thank Karen Ferree, Miles Kahler, Mat McCubbins, Branislav Slantchev, and Phil Roeder, and my colleagues in international relations and comparative politics at UCSD, including Scott Bailey, Kyle Beardsley, Rob Brown, Barak Hoffman, Alejandra Rios-Cázares, Idean Salehyan, and Heather Smith.

David Lake was my advisor and remains my mentor and my friend. I cannot thank him enough for all of his help, advice, comments, and support, and hope that I can someday do for someone what he has done for me. Emily Beaulieu, Carew Boulding, David Cunningham, Kathleen Cunningham, Irfan Nooruddin, and Elizabeth Saunders have endured all of the ups and downs with me and helped me work through every (important and unimportant) detail. This project wouldn't have been half as fun without them. I also thank Michael Barnett, Karisa Cloward, Suzanne Katzenstein, Judith Kelley, Sharon Lean, Tom Legler, Alberto Simpser, Jack Snyder, Zach Zwald, and my collaborators on other research projects: Mike Alvarez, Thad Hall, Emilie Hafner-Burton, and Angel O'Mahony.

In addition, this book benefited from the advice, comments, and encouragement from faculty and graduate students participating in a number of workshops and seminars.

The project would not have come to fruition without the assistance of many members of the election observation community. Eric Bjornlund, David Carroll, David Pottie, and Avery Davis-Roberts deserve special thanks and have each had an enormous influence on my thinking on the subject. I also thank Glenn Cowan, Anders Erikson, Pat Merloe, Gerald Mitchell, Shelley McConnell, Jennifer McCoy, Vladimir Pran, and many others whom I cannot thank here.

My parents and brothers have been a constant source of support. Annie helped me and this book along at a particularly crucial time. Most of all, I thank my partner of ten years, Sean Smith, for sharing this adventure with me, pushing me further than I would have gone on my own, listening to all my complaints, celebrating my successes, and being proud of me throughout.

THE PSEUDO-DEMOCRAT'S DILEMMA

INTRODUCTION

In October of 1958, the Cuban dictator Fulgencio Batista was one of the first leaders to seek international observation of his country's elections. Facing declining U.S. support of his regime, pressure from the United States to hold elections, and a growing threat from Fidel Castro's revolutionary forces, Batista scheduled elections, announced he would not run again, and attempted to invite international observers from the Organization of American States and the United Nations. Both organizations refused to send monitors, stating that they lacked the "facilities to supervise elections."[1] The November 1958 elections were widely viewed as a charade.[2] Shortly after these discredited elections, Batista resigned and fled into exile, clearing the way for Fidel Castro's rise to power.[3]

Fifty years later, the idea that governments should invite foreign election observers had become so widely accepted that the Iranian government's refusal to invite international observers to its 2009 elections was interpreted around the world as evidence that the Iranian elections had been stolen. Responding to questions about the conditions under which he would accept the announced results, U.S. President Barack Obama expressed doubts about the quality of the elections, stating that "we didn't have international observers on the ground" and that therefore "we can't say definitively what happened at polling places throughout the country."[4] German Chancellor Angela Merkel called for a recount of the votes under international observation as a way for Iranians to "eliminate doubt" and

1. "Doubtful Future Confronts Cuba: Tomorrow's Elections May Begin Uncertain Era—Rebels Ask Boycott," *New York Times*, October 31, 1958.
2. Ibid.
3. "Cuba Will Accept Voting Observers," *New York Times*, October 18, 1958.
4. "Text of President Obama Tuesday," Associated Press, June 28, 2009.

increase trust.[5] Explaining why he believed the Iranian elections to be sto-len, U.S. Senator Joseph Lieberman said that "one thing we know is that Iran would not let international monitors in, which most every country in the world does to supervise the elections."[6] The *Bangkok Post* in Thailand editorialized that the Iranian government was culpable in part because it had harassed foreign journalists and barred election observers.[7] Iranian Nobel Peace Prize winner Shirin Ebadi called for European sanctions against the Iranian government and argued that "a new election must be held and this time it should be under the monitoring of international organizations."[8] This sentiment was echoed widely in forums as diverse as the editorial pages of the *Jordan Times*, *USA Today*, and the *Washington Post*, and by the Iranian League for the Defense of Human Rights.[9]

Between the 1958 Cuban elections and 2009 elections in Iran, invit-ing international election monitors had become an international norm.[10] Cuba's attempt to invite observers was anomalous, and international actors refused to send observers, but views regarding election monitoring had changed dramatically by the end of the 1990s; by then, the few govern-ments choosing not to invite international observers were assumed to be hiding electoral manipulation.[11] As of 2006, more than 80% of elections

---

5. "Germany's Merkel urges Iranian Election Recount," Reuters, June 21, 2009.

6. Lieberman, "Interview with Senator Joseph Lieberman," June 15, 2009.

7. BBC Monitoring, "Thai Paper Says Iran Must Let 'Outsiders' Monitor Poll Probe," June 17, 2009.

8. Deutsche Presse-Agentur, "Iranian Nobel Peace Prize Winner Ebadi Calls for New Polls," June 17, 2009.

9. "Iran's Fishy Election Results," *USA Today*, June 15, 2009; "Iran Needs Another Elec-tion," *Jordan Times*, June 23, 2009; "Iran: Confiscated Election, FIDH and LDDHI Fear a Bloody Repression," *News Press*, June 17, 2009; Medhi Khalaji, "Khamenei's Coup," *Wash-ington Post*, June 15, 2009.

10. Below, I define an international norm as a shared "standard of behavior appropriate for actors with a given identity." Finnemore and Sikkink, "International Norm Dynamics and Political Change," 891.

11. There are several borderline cases that precede the Organization of American States' election observation in 1962, including internationally observed plebiscites before World War II. See Wambaugh, *A Monograph on Plebiscites;* Wambaugh, *Plebiscites since the World War.* In addition, at least one internationally observed election was held in the immediate aftermath of World War II, although the international agreements pertaining to the case are unique and it is not referenced by later missions as a precedent. Citing the Yalta Declaration on Liberated Europe and the provision that the Allied powers would assist Axis-occupied countries in order "to form interim governmental authorities broadly representative of all democratic elements in the population and pledged to the earliest possible establishment through free elections of governments responsive to the will of the people; and to facilitate where necessary the holding of such elections," the Greek government invited international observers from the United States, France, and Great Britain to the March 1946 elections.

in the world were internationally monitored. Even the most committed electoral autocrats—Russia's Vladimir Putin, Zimbabwe's Robert Mugabe, Belorussia's Alexander Lukashenko, Peru's Alberto Fujimori, and Yugoslavia's Slobodan Milošević—sought reputable international observers to judge their elections. Many of these leaders went to great lengths to manipulate the elections and the monitors, and they were internationally condemned for election fraud. Why did incumbent governments begin inviting observers, and why do they continue to do so in such impressive numbers? Why did election monitoring become an international norm, even though it is costly for many governments to invite foreign election observers?

That states comply with international norms when it is consistent with their material interests is not a particularly controversial claim. When an international norm contradicts what would otherwise be viewed as a state's rational self-interest, however, its creation is a puzzle. In this book, I present an alternative theory of norm creation, focused on explaining the mechanism by which costly behaviors are initiated, diffuse, and become internationally expected behaviors, or international norms. In my theory, states seeking international benefits are motivated to send externally credible signals that they possess certain characteristics when they perceive that doing so will increase their share of internationally allocated benefits, such as foreign aid, increased foreign investment, tourism, trade, membership in international organizations, and legitimacy and prestige. When other states imitate successful benefit-seeking signals, new behaviors become widespread, even in the absence of overt pressure on states to adopt the new behavior. If a signal is accepted by other international actors as a behavior common to all states possessing a valued characteristic, it becomes a new international norm. These unintended norms are more likely to exist in issue areas for which pressure from international activists or powerful states is insufficient to motivate governments to adopt new behavior, and typically there is no coalition of individuals or states pushing for the norm. In general, I suggest the conditions for norm generation and diffusion exist when any regime has the incentive and the ability to signal its characteristics to international audiences in order to increase its share of international benefits. In contrast to existing explanations that focus on how norms can be generated despite their costs to states, or explanations

---

The mission included 1,155 observers and 240 teams from the three countries, the majority of which were military "acting in civilian capacity" (Joseph Coy Green Papers, Seeley G. Mudd Manuscript Library, Princeton University, Princeton, NJ., *Report of the Allied Mission to Observe the Greek Elections.*)

that focus on mutually beneficial norms, my argument explains that international norms are generated in part *because* compliance with the new behavior is costly.

Within international politics, states engage in many puzzling behaviors, some of which become widely adopted practices and international norms.[12] Inviting international election observers is one example of a consequential international norm. This book focuses on election observation because it is a substantively important form of democracy promotion and international intervention in the domestic politics of sovereign states. My account of norm formation is useful to explain a variety of other similar empirical puzzles. For example, why have so many developing countries moved to create independent central banks, reduce capital controls, and adopt fixed exchange rates? Why are countries such as Iraq and North Korea expected to allow the presence of international weapons inspectors and assumed to have illicit weapons if they do not? What explains the rapid adoption of bilateral investment treaties to ensure property rights protection for foreign investors? Why do all but a handful of countries in the world now hold national elections? Why have dozens of countries adopted legislative gender quotas, even in electoral autocracies?[13] Why has hiring private credit-rating agencies become a necessary step for countries wishing to issue sovereign bonds? Why do some of the worst violators of human rights sign human rights treaties?[14] Some of these examples are more controversial than others, but in each of these cases a convincing argument can be made that these practices would not have become normalized state behavior if individual states were not attempting to find credible ways to signal to international or domestic audiences.

Motivated by the puzzle of how international norms are generated when compliance is costly, I explain why election monitoring became an international norm. I show that international norms are generated through a process that is endogenous to strategic interaction among international actors and that costly signaling leads to unintended and consequential international norms. Although this signaling theory of norm formation is generalizable to other areas of international relations, it was generated to better understand the consequences of international democracy promotion and explain international election observation as an overt and

---

12. Hurd, "Legitimacy and Authority in International Politics."
13. Bush, S., "International Politics and the Spread of Quotas for Women in Legislatures"; Goertz and Diehl, "Toward a Theory of International Norms."
14. Hafner-Burton and Tsutsui, "Human Rights in a Globalizing World"; Hathaway, "Do Human Rights Treaties Make a Difference?"

substantively important form of international involvement in the domestic politics of sovereign states.

Defining the Norm of Election Observation

Throughout this book, I follow the majority literature in defining international norms as shared "standards of appropriate behavior for actors with a given identity."[15] This book focuses on the norm, or shared standard of appropriate behavior, that for all national elections, leaders committed to democratization should invite international observers and receive their endorsement, particularly when there is uncertainty about the government's commitment to democracy.[16]

Not all internationally observed elections are democratic. Rather, the norm is the shared belief that all potentially democratic elections are internationally observed and any nonobserved election is not democratic. International election observers are official delegations of foreigners invited to observe and report on the credibility of the electoral process. Since at least the early 1990s, observers are typically credentialed by the host government and permitted access to the entire electoral process, including registration of voters, campaigning, distribution of electoral materials, and most notably, observing activities in and around polling stations, vote counting, and vote aggregation centers during the election period. They are officially nonpartisan and are intended to be objective third-party observers.

Uncertainty about the commitment of some governments to democracy was a necessary condition for the initiation and diffusion of the norm. For some states, there is little uncertainty about the incumbent government's commitment to democracy. On the autocratic end of the spectrum of regimes, governments holding uncontested elections are not expected to invite observers when the characteristics of the election eliminate the possibility of electoral competition. Countries with only one legal political party, with severe restrictions on candidate entry, and with totalitarian political structures would be understood as holding authoritarian elections

---

15. Finnemore and Sikkink, "International Norm Dynamics and Political Change," 891.

16. Throught the book, I use the terms "election observers" and "election monitors" interchangeably. Some organizations and governments prefer to avoid the term "monitor" because they argue that it implies a more interventionist practice, or a practice that involves more direct cooperation with the government. However, interventionist monitoring exists very rarely in practice, the distinction between the terms is not particularly useful outside of diplomatic circles.

even if they invited international observers; thus, they stand to gain little by inviting observers.

As the norm diffused in the 1990s, countries that were widely considered to be consolidated democracies, such as those in Western Europe and North America, held elections but were not expected to invite observers. Other states "graduated" by demonstrating their democratic credentials. For example, at the end of a seventeen-year period of dictatorship and as part of the country's transition back to civilian rule, the Chilean government invited observers to the 1988 referenda on the continued rule of General Augusto Pinochet and to the 1989 general elections. Because the country is now widely perceived to have successfully transitioned to democracy, it is no longer expected to invite international monitors. Similarly, new European Union (EU) members are widely perceived as democracies after meeting the EU accession criteria and frequently are not expected to invite international observers.

However, reflecting the diffusion of the norm, this trend has changed slightly in more recent years, with observers from the Organization for Security and Cooperation in Europe's Office for Democratic Institutions and Human Rights (OSCE/ODIHR) observing elections in Belgium (2007), Canada (2006), Finland (2007), France (2002, 2007), Iceland (2009), Ireland (2007), Italy (2008), the Netherlands (2006), Portugal (2009), Spain (2008), Switzerland (2007), the United Kingdom (2003, 2005), and the United States (2002, 2004, 2006, 2008). It is not yet clear whether other, similar democratic states will follow their lead and invite observers even when their status as a democracy is unquestioned. It is also unclear whether organizations sponsoring international observation would be willing to allocate scarce resources to observing elections in countries that are already considered stable democracies.

The Puzzling Norm of International Election Observation

There is no global government to enforce the norm of election observation, and inviting observers remains the choice of election-holding governments. Additionally, international monitors observe elections only when they have been officially invited by the host government. The incumbent may delegate this decision to another domestic actor, such as the foreign minister or the election commission, but the incumbent maintains the right to refuse entry to foreign observers. Without formal credentials from the host government, it is nearly impossible for observers to engage in credible election observation, a standard now enshrined in numerous international documents, including the 2005 *Declaration of Principles for International Election Observation.*[17]

Leaders apparently face an easy choice: invite observers when they know their elections will be clean and prohibit them when election fraud is likely to be discovered. The creation of an internationally held norm of election observation, however, has made the choice for leaders much less simple. Pseudo-democrats, or governments willing to engage in election manipulation, face a dilemma. On one hand, the norm generates consequences for not inviting observers. Although noncompliance with the norm is rarely tested (arguably a sign of its strength), those leaders who do not invite foreign observers are assumed to be holding undemocratic elections, as in the Iranian example discussed above.[18] Similarly, Egypt's refusal to invite international observers to its 2005 presidential elections led many external groups to conclude that the election would be a charade before it took place, even though opposition presidential candidates were permitted for the first time. Commentators on Hosni Mubarak's decision to refuse foreign observers argued that the absence of international monitors was "proof that the...election will be no different than preceding ones" in which the president allowed no opposition candidates and voters were given the opportunity only to vote yes or no on Mubarak's continued rule.[19] Holding internationally monitored and endorsed elections has also become a necessary step before countries under economic sanctions can resume normal bilateral relations with many Western governments. For example, U.S. President George Bush challenged the Cuban government to hold free and fair elections in 2003, saying that "once the 2003 elections are certified as free and fair by international monitors, once Cuba begins the process of meaningful economic reform, then and only then will I explore ways with the United States Congress to ease economic sanctions."[20]

17. Carter Center, *Building Consensus on Principles for International Election Observation;* United Nations, *Declaration of Principles for International Election Observation and Code of Conduct for International Election Observers.*

18. To illustrate, countries that are not already considered consolidated democracies but that refused to invite observers to all elections after 2000 include Bahrain, Cuba, Egypt, Guinea, Iran, Jordan, Kuwait, Laos, Malaysia, North Korea, Oman, Syria, Turkmenistan, and Vietnam. Countries that refused observers to some but not all elections after 2000 include Benin, Equatorial Guinea, Ethiopia, Gabon, Iraq, Madagascar, Mauritania, and Singapore.

19. "Arab Observers Warn of Egypt Election 'Masquerade'," September 6, 2005, Agence France Presse.

20. G. Bush, "Remarks on the 100th Anniversary of Cuban Independence in Miami, Florida," May 20, 2002.

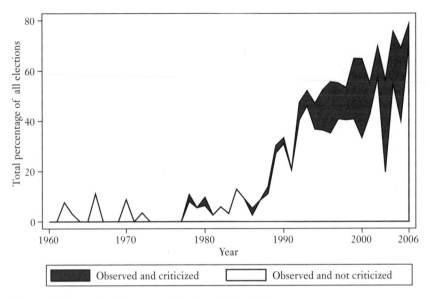

Figure I.1. Internationally observed elections, 1960–2006
Source: Author
Note: Includes 1,759 election events in 157 independent states, excluding those with population < 250,000.

On the other hand, choosing to invite observers and complying with the norm is also risky. For those leaders wishing to manipulate elections, both the chances of getting caught and the consequences of a negative report have increased with the spread of election observation. Negative reports from election monitors have been linked to domestic uprisings and electoral revolutions, reductions in foreign aid, exclusion from international forums, and other forms of internationally imposed sanctions.[21]

Figure I.1 illustrates the rate of observed elections and internationally criticized elections over time and shows that negative reports from international observers have not reduced the rate of internationally observed elections, as we would expect if leaders invited observers to only those elections likely to be clean. To explain the norm of election monitoring, I focus on the decision by leaders to invite international observers. The norm of

21. This topic has not yet been treated in the international relations literature with rigorous cross-national quantitative methods, but a thorough reading of cases in which fraud is alleged by international observers highlights many well-publicized cases in which the government faced internationally imposed costs because of election manipulation. The issue is explored in greater detail in chapter 3.

election observation is particularly useful as an empirical case because it is not well explained by existing theories of norm formation, and I use it to develop a distinct causal explanation for why individually costly behaviors diffuse and become new and self-enforcing international norms.

Signaling and International Norms

In part, my argument is based in economic theory. In the "market for lemons," famously described by economist George Akerlof, when consumers possess little information about the quality of a product, such as used cars, and the quality of the product is known to vary, the market fails.[22] Consumers prefer to avoid cars that are "lemons," but they cannot, by themselves, distinguish between high- and low-quality products. The price that they are willing to pay reflects the uncertainty of a market containing both (indistinguishable) types of products. Sellers of high-quality used cars cannot command a sufficiently high price and so choose not to sell their vehicles, thus lowering the expected quality of used cars on the market and eventually causing only undesirable lemons to be for sale. Rather than risk a lemon, buyers in this market avoid used cars entirely.

Information between international actors is similarly asymmetric: states possess accurate information about their own type, but international actors can have difficulty judging whether another state is an undesirable type, or a so-called lemon. In the absence of better information about the true characteristics of states, the international-level equivalent of consumers may prefer to avoid risk and interact primarily with states that already have credible reputations as desirable types. In addition, states also benefit from promoting certain types of characteristics among other states in the international system, and they do so by rewarding states that are believed to possess valued characteristics. For states possessing valued characteristics but lacking a matching reputation, this type of international market gives them the incentive to find credible ways to signal their type to external audiences.

To describe this dynamic in other terms, many states in the international system seek international benefits—such as increased investment, trade, foreign aid, military support, membership in international organizations, and legitimacy and prestige. These international benefits are frequently targeted toward states possessing valued characteristics and withdrawn

---

22. Akerlof, "The Market for 'Lemons'."

from states that are revealed not to possess them. Benefit-seeking leaders, like sellers of used cars, possess more information about their own characteristics than other international actors. Even when influential international actors prefer to interact with specific types of states, they cannot always distinguish good types from bad types and, all else equal, prefer to avoid rewarding states of uncertain type. Benefit-seeking states, like owners of high-quality used cars, are motivated to find a solution to this market failure. A credible signal of their type to other international actors represents such a solution.[23]

Within international politics, it is well known that states vary in their type. In fact, Akerlof's 1970 paper was motivated by a desire to explain why business in "underdeveloped" countries is difficult and not, despite its title, to explain the used car market. Yet in part because of the diffuse nature of the international system, it is rarely articulated exactly how states that possess desirable characteristics but lack a matching reputation might credibly signal their type. Credible signals are not necessarily mandated or articulated by benefit-giving actors; they must instead be discovered by benefit-seeking states. Before election monitoring became a norm, for example, it was clear that the value of democratic political institutions was increasing and that democratizing states wanted such support to increase, but international actors did not specify exactly how states that were not already considered consolidated democracies could demonstrate their commitment to democratization.

Similarly, increasing globalization and the preferences articulated by powerful states and international organizations for neoliberal economic policies gave many states the incentive to signal their valued characteristics in order to attract increased international investment, help negotiate better trading arrangements, and enhance their stature relative to other countries. Across a variety of issue areas, if a given signal is successful in communicating that a state is a valued type, other states will have the incentive to adopt the signal. If all "good" types are believed to send a given signal, even states that do not actually possess the valued characteristic should attempt to fake that signal.

Signaling behaviors have been linked to social norms by Robert Axelrod, who argues that individuals follow existing social norms in part because "violating [the norm] would provide a signal about the type of person you are."[24] Dressing sloppily at a formal dinner, he argues, not only draws dis-

---

23. Spence, "Job Market Signaling."
24. Axelrod, "An Evolutionary Approach to Norms," 1107.

approving stares from other diners but may lead them to conclude more generally that you are a lazy, cheap, or rude person. Axelrod links this concept to the creation of new social norms, which grow out of "behavior that signals things about individuals that will lead others to reward them" and that "as more and more people use the signal to gain information about others, more and more people will adopt the behavior that leads to being treated well."[25]

States seeking international benefits, in my theory, are similar to individuals seeking social approval in Axelrod's argument. A signal becomes a norm when the relevant audience assumes that all desirable types of states likely engage in a specified behavior. The norm creates incentives for other, less-desirable types to try to mimic the signal. Thus, if it is possible to simulate a signal, even if it is costly for undesirable types to do so, signaling behaviors spread and become new international norms when they become linked to desirable characteristics. This diffusion can take place even in the absence of explicit advocacy, overt pressure from powerful states, or incentives for cooperation. Adoption of the behavior as an international norm reinforces the incentives for governments of uncertain type to continue sending the signal and may create incentives for international actors to raise the stakes for undesirable types by increasing the costs of mimicry.

This process has strong parallels to solutions for the market failure identified for Akerlof's market for lemons. Similarly, in Michael Spence's well-known education game, workers are willing to pay the costs of obtaining an education because education represents a credible signal to employers that workers are worth a higher wage, even if more years in school do not add to their productivity.[26] In relation to international credit markets, Sylvia Maxfield argues that "politicians use central bank independence to try to signal their nation's creditworthiness to potential investors."[27] To gain international credit, states are willing to invite (and pay for) sovereign bond ratings from reputable firms, even when they are likely to get a less than perfect rating. Now that credit-rating agencies are widely accepted, countries have difficulty issuing sovereign bonds if they have not been rated by one of the three major agencies.[28] Higher ratings should attract better investors, yet because of the international expectation that

25. Ibid.
26. Spence, "Job Market Signaling."
27. Maxfield, *Gatekeepers of Growth*, 4.
28. Although credit rating agencies have been criticized and their reputations were damaged by the 2008 financial crisis, countries cannot forgo credit ratings entirely.

all creditworthy states receive a credit rating, a poor credit rating is better than none at all.

For this theory to work, it is not necessary that signals communicate an actor's type with certainty. Signals, even when they become accepted as norms, are not always perfectly informative. In the corporate job market, for example, it is logically possible that a very intelligent, educated, and productive job applicant could lack an MBA. It is also possible that a high-quality used car could be for sale without a factory-certified warranty. Or a creditworthy country likely to repay its debts could refuse to obtain a sovereign bond rating. However, the widespread acceptance of these signals has made it unlikely that any good types will refuse to signal. When such signals become norms, the relevant audience believes that all good types send the signal, and the act of refusing to signal itself becomes a source of information about an actor's type: all else equal, used cars with factory-certified warranties are perceived as more reliable than those without, individuals with MBAs or other advanced degrees are perceived as more qualified job applicants than those without, and internationally observed and certified elections are perceived as more democratic than those that are not observed.

In all these cases, the signal is useful and becomes accepted because there is some existing uncertainty about the characteristics of a subset of actors, the process of signaling reveals additional information about the signaling actor, and sending the signal is more costly to bad types. Some warranties are limited or cover a short period of time, some graduates receive poor grades, some countries earn low sovereign bond ratings, and some reports from international election observers criticize elections as fraudulent.

Not all international signals become international norms. At the international level, a norm is generated only if a signal becomes widely accepted as a useful source of information about a state or leader's type, and benefit-seeking actors develop the belief that all good types of leaders send the signal. Domestic actors may also accept the signal as credible, a change that becomes more likely as a new behavior becomes an internationally held norm. Although domestic actors may pressure some governments to adopt a new norm after it has been initiated in another state, it is important to note that in the absence of a transnational advocacy network[29] domestic pressure does not explain the international diffusion of a norm. Especially in the case of international election observation,

---

29. Keck and Sikkink, *Activists beyond Borders.*

domestic audiences react to the signal by the incumbent government in crosscutting ways. More important, pressure from domestic audiences does not necessarily provide a common exogenous shock that can explain international diffusion of a behavior. Without such a common shock, such as a change in the allocation of international benefits, it is more difficult to explain the global diffusion of a new behavior.

In the case of election observation, the signal requires inviting international observers *and* receiving their endorsement of the election. Governments that invite observers and receive negative reports fail to signal to both domestic and international audiences that they are holding plausibly democratic elections. Normalization of a signal reinforces the behavior by generating costs for noncompliance. When the belief is accepted that all valued regime types send the signal, then choosing not to signal indicates that a state is not a valued type, further increasing the incentives for other international actors to imitate the signal.[30]

My theory of norm development is therefore characterized by a change in benefits available to democratizing states, governments attempting to signal to external audiences, mimicry of successful signals by other governments, acceptance of the signal by prominent international actors, and enforcement of the norm by those who benefit from improved information about governments' types. International norms in a variety of issue areas could be explained by this theory, as I explore later. Distinctions among states regarding property rights protections, domestic political institutions, levels of corruption, civic and media freedoms, independence of central banks, or the presence or absence of specific military weapons are all sources of variation that have been rewarded by various international actors. The theory can help explain why most countries now have neo-liberal economic institutions; why nearly all countries in the world hold national-level elections even where few believe that the process is democratic; why countries such as Iraq and North Korea are willing to allow weapons inspectors; and, returning to the question motivating this book, why most leaders now invite foreign monitors to evaluate their elections.

Democracy and the Norm of International Election Monitoring

This book presents an alternative causal path to the development of international norms and explains the rise and persistence of international election observation as a consequential form of international involvement

---

30. This emphasis on the costs of norm-violating behavior is similar to Axelrod, "An Evolutionary Approach to Norms."

in the domestic affairs of sovereign states. The norm of inviting observers, I argue, was initiated by leaders of developing countries in an effort to attract increased international support for democratic and democratizing governments. When powerful states expressed a general preference for supporting democratic regime types, initially in the early 1960s and overtly in the 1980s, the premium for being identified as a democratizing regime gave "true democrats" an incentive to signal their democratic credentials to international audiences.[31] Although there were other possible signals of democratization, such as an opposition candidate victory or opposition party acceptance of the results, these leaders chose to invite observers as an action that distinguished their regime as one committed to democratization but that did not necessarily require them to give up power.

As the potential rewards for demonstrating a commitment to democracy increased and as international actors developed the belief that all governments holding potentially democratic elections would invite international observers, other benefit-seeking leaders imitated the signal even when they were not committed to democratization. This widespread and repeated behavior, coupled with the growing importance of democracy to international actors, changed international expectations such that inviting observers became an international norm. The norm holds that pro-democracy actors believe that all good types invite observers and receive their endorsement. Given uncertainty about the government's commitment to democracy, failing to hold internationally certified elections necessarily became a signal that a government was not holding democratic elections. Pro-democracy actors, primarily those at the international level but also domestic actors, began to rely on election monitoring to evaluate the democratic credentials of states and tied foreign aid and other targeted benefits to internationally certified elections. For example, following coups or other interruptions of democratic rule, Western aid donors

---

31. The international emphasis on democracy is a consequential and relatively unexplored variable within international relations. See McFaul, "Democracy Promotion as a World Value." It is more thoroughly explored in the international law literature on the emerging right to democratic governance: Fox and Roth, "Democracy and International Law"; Rich, "Bringing Democracy into International Law"; Franck, "The Emerging Right to Democratic Governance." See also the literature on the international dimensions of democratization, including Burnell, *Democracy Assistance*; Crawford, *Foreign Aid and Political Reform*; Drake, "The International Causes of Democratization"; Gleditsch and Ward, "Diffusion and the International Context of Democratization"; Levitsky and Way, "International Linkage and Democratization"; Mansfield and Pevehouse, "Democratization and International Organizations"; Pevehouse, *Democracy from Above*; Pevehouse, "Democracy from the Outside-In?"; Starr, "Democratic Dominoes"; Vachudova, *Europe Undivided*; Whitehead, *The International Dimensions of Democratization*.

frequently required internationally certified elections before normal bilateral relations could be restored. By the late 1990s, a government's refusal to invite observers became a conspicuous signal that the election was not legitimate, further constraining election-holding leaders throughout the developing world.

Alternative Explanations

This book outlines a new theory of international norm formation. The majority of existing work on international norm creation focuses on two causal pathways: norms that result from the work of committed activists, commonly referred to as norm entrepreneurs, and norms that result from attempts to facilitate international cooperation.[32] Although not focused on norm formation, the literature on the international diffusion of policies also provides a potential alternative explanation for the spread of election monitoring.[33] I provide a brief summary of these general theories and contrast them with my argument.

Advocacy and Norm Entrepreneurs

The most prominent theory of norm development in international relations offers one possible explanation for the creation of norms under which compliance is costly. According to this theory, initiated by constructivist scholars of international relations, new and more controversial international norms are generated because coalitions of activists or powerful states pressure other actors to change their behavior. Activist pressure changes the decision calculus for leaders, and as a result state leaders are motivated to comply with the new norm. This activist-centered theory is

---

32. For representative works involving norms and international cooperation see Katzenstein, Keohane, and Krasner, "International Organization and the Study of World Politics"; Krasner, "Structural Causes and Regime Consequences"; Keohane, "Reciprocity in International Relations"; Keohane, *After Hegemony;* Schelling, *The Strategy of Conflict.* For a sample of widely recognized work on norm entrepreneurs, see Klotz, *Norms in International Relations;* Finnemore, "International Organizations as Teachers of Norms"; Risse-Kappen, Ropp, and Sikkink, *The Power of Human Rights;* Price, "Reversing the Gun Sights"; Thomas, *The Helsinki Effect;* Finnemore and Sikkink, "International Norm Dynamics and Political Change"; Nadelmann, "Global Prohibition Regimes."

33. Elkins, Guzman, and Simmons, "Competing for Capital: The Diffusion of Bilateral Investment Treaties, 1960–2000"; Gleditsch and Ward, "Diffusion and the International Context of Democratization"; Simmons and Elkins, "The Globalization of Liberalization"; Simmons, Dobbin, and Garrett, *The Global Diffusion of Markets and Democracy.*

most clearly articulated by Martha Finnemore and Kathryn Sikkink: in the first stage of norm initiation, "norm entrepreneurs attempt to convince a critical mass of states (norm leaders) to embrace new norms." Norm leaders then pressure other states to become norm followers, causing a "norm cascade" in which increasing numbers of states adopt the new norm. In the third stage of their theory, norms can become internalized and compliance with the norm becomes automatic.[34]

Although instrumental logics play a part in this theory and many related arguments—the work of activists may be intended to, for example, generate costs for actors who fail to comply with the new norm—norm entrepreneurs are central in initiating and spreading the new behavior. Without this pressure, the activist-centered theory implies that states or other international actors that are better off not complying with the potential norm would not be motivated to change their behavior. Therefore, unless advocates for a new norm are sufficiently powerful, influential, or persuasive, attempts to change state behavior and generate new international norms are unlikely to succeed.

Like Finnemore and Sikkink, Richard Price highlights the work of transnational activists in the global campaign to generate a norm against the use of antipersonnel landmines.[35] Norm entrepreneurs and activists lobbied governments, generated international media attention against mine-producing states, mobilized domestic populations, and campaigned for the UN treaty banning the production and sale of landmines. Similarly, Nina Tannenwald argues that in addition to nuclear deterrence, a post–World War II international norm against the use of nuclear weapons explains the absence of nuclear weapon use since 1945. This norm was created, she argues, in part because of the work of a global and morally motivated network of activists who campaigned against the use of nuclear weapons and raised moral objections against them.[36] The work of activists, which may include networks of committed individuals, nongovernmental organizations (NGOs), or states, is intended to "mobilize popular opinion and political support both within their host country and abroad" and ultimately to motivate international actors to change their behavior.[37]

The pattern of election observation over time closely tracks the pattern of norm development described by Finnemore and Sikkink, including

34. Finnemore and Sikkink, "International Norm Dynamics and Political Change," 896.
35. Price, "Reversing the Gun Sights."
36. Tannenwald, "The Nuclear Taboo."
37. Nadelmann, "Global Prohibition Regimes," 482.

norm initiation, norm cascade, and norm internalization.[38] It is tempting to conclude that the causal mechanism is the same and that norm entrepreneurs advocated the practice of election monitoring, causing it to spread, and lobbied powerful states to pressure noncomplying states to change their behavior. Finnemore's and Sikkink's theory is so widely accepted as the dominant explanation for norm development that when encountering a new international norm, some scholars assume that it must have been generated through activist pressure. This is clearly a tautology that Finnemore and Sikkink did not intend, but it highlights the dominant influence of their theory.

Advocacy-based theories of norm creation have been useful in explaining a number of now-prominent international norms governing state behavior, including the targeting of civilians in war, the production and use of landmines, trafficking in slaves, as well as those international norms proscribing individual behavior within states, such as international norms against child labor, killing endangered species, and discriminating against ethnic and religious minorities.[39] They have also been useful in demonstrating that international norms matter and that states may comply with international norms even when it is costly for them to do so.[40] Yet the activist theory of norm development does not—nor was it intended to— explain all international norms, nor all norms that are consequential.

Finnemore and Sikkink argue that "norms do not appear out of thin air; they are actively built by agents having strong notions about appropriate or desirable behavior in their community."[41] It is this feature of the Finnemore and Sikkink theory that most clearly distinguishes it from my argument in this book. By providing a theory of norm initiation and diffusion that does not require activism or imposition by powerful states, I focus explicitly on norms that are generated primarily through diffusely motivated strategic action and that can be created even in the absence of activist pressure.

Judith Kelley adopts the Finnemore and Sikkink model to explain the norm of election monitoring.[42] In contrast to the more general theory and Kelley's explanation of election monitoring,[43] I argue that the primary

---

38. Finnemore and Sikkink, "International Norm Dynamics and Political Change."

39. Checkel, "International Norms and Domestic Politics"; Klotz, *Norms in International Relations;* Payne, "Persuasion, Frames and Norm Construction"; Nadelmann, "Global Prohibition Regimes"; Thomas, *The Helsinki Effect.*

40. Katzenstein, *The Culture of National Security.*

41. Finnemore and Sikkink, "International Norm Dynamics and Political Change," 896.

42. Kelley, "Assessing the Complex Evolution of Norms."

43. Ibid.

motivation for the initiation, spread, and acceptance of international norms is not activist pressure but the incentive of individual states to signal their type and avoid being viewed as pseudo-democrats by influential international actors.

In the case of election monitoring, as I document in chapter 2, norm entrepreneurs and activists were conspicuously absent when election observation was initiated and began to spread, and regimes seeking international benefits, rather than activists, were the first movers in initiating election monitoring. Some scholars infer the existence of norm entrepreneurs because election observation is now an international norm, but evidence of norm entrepreneurship in election observation is nearly all present after the end of the Cold War, and well after election observation was initiated and diffused widely, undermining confidence in its explanatory potential.[44] Even prominent election observers such as former U.S. President Jimmy Carter were at first reluctant to engage in election observation. Carter grew willing to participate as an international monitor only after being invited by sovereign leaders as part of a broader peace process in Haiti and Nicaragua. Even after these elections, the Carter Center continued to emphasize that they would observe elections only if invited by the host government and opposition parties. Providing an even clearer example of international reluctance to engage in election monitoring, from the 1950s to 1990 the United Nations refused numerous invitations to monitor elections on the grounds that the practice violated sovereignty and constituted undue influence in the domestic affairs of member states. Even the Organization of American States, the first international organization to adopt international monitoring as a common practice, initially refused to send election monitors after being invited on multiple occasions by leaders of member states.

Norms and Incentives for Cooperation

Within international relations theory, one of the dominant approaches—frequently referred to as "rationalist" or "neoliberal institutionalism"—typically discusses norms as embedded within international institutions, and therefore generated along with them, frequently as a result of demand for interstate cooperation or through imposition by powerful states.[45] This second alternative theory of norm development is similar to my argument

---

44. Ibid.
45. Keohane, *After Hegemony*; Krasner, *International Regimes*; Young, "Regime Dynamics: The Rise and Fall of International Regimes."

in that both focus on strategic interaction between international actors; however, the institutionalist theory is not intended to explain the formation of costly norms or norms that are not intended to facilitate cooperation within international institutions. The types of norms discussed by institutionalists—such as those governing the flow of goods across borders—are distinct in that they contribute to or result from mutually beneficial international cooperation. Any risks associated with the norm must therefore be outweighed by the benefits of cooperation. Cooperative norms (also called conventions) can result from simple coordination dilemmas, such as a community's decision to drive on one side of the road or the adoption of international aviation control regulations. Defection is automatically punished, and the gains from following the norm are clear. Norms may be sticky or path dependent and may persist after the incentives that generated them change, but in general, the substantive focus is on norms that facilitate international cooperation by providing focal points and common knowledge or by constraining or ordering preferences.[46] Similarly, scholars in economics and international law have argued that norms and other social conventions can develop spontaneously as a result of repeated interactions and persist because they are Nash equilibria, with no actor having the incentive to deviate from the norm.[47]

My argument presents an alternative causal explanation for the creation of international norms and shows how consequential international norms can be generated unintentionally in a process that is endogenous to strategic interaction. Nevertheless, the interests of powerful states and pro-democracy advocates were important in raising the profile of democracy during the Cold War and generating the near-universal support for democratic governments within international organizations. International pressure for democracy or democratization, however, does not necessarily include pressure for monitoring of elections, and my argument is that the norm of election monitoring was generated primarily because states seeking international benefits reacted to growing international support for democratic states. I find little historical evidence to show that early advocates attempted to pressure other governments to invite observers. Across other issue areas, signaling-generated norms may coexist with advocacy, norm entrepreneurs, pressure from powerful states, and incentives

---

46. Schelling, *The Strategy of Conflict*; Katzenstein, Keohane, and Krasner, "International Organization and the Study of World Politics."

47. Sugden, "Spontaneous Order"; Koh, "Why Do Nations Obey International Law?"; Axelrod, "An Evolutionary Approach to Norms."

for cooperation, although I emphasize the distinction to make my theoretical contribution clear.

In relation to election monitoring, even in a counterfactual world in which the United States demanded that all democratizing countries invite observers, or if a transnational advocacy network developed with the objective of pressuring or shaming states into inviting international election observers, there are several reasons why it was unlikely they could have persuaded state leaders who were not already committed to democracy to begin allowing such an intrusion into their domestic political affairs. Invitations to international election monitors from sovereign governments motivated to improve their country's democratic credentials were a necessary first step. Additionally, international organizations such as the United Nations and the Organization of American States initially objected quite strenuously to the practice of election monitoring as a violation of the organizations' commitment to nonintervention. In the absence of repeated invitations from sovereign leaders, it is not clear that they would have been persuaded to not only send observers but also to initiate election observation, pressure countries to invite observers, and force observers upon unwilling states. Finally, pressuring governments to invite observers would have been unlikely to succeed for a very practical reason. Without government permission, it is extremely difficult for foreigners to engage in effective election monitoring because they can be denied entry to the country and access to important parts of the electoral process. In the case of election monitoring, and in other similar cases, my contention is that election observation would not have spread so widely had it not been initiated by state leaders in an effort to (sometimes falsely) signal the democratic quality of their elections. International pressure for democracy, democratization, human rights, and self-determination played a role in motivating states to find a signal of their commitment to democratization, but the norm of election monitoring would not have developed without the incentives generated by the dynamic signaling process.

Diffusion of Policies across Time and Space

An additional alternative explanation for the norm of election monitoring is suggested by the literature on international diffusion of policies. Although the policy diffusion literature is not intended to explain international norm formation, it is similar to my argument in several ways. Like my argument, recent theories of policy diffusion also focus on instrumental motivations in explaining the spread of behaviors among states. For example, Beth Simmons and Zachary Elkins argue that the diffusion of neoliberal economic policies, including capital account liberalization, exchange rate policy unification, and current account liberalization, have taken place in part because of international factors that influence information and the available set of policy choices. They argue that the incentives for a given state to adopt a particular policy are influenced by the foreign policy choices of other states and the information used by governments to make policy choices is also altered by policy choices in other states.[48] Similarly, Simmons, Frank Dobbin, and Geoffrey Garrett theorize that policies diffuse between states by four processes: coercion, competition, learning, and emulation.[49] Competition, learning, and emulation are all elements of my signaling model of norm formation and diffusion, although my theory can be considered a more specific version of a diffusion model and one that focuses on a particular causal mechanism. Kristian Gleditsch and Michael Ward highlight international factors in explaining the global diffusion of democratic political institutions.[50] In addition to domestic causes of democratization, they demonstrate that a democratic transition is more likely in a given nondemocracy if neighboring countries also democratize and "firmly reject the idea that institutional change is driven entirely by domestic processes and unaffected by regional and international events."[51] However, like Simmons, Dobbin, and Garrett, they do not go into great detail about the casual mechanism underlying how international variables affect democratic transitions.

Across the literature on international policy diffusion, international norms are treated as a potential explanatory variable rather than a topic to be explained, and scholars in this literature tend to present norm-based explanations for the diffusion of policies as an alternative to those that focus on strategic behavior. For example, Gleditsch and Ward present the argument that "norms and values...favor the development and durability of democratic rule" as an alternative to their interpretation.[52] Simmons and Elkins argue that one way that the policy choice payoffs can be altered are "ideational" and "works through the more subjective pressures of prevailing global norms."[53] As I discuss in the next section, this contrast presents an incomplete picture of the role of international norms

---

48. Simmons and Elkins, "The Globalization of Liberalization."
49. Simmons, Dobbin, and Garrett, "Introduction"; Simmons, Dobbin, and Garrett, *The Global Diffusion of Markets and Democracy.*
50. Gleditsch and Ward, "Diffusion and the International Context of Democratization."
51. Ibid., 930.
52. Gleditsch and Ward, "Diffusion and the Spread of Democratic Institutions," 263.
53. Simmons and Elkins, "The Globalization of Liberalization," 172.

when accounting for the widespread diffusion of a variety of policies and practices among states. Although these scholars do not attempt to explain international norms, I believe that many of the substantive topics they explore can be better understood if viewed through the lens of international norm formation, as I discuss in greater detail below.

Election Monitoring Is Costless?

A final alternative explanation, and a challenge to my argument and the overall theme of this book, would be that election monitoring does not matter: if it is costless to invite observers, then it would be easy for all state leaders to mimic the trend even if they are engaging in widespread election fraud, and election monitoring would be relatively uninteresting as a topic. Therefore, in order to evaluate my argument, it is also necessary to evaluate whether election monitoring matters in substantive ways.

Several consequences of election monitoring are implied directly by my theory. The signal of inviting observers must be more costly for pseudo-democrats than for leaders committed to holding democratic elections. There are at least three ways that election monitoring matters for the domestic politics of inviting states and that make election monitoring more costly for pseudo-democrats. First, the existence of the norm of election monitoring may reduce international benefits for those who invite monitors and are caught cheating, as well as for those pseudo-democrats who do not invite them at all. Second, election monitors may reduce fraud directly and cost pseudo-democrats a percentage of their fraudulently obtained vote share. Third, the dynamics of signaling and norm creation triggered an evolving game of strategy between international monitors attempting to evaluate the quality of elections and incumbent leaders seeking international certification of their elections. Taken together, the potential costs of election monitoring act as a set of diverse constraints on governments, making it more difficult for leaders to hold elections without risking their hold on power and also illustrating why international monitoring is an important—although imperfect—element of democracy promotion.

Caveats for International Norms

International norms are often mischaracterized or misunderstood by political scientists, and it is helpful to clarify several points. First, I focus on international norms that are generated unintentionally, in the absence of advocates, but that are also puzzling because compliance with them can be costly. The current literature provides few examples of norms that are both consequential (i.e., noncooperative norms) *and* that are generated without norm entrepreneurs, incentives for cooperation, or imposition by powerful states.[54]

Second, my theory is not about moral or ethical motivation, which is typically used to explain the commitment of activists and is assumed by some to be a necessary component of international norms. Although international norms or "shared standards of appropriate behavior" must be expected to possess a quality of "oughtness," they need not be based in morality to be international norms.[55] Nevertheless, the substantive focus of many studies, such as those on torture, the slave trade, landmines, child labor, female genital mutilation, treatment of medical personnel in war, the use of nuclear weapons, and other similar cases of international norm formation may lead one to conclude otherwise. My view of international norms, following a widely used definition in the literature, is more general and can be applied to shared expectations of appropriate behavior across issue areas, regardless of the moral dimension.

Third, although I present an overtly instrumental or "rational" theory of norm formation and diffusion that is distinct from existing theories, it is far from the only theory of norm creation to include some element of strategic interaction or rational behavior. The debate about international norm formation is sometimes misperceived as a debate between rationalists and constructivists over whether norms matter. This perceived debate is outdated, at best, and by some accounts it never took place. Highlighting constructivist attention to rational action, Finnemore and Sikkink label the process of norm formation "strategic social construction" and argue that "rationality cannot be separated from any politically significant episode of normative influence or normative change, just as the normative context conditions any episode of rational choice."[56] Peter Katzenstein, Robert Keohane, and Stephen Krasner argue that although constructivists and rationalists disagree on ontology, "on issues of epistemology and methodology, however, no great differences divide constructivists from rationalists."[57] Similarly, James Fearon and Alexander Wendt complain

---

54. Some coordination norms are generated without activists, but because they generate gains from cooperation, compliance with such norms is not controversial. See Sugden, "Spontaneous Order."

55. Goertz and Diehl, "Toward a Theory of International Norms."

56. Finnemore and Sikkink, "International Norm Dynamics and Political Change," 888.

57. Katzenstein, Keohane, Stephen Krasner, "International Organization and the Study of World Politics," 675.

that rationalism and constructivism are often falsely pitted against one another, and some scholars mistakenly argue that "rationalists believe that people are always acting on material self-interest, and constructivists believe that people are always acting on the basis of norms and values."[58] They go on to argue that this widely held misperception is due to misunderstanding of rationalism, not to any fundamental theoretical conflict between rationalism and constructivism.

Additionally, a number of prominent scholars focused on international norms have now highlighted that rational choice and constructivism complement each other more often than not and that rational or strategic action is closely tied to norm initiation and norm compliance.[59] For example, in relation to the norm of Arabism governing the international relations of Arab states, Michael Barnett argues that changes in this norm were generated through "social and strategic interactions" between rational and self-interested Arab states. In explaining state acceptance of the norm of territorial integrity, Mark Zacher argues that instrumental motivations played a large part in driving states to accept the norm, in addition to democratic ideals promoted through international organizations.[60]

A final clarification relates to which actors must hold an international norm in order for it to exist. It is not necessary for those actors who are expected to comply with the norm to share it. Rather, it is entirely possible for one group of states—such as the Western developed democracies—to share expectations about the appropriate behavior of a second group of states—such as developing countries. Continuing with Zacher's territorial integrity norm, it is not necessary for all states to believe that the norm is legitimate in order for it to be enforced.[61] It only must be true that some sufficiently powerful states share the norm of respect for territorial integrity and are willing to enforce it against potential aggressors. The fact that many powerful states and most international organizations now share the norm of election observation is sufficient to motivate change in state behavior; it is not necessary that every state leader choosing to invite

---

58. Fearon and Wendt, "Rationalism v. Constructivism," 58.

59. Abbott and Snidal, "Values and Interests: International Legalization in the Fight against Corruption"; Barnett, *Dialogues in Arab Politics*; Finnemore and Sikkink, "International Norm Dynamics and Political Change"; Fearon and Wendt, "Rationalism v. Constructivism"; Kelley, "Assessing the Complex Evolution of Norms: The Rise of International Election Monitoring"; Zacher, "The Territorial Integrity Norm."

60. Zacher, "The Territorial Integrity Norm."

61. Ibid.

observers does so out of a belief in the appropriateness or legitimacy of the norm.[62]

In my theory, only after the norm exists are costs imposed for noncompliance. If the norm, and the associated costs of noncompliance, did not exist, improvements in the accuracy of the signal (the quality of election monitoring) would mean that leaders could stop playing the game without fear of sanctions (losing only potential benefits from successful signaling). With the international norm and the expectation that all true democrats invite international observers to their elections, the costs of noncompliance reinforce the incentives for states to participate in the signaling game, even when compliance with the norm becomes more costly. The norm makes it more likely that domestic and international democracy promoters will react to a negative report or a country's failure to invite observers.

States' leaders may, of course, still choose to comply with the norm because they have internalized it or because they believe it is legitimate, and for most purposes it is not productive to debate whether states comply with international norms out of instrumental or norm-based reasons. As Fearon and Wendt argue, the answer could always be "both."[63] In the case of election monitoring, by distinguishing between norm-compliers and those who hold the norm, however, I am able to show how norms generate costs for noncompliance that would otherwise not exist and argue that the international norm causes states to continue inviting observers when it would not otherwise be in their interest to do so.[64]

Outline of the Book

In chapter 1, I present this argument in greater detail, working up to a set of empirical implications about the causes and consequences of the norm of election monitoring that are evaluated in chapters 2–5. In chapter 2, I focus on changes over time in the reasons why leaders invite international election observers. I provide a detailed narrative description

---

62. This point is similar to the "logic of appropriateness" and "logic of consequences" arguments outlined by March and Olsen in "The Institutional Dynamics of International Political Orders." Actors sharing the norm are motivated by a "logic of appropriateness," but actors that comply with a norm may be doing so not because they believe it is right but rather based on a "logic of consequences."

63. Fearon and Wendt, "Rationalism v. Constructivism."

64. For a discussion of the differing motivations to comply with new norms, see Hurd, "Legitimacy and Authority in International Politics."

of the governments that initiated election monitoring and present a new dataset documenting the trend of election monitoring over time. Using descriptive statistics and regression analysis, I use original data to evaluate whether my theory about the causes of internationally monitored elections is consistent with the cross-national empirical evidence. I also compare my argument to the alternative explanations outlined above, for which I find only limited support.

Chapter 3 considers the supply side of election monitoring and documents changes in international democracy promotion as well as the change in democracy-contingent benefits associated with the norm of election observation, providing quantitative and qualitative evidence in support of my argument. I show that pro-democracy actors are responsive to the reports of observers and that the reports of observers are now used in many prominent indices, such as Freedom House, that quantify a country's political institutions. I also document changes in international benefits over time in several illustrative cases, providing clear evidence of the connection between international benefits and internationally certified elections.

In chapter 4, I use experimental evidence to document that election monitoring is costly for pseudo-democrats in a way that it is not for true democrats. At a minimum, monitoring reduces election day manipulation, thus making it harder or more expensive to steal an election outright. For those holding clean elections, the same cost does not exist, an empirical finding that buttresses my theoretical argument.

In chapter 5, I explore the game of strategy between international observers and incumbent governments that are intent on manipulating the election and evading the consequences of a negative report. Using qualitative evidence, documented changes in observation methodology, and details from hundreds of election observation reports, I illustrate how the types of election manipulation have changed over time, in part responding to improved methods of election observation and increased willingness by other international actors to tie benefits to the reports of observers.

Even as it became more costly for many leaders to comply with the norm, the growing international emphasis on democracy meant that the norm was reinforced rather than weakened. So long as democracy remains a characteristic valued by other states in the international system, the norm will reinforce itself. However, should democracy become unimportant to powerful states and international organizations, the norm will weaken, and pseudo-democrats would be the first to stop inviting international election monitors.

In the concluding chapter, I briefly extend the argument to several other issue areas, including international weapons inspection, bilateral investment treaties, and the diffusion of a variety of neoliberal economic policies. I then discuss the implications of this study for future research on international norm formation, election manipulation, and international constraints on pseudo-democratic leaders. In terms of policy, I outline the implications of this project for international election monitoring and for democracy promotion and international pressure more generally.

Indirect Pressure, Diffusion, and Norm Formation

This book presents a theory of norm development that explores how states in the developing world respond to the preferences of powerful states. Regardless of where these preferences originate, the overarching implication of this theory is that leaders respond to the changing preferences of more powerful actors within the international system. A corollary to this theory is that it is not necessary for powerful states to impose their will on less-powerful actors for new international norms, rules, and institutions to be generated. Rather than requiring the work of advocates, imposition by powerful states, or mutually beneficial coordination, these rules and norms can result from diffusely motivated reaction to anticipated international benefits. States respond to the availability of international benefits, and successful responses are mimicked. When signals diffuse in such a manner because of their relationship to characteristics that are valued or rewarded, signals can quickly become international norms, even when no relevant actors pressure for a new norm.

This project covers the global development of international election observation from 1960 through 2006. The central argument is presented as a signaling game between incumbent leaders and democracy promoters. The empirical implications derived from this model are evaluated using several types of evidence, including original cross-national data on elections and election observation throughout the developing world, natural and field experiments involving the random assignment of international observers, and qualitative evidence about the dynamics between leaders, international observers, and pro-democracy international actors. By moving from a macro-level theory explaining the new norm of election observation to cross-national, qualitative, and micro-level tests of the implications of this theory, I provide a comprehensive examination of why election monitoring has become an international norm as well as the consequences of the norm for governments throughout the world.

1

SIGNALING DEMOCRACY AND THE NORM OF INTERNATIONALLY OBSERVED ELECTIONS

Since the end of the Cold War, international election observation has attracted significant attention from policymakers and practitioners of foreign aid, democracy promotion, and postconflict political development as a useful and widely accepted tool to help facilitate democratic elections. For scholars of international relations and comparative politics, especially those interested in the consequences of international pressure on government behavior, election observation also represents an ideal case of international norm formation. This chapter presents my argument in detail, providing a theory of international norm creation in which strategic interaction between state leaders and powerful international actors generates new and consequential international norms. I present a stylized model of the interaction between governments seeking international benefits, democracy promoters, and international election observers. Election monitoring became a norm in part because compliance is perceived to be costly for a well-defined subset of governments: those that engage in significant election manipulation. By inviting independent third-party observers to judge their elections' quality, governments holding rigged elections risk heightened international and domestic exposure of their corrupt practices. Because election monitors can deter fraud directly or make fraud more difficult, inviting observers is more costly for leaders who engage in election manipulation. These costs, in turn, are precisely what make election monitoring a useful and informative signal.

The argument is presented in four parts. First, I introduce the relevant actors, including true democrats, pseudo-democrats, democracy promoters, and international election observers. The creation of the norm of election observation hinged in part on the perceived existence of two types of leaders: those who are committed to genuine democratization and those who hold elections but are not necessarily willing to abide by democratic rules.[1] Second, I argue that changes in the international environment generated a common shock, exogenous to domestic political developments, that increased benefits for some state leaders who signaled their commitment to democracy. Although election monitoring was just one of many potential signals that governments could have used, it spread in part because democracy promoters began to recognize and reward positive reports from foreign election observers as an informative signal of a government's intention to democratize.

Third, focusing on the decision to invite election observers, I argue that efforts by state leaders to gain democracy-contingent benefits led to a change in the expectations among democracy-promoting actors and ultimately generated an international norm of election observation.

The norm is unintended in the sense that no constituency or group lobbied for the norm, nor do I find evidence that it was imposed by a global or regional hegemon. The signal of inviting international election observation was initiated by leaders wishing to demonstrate their commitment to democratization, not by leaders seeking a new norm, and was imitated by pseudo-democratic leaders when the "democracy premium" grew sufficiently large. Repeated invitations from many state leaders led to the normalization of election observation and its explicit use as a method to evaluate the democratic credentials of other states.

Finally, I outline the empirical implications of this theory and summarize the approach used to evaluate them in the subsequent chapters of the book. The analysis includes a global dataset of elections and election observation, detailed information on changes in democracy promotion and international benefits, evidence from election observer reports, and natural and field experimental tests of the effects of election monitoring on domestic political behavior.

International Incentives and the Decision to Invite Observers

Although states are sovereign within the international system, they do not act in isolation. The decisions of leaders and the behavior of domestic political actors are subject to a variety of external influences. I focus in

---

1. Note that these are ideal types, and even leaders who are committed to democratization may be willing to bias the election in their favor. The important distinction between types of leaders is whether the recipients of the signal—in this case democracy-promoting actors—perceive that the distinction between types exists and if they think that they are better off supporting governments that are true democrats.

particular on one form of international influence: powerful international actors hold preferences about the characteristics of other states and encourage these characteristics indirectly through the allocation of international benefits. This hierarchical relationship between more and less influential international actors provides the foundation for my theory.[2] Economic and political stability, strategic location, transparency, and democratic political institutions are examples of valued and rewarded state-level characteristics. Countries such as Egypt and Israel receive high levels of foreign support from the United States primarily because they are strategically important, and the United States seeks to encourage such allies through military and financial support. Countries such as Singapore and Costa Rica attract high levels of foreign direct investment in part because they are perceived as stable. Economic and political stability is a state-level characteristic that is rewarded by many international actors. Across a variety of issues areas, however, influential international actors frequently do not define exactly how states should prove that they are transparent, stable, or possess other desirable characteristics. Instead, for powerful states, it is frequently a safer strategy to interact with and reward those states whose "type" is clear from their behavior. Leaders of benefit-seeking states without established reputations must find a way to demonstrate their country's qualifications in the absence of clear directives, an environment that gives them the incentive to identify credible signals of their type.

Given a change in the preferences of powerful international actors about the characteristics of other states—such as an increase in the emphasis on democracy—states that are not already perceived to possess the characteristic have an increased incentive to modify their behavior in order to gain more international benefits and to signal their commitment (or type) to skeptical or indifferent audiences. International benefits are diverse and fungible and include international investment, foreign aid, preferential trade agreements, membership in international organizations, military support, increased economic exchange, and legitimacy and prestige. New behaviors that become recognized as credible signals of a government's type produce dynamic effects. Because such signals increase the incentives for other states to imitate the new behavior, the new behavior spreads. In addition to generating imitators, success of a given benefit-seeking signal indicates that some international actors have accepted the signal and therefore increases the demand for the signal among

---

2. Lake, *Hierarchy in International Relations.*

its intended recipients. If the signaling game becomes institutionalized such that international actors believe that all good types of states send a given signal, the new behavior becomes a norm. Only bad types refuse to signal. Therefore, if there is some probability that bad types can mimic the signal, this dynamic generates pressure on all benefit-seeking states to comply with the norm.

This process is most likely when benefit-giving actors want to encourage or reward a characteristic that is not readily observable. Because some governments may attempt to mimic democratic political institutions, it is difficult for external actors to judge a regime's commitment to democracy. In the context of democracy promotion, pro-democracy actors prefer to support states committed to democratization and, all else equal, attempt to avoid supporting states that are not committed democrats.

True and Pseudo-Democrats

A common assumption in political science research is that the primary goal of incumbent politicians is to maintain power. This is often a useful assumption, but it can be misleading when applied to countries without established political institutions that help "enforce" democracy.[3] For some leaders in transitional countries, the goal of democratization trumps the goal of staying in power at all costs. Throughout democratic history, during periods of institutional instability some leaders have put their desire to lead their country toward democracy ahead of their desire to stay in office. U.S. President George Washington was one of the first prominent politicians to do so, and he transferred power to an elected successor despite popular opinion that he should serve indefinitely. Since that time, a number of incumbent politicians have risked their own political future in order to help their country progress toward democracy, including one of the first leaders on record to invite international observers to elections in a sovereign state: José Figueres of Costa Rica, a man referred to upon his death as his country's "father of democracy."[4]

State leaders condition their behavior on anticipated international benefits. Benefit-seeking behavior is common in the developing world, where foreign aid and other forms of external support are frequently used for political purposes. Not all benefit-seeking leaders are equally committed

---

3. Przeworski, *Democracy and the Market*; Weingast, "The Political Foundations of Democracy and the Rule of Law."

4. "José Figueres, Father of Costa Rican Democracy, Dies." United Press International, June 8, 1990.

to democratization, even when they hold elections, as electoral autocrats such as Alberto Fujimori, Vladimir Putin, and Robert Mugabe illustrate. This distinction between types of leaders means that, given some level of international benefits tied to democracy and uncertainty about some governments' commitment to it, those leaders who are actually committed to democratization are motivated to signal their type to domestic and international audiences.

Throughout this book, national leaders of transitional countries are referred to as "incumbents" or "governments." This assumed actor can be one individual or a group of leaders, depending on the regime type. Once elections are announced, all incumbents choose the degree to which they (and usually their party and supporters) will abide by the rules of a democratic election. In institutionalized democracies, a free and independent media, an independent judiciary, rule of law, and an informed and active citizenry mean that—at least in theory—leaders are bound to democratic rules by predictably severe consequences.[5] In countries in which democracy is not institutionalized, some of the mechanisms of self-enforcing democracy may be weak or limited, and leaders are not so constrained. Incumbents may choose to delegate authority to an independent electoral commission, but one may assume that they always maintain ultimate authority over the degree to which elections are manipulated.

Within this environment, there are two general types of incumbents: true democrats and pseudo-democrats. True democrats are those incumbents who obey the letter and the spirit of electoral laws: they follow rules regulating electoral competition (they do not commit electoral fraud) and comply with expected behavior following an election (if they lose, they peacefully transfer power). Put simply, they act like leaders in established democracies, working to maintain power within the confines of democratic institutions.

For other leaders of countries in transition, power-hungry politicians will attempt to stay in office at all costs, including through undemocratic means. Although pseudo-democrats agree to hold elections, and will even hold free and fair elections if they believe that they are popular enough to win outright, they manipulate the election or the electoral process when they are not otherwise sure of their victory. The crucial differences between true democrats and pseudo-democrats are that, first, pseudo-democrats will cheat in order to win and, second, if they are defeated, they do not willingly transfer power to another party.

---

5. Weingast, "The Political Foundations of Democracy and the Rule of Law."

I do not attempt to classify each and every leader as a true or pseudo-democrat because it is frequently impossible to do so before elections take place.[6] Some leaders may change during their tenure, such as dictators who rule unelected for decades but peacefully leave power after allowing—and losing—democratic elections. Kenneth Kaunda, the president of Zambia from 1964 to 1991, is such an example. Other leaders persist in holding elections long after they are widely perceived as dictators or "electoral autocrats." Still others appear to oscillate between gross violations of democratic procedures and respecting democratic processes even when they lose, such as Hugo Chavez of Venezuela or Daniel Ortega of Nicaragua.

Variation in the degree to which leaders are willing to abide by the rules of democratic elections is essential in explaining why election monitoring became an international norm. Even China claims to be democratizing, and even North Korea and Turkmenistan hold elections. There are also a number of countries such as Chile, Ghana, and Indonesia that transitioned to democracy under great uncertainty about the commitment of their leaders to democratization. Judging which governments are actually democratizing is difficult because verbal commitments by leaders claiming to democratize and even the decision to hold elections are cheap talk. Many autocrats pay lip service to democratic values and hold rigged elections without serious risk to their power. As I argue in this chapter, international election monitoring spread widely because an endorsement from reputable international observers became internationally recognized as a signal that a leader was committed to holding democratic elections, because it is costly but not impossible for pseudo-democrats to imitate this signal, and because observation itself generated valuable information for democracy-promoting states.

Democracy Promoters

The other major actor in the development of election observation is the democracy-promoting community, represented primarily by powerful Western states. In some cases, the coalition of democracy promoters also includes domestic forces within a potentially democratizing country, although domestic pro-democracy forces are not necessary for governments to have the incentive to respond to foreign democracy promoters. In

---

6. Przeworski et al. code a binary democracy variable based on whether democratic elections are possible, although the coding rules make it difficult to apply to these rules to election monitoring (*Democracy and Development.*)

reality, democracy promoters are an amalgamation of states, international organizations, and other actors, all of whom act independently from one another. I refer to these actors in the aggregate in order to examine how a leader's decision to invite election monitors is influenced by the expected response among democracy promoters. This type of assumption is not without precedent. For example, as Michael Tomz has shown in relation to state reputation in international capital markets, coordination is not necessary for diverse international actors—such as investors or democracy promoters—to develop common beliefs and responses to the behavior of governments.[7] Simply put, the behavior of leaders can be influenced by the anticipated reaction of the pro-democracy international community, even when the international community is a diffuse set of actors without a formal mechanism to coordinate their response.[8]

International Election Observers

International election observers are official delegations of foreigners who are invited by the host government to observe and report on the electoral process. Election observation missions are deployed or sponsored by international organizations, such as the Organization of American States (OAS), the Organization for Security and Cooperation in Europe's Office for Democratic Institutions and Human Rights (OSCE/ODIHR), and the European Union (EU), and nongovernmental organizations (NGOs), such as the Carter Center and the Asian Network for Free Elections (ANFREL). Some NGOs such as the National Democratic Institute and the International Republican Institute are nominally independent but are primarily funded by individual governments. International election observers are central in my theory, yet their role is straightforward. Although there are several notable exceptions, the primary role of international observers at an election is to evaluate its quality and to provide recommendations for improvements to the electoral process. In this stylized model of election observation, their report on election quality is not determined by the expected response of other actors but rather is determined only by the quality of the election.[9]

In this sense, the reports of observers on election quality are not strategically motivated, although I will show later that as the norm became

---

7. Tomz, *Reputation and International Cooperation.*
8. This point is also made clearly by Goertz and Diehl in relation to diffuse sanctioning of norm violators in "Toward a Theory of International Norms."
9. But also see Kelley, "D-Minus Elections."

more widely accepted, organizations supporting international observers invested in improving observation technology.[10] For now, it is important to note that in my theory, international observers do not by themselves confer international costs or benefits.[11] They primarily serve an informational role, and their reports matter to the extent that other actors rely on them to evaluate the quality of elections.

The quality of observers varies considerably over time and between organizations. Since observers began criticizing elections in the 1980s, a subset of observer organizations have developed reputations as being more professionalized and more willing to call out problematic elections. As I discuss in chapter 5, this fact has been exploited by pseudo-democrats in the game of strategic manipulation played with observers.[12] Other organizations are unlikely to be explicitly critical and do not invest resources in improving monitoring techniques.

The International Environment and the Democracy Premium

Countries seeking international benefits respond to the preferences of other international actors, such as a preference among powerful states for democratic political institutions to be present in states receiving their support. The skeptic may doubt that such a "democracy premium" exists in practice because there are many examples in which nondemocratic regimes continue to receive external support from pro-democracy actors. It would be naive to assert that influential actors promote democracy at all costs or that democracy promotion trumps all other interests of powerful states. At best, promoting democracy is just one of many foreign policy goals, and its importance relative to other objectives changes over time within individual countries and international organizations. Nevertheless, there is much evidence to suggest that international pressure for democracy exists and that benefit-seeking states respond to this pressure.[13] For

10. There are several counter examples in which international observers are pressured to reach a predetermined conclusion about the election or to base their conclusion on which party won rather than the quality of the process, but these examples are, at this point, exceptions.

11. It is possible that there is a direct psychological effect on leaders as a result of praise or criticism, although this is not included in my theory.

12. Beaulieu and Hyde, "In the Shadow of Democracy Promotion"; Simpser, "Unintended Consequences of Election Monitoring."

13. States promote democracy for many reasons ranging from the ideological to the strategic. I set aside the question of why states promote democracy, and I discuss the empirical

such international pressure to influence the behavior of leaders, it is only necessary that not-yet-democratic states have reason to believe that they may be rewarded for appearing to democratize.

Leaders vary in the types of international benefits they seek, and they may desire benefits such as international legitimacy, foreign aid, membership in international organizations, and increased foreign direct investment. International benefits can also be withheld or withdrawn as a penalty for various reasons, including actions related to democratic reversals. Individual states or leaders may prefer different types of benefits and may seek material or less tangible benefits, such as international legitimacy or prestige. As I discuss in chapter 2, the fact that international benefits are fungible makes measurement more challenging, but it is unnecessary to assume that leaders seek only material benefits or nonmaterial benefits such as legitimacy.[14]

During the Cold War, democracy promotion was closely tied to U.S.- and Western-aligned states. Although anti-communism was clearly the most important characteristic to the United States, and frequently trumped democracy, allies were periodically encouraged to liberalize politically and were promised increased support if they did so.[15] The end of the Cold War brought democracy promotion closer to the top of the foreign policy agendas of many powerful states, and the issue of democracy gained prominence in a number of international organizations.[16] Even after the end of the Cold War, however, the widespread movement toward overt and multifaceted democracy promotion by powerful international actors did not displace other foreign policy objectives, but rather it grew in importance relative to anti-communism. Pressure for democracy continues to vary across states and regions depending on other geopolitical concerns.

In presenting this theory, I make the basic assumption that international actors prefer to support countries that they judge to have high value and that the characteristics valued by international actors change over time. More than one characteristic of a given state can be rewarded or punished, even if they sometimes conflict, and the relative weight of individual

---

evidence of democracy promotion efforts and the international benefits tied to democracy in chapter 3.

14. Kelley argues that leaders are primarily seeking legitimacy when they invite observers, although she highlights both instrumental and normative reasons in "Assessing the Complex Evolution of Norms."

15. Smith, *America's Mission.*

16. Donno, "Defending Democratic Norms: Regional Intergovernmental Organizations, Domestic Opposition and Democratic Change"; Pevehouse, *Democracy from Above;* Mansfield and Pevehouse, "Democratization and International Organizations."

characteristics changes. For example, during the Cold War, a communist-aligned government could not gain support from democracy promoters because its position on communism would have outweighed its other characteristics, even if the country's government was genuinely committed to democratization. An anti-communist government, however, could lobby to increase its share of international benefits by signaling its commitment to democracy. Also according to this model, a strategically important autocrat may continue receiving support from democracy-promoting states so long as the value of its geopolitical position outweighs its lack of political liberalization.

State-level characteristics may change in value relative to each other. When anti-communism was the most important factor in allocating international benefits during the Cold War, increasing a state's commitment to democracy would lead to only a small boost in international benefits, and becoming more democratic could not outweigh the negative value attached to a communist-sympathizing government. Compared to the value associated with anti-communism, the weight of democracy was small. After the Cold War, the weight given to democracy increased relative to other characteristics, giving more leaders the ability and incentive to seek democracy-linked benefits.

Two simple but important implications follow from this basic model. First, it is not necessary that democracy is the state's most important characteristic for it to factor into the decision-making behavior of benefit-seeking incumbents. Second, for each government seeking international benefits, any change in the relative weight given to democracy in the allocation of international benefits changes the corresponding expected benefits of being internationally recognized as democratic.

Although this emphasis is redundant, scholars and public commentators often make the point that democracy promotion cannot be effective if it is inconsistently applied across states or if other characteristics are also valued.[17] In contrast, I argue that inconsistent democracy promotion, or democracy promotion conditioned by geopolitical interests, can still have important effects in motivating changes in the behavior of benefit-maximizing leaders. Counterintuitively, this argument also suggests that some ambiguity in the motivations of powerful democracy-promoting states increases the number of leaders willing to risk political liberalization and invite international exposure. If all leaders expected that foreign commitments to enforce democracy were absolute, the governments most

17. Roth, "Despots Masquerading as Democrats."

likely to violate democratic institutions would be the least willing to risk political liberalization to gain democracy-contingent international benefits. In a world of sovereign states, the promotion of democracy at all costs would decrease the incentives for pseudo-democrats to invite observers and therefore decrease international scrutiny where it is most interesting: governments that are most likely to be manipulating their elections and constraining political liberalization.

Signaling Commitment to Democracy

Assuming that a democracy premium exists and that democratic governments receive some increase in their expected level of foreign support, how might a government of an uncertain type send a credible signal of its commitment to democratization? Historically, scholars and policymakers have applied various standards to democratizing countries in order to judge when they can be considered democratic. One such standard is the "two-turnover test," in which a country is considered democratic after two peaceful transitions in power through elections, a standard that leaders or parties who wish to remain in power would clearly not prefer.[18] Another popular standard defines an election as democratic if all political parties accept the results. Opposition acceptance of the results is an unreliable indicator because opposition political parties may act as sore losers, protesting even democratic elections. Similarly, governments may credibly threaten to crack down on protest following rigged elections and successfully intimidate losing parties. Such a credible threat of retribution would falsely give the appearance that opposition parties had accepted the results.

These standards are not ideal from the perspective of true democrats seeking recognition as such: a country could theoretically be democratic before experiencing two turnovers, as Arend Lijphart has argued in the cases of Germany, Luxembourg, the Netherlands, and Switzerland,[19] or countries could experience democratic backsliding even after two or more turnovers in power, as in Nicaragua or Peru. Before democracy is institutionalized, suspicion between political actors and an absence of credible information make it difficult for leaders to signal whether an election is democratic. This idea was neatly summed up by a Chilean general before the internationally observed 1988 plebiscite on the continued rule of

18. Huntington, *The Third Wave of Democratization*.
19. Lijphart, *Patterns of Democracy*.

Augusto Pinochet: "If the government's candidate wins everyone will say it was fraud. If he loses everyone will say it was a fair election. So it is more in our interests than anyone else's to be able to show it was an absolutely fair election."[20]

Following an increase in democracy-contingent benefits, benefit-seeking states have the incentive to signal their type rather than rely on the judgment of powerful states. Other potentially credible signals, such as opposition victory, require leaders to give up power. By proactively signaling their commitment to democratic elections, state leaders who initiated election observation could make it more likely that their country was accurately recognized as a democratizing state, potentially decrease suspicion among domestic opposition parties, and increase their likely share of international support from the West. International election monitoring is a credible signal because it is more costly for pseudo-democrats than for true democrats, yet both types of leaders can signal their commitment to democracy by holding internationally monitored and endorsed elections.

Simply extending an invitation to international observers is not a sufficient signal: elections must also receive a positive report from observers. As election monitoring spread, pro-democracy actors, including true democrats, increased the cost of the signal to pseudo-democrats by expanding the mandate of election monitoring and improving the quality of observation: governments increasingly had to allow more observers; give them unfettered access to the entire electoral process throughout the country before, during, and after the election; and avoid manipulating the election in a manner that observers would criticize.

The dynamics of this interaction, including the diffusely motivated behavior of states acting in their own best interest, caused the new behavior—inviting international election monitors—to spread widely. Because these state leaders were successful in advocating a connection between election monitoring and democracy, initially reluctant international actors began to accept the signal of inviting observers in some regions. Over time, these pro-democracy actors began to expect that all leaders holding potentially democratic elections would invite international election monitors unless they were not committed to democracy.[21] This change in international

---

20. General Fernando Mattei on Pinochet's "insoluble dilemma," quoted in Huntington, *The Third Wave*, 84.

21. On the norm of election observation see Bjornlund, *Beyond Free and Fair*; Kelley, "Assessing the Complex Evolution of Norms"; Rich, "Bringing Democracy into International Law"; Santa-Cruz, "Constitutional Structures, Sovereignty, and the Emergence of Norms."

expectations about the behavior of governments has been noted by other scholars. As Roland Rich argues,

> International observation of national elections and referendums in countries claiming to be democratic has become the norm. The rejection of foreign electoral observers has come to be taken as a signal that the country concerned is not prepared to open itself to international scrutiny and is not interested in the international legitimacy that a positive report would bestow.[22]

And, as Eric Bjornlund writes, "in democratizing and semiauthoritarian countries, election monitoring has become the norm and is now effectively a prerequisite in such countries for elections to be viewed as legitimate."[23] Judith Kelley similarly highlights the change in internationally held expectations, arguing that because "honest governments always had the incentive to invite monitors...[t]he international community could therefore infer that incumbents who refused monitors must have intended to cheat."[24]

In recent years, the norm has spread even among developed democracies. Until 2000, few countries invited observers if they had established their type and their commitment to democracy. But as election observation became normalized, some pseudo-democratic governments complained of hypocrisy and paternalism in the application of election observation, and partly in response, European and North American democracies began to invite foreign observers.

The Dynamics of Norm Initiation and Diffusion

Why did state leaders choose to invite international scrutiny of what used to be an entirely domestic political process? Why did leaders who planned to commit election fraud begin inviting observers? Why did inviting observers become an international norm rather than a fleeting phenomenon, and why do states continue to comply with the norm even when it is clear that they will be caught manipulating the election?

Explaining the global diffusion of election monitoring requires explaining the decision by individual leaders to invite observers or not. My theory is based on a signaling game.[25] Scholars of international norms and game

---

22. Rich, "Bringing Democracy into International Law," 26.
23. Bjornlund, *Beyond Free and Fair*, 31.
24. Kelley, "Assessing the Complex Evolution of Norms," 231.
25. For discussion of signaling games in international relations, see Morrow, "The Strategic Setting of Choices: Signaling, Commitment, and Negotiation in International Politics."

theorists rarely engage one another, although some concepts have strong parallels in both literatures.[26] Because the setup and implications of the game are relatively straightforward, the formalization of the game is confined to the appendix and the model is described entirely in words. When it is useful, I link the argument to game-theoretic concepts, and familiarity with game theory is helpful but not necessary to understand this part of my argument.

Incumbent governments choose whether to invite observers and attempt to gain their endorsement. This decision is modeled as a signaling game played by incumbents of uncertain type: unambiguous autocratic regimes such as Saudi Arabia or North Korea are not expected to play the game, and unambiguously democratic regimes such as Australia, Belgium, or Canada were not expected to invite observers until the norm had diffused widely.[27] For such governments, it is unlikely that the signal of inviting observers and receiving their report would change other actors' beliefs about regime type, making it unlikely that they will attempt to play the game.

Given that elections are being held in a country that is not unambiguously autocratic, I assume that the incumbent leader can be a true democrat or a pseudo-democrat. Both types of leaders decide whether to invite international observers. Before making this decision, leaders evaluate their likely share of international benefits and the available (potential) benefits tied to democracy. Other country-level characteristics known to the incumbent and democracy promoters, such as strategic location, alliances, or any number of other characteristics, also factor into the anticipated benefits that incumbents perceive before deciding whether to invite observers. In choosing whether to invite observers, governments also consider whether and how they will attempt to manipulate the election in their favor. More manipulation is more expensive and more likely to be caught when observers are invited. Methods of manipulation that are less likely to be caught by observers are assumed to be more expensive, because additional effort must be devoted to concealing manipulation or manipulating the election using legal or indirect tactics.

See also Schelling, *The Strategy of Conflict*; Schultz, *Democracy and Coercive Diplomacy*; Schultz, "Domestic Opposition and Signaling in International Crises"; Milner, *Interests, Institutions, and Information*; Fearon, "Rationalist Explanations for War."

26. Katzenstein, Keohane, and Krasner, "International Organization and the Study of World Politics"; Morrow, "When Do States Follow the Laws of War?"; Fearon and Wendt, "Rationalism v. Constructivism"; Finnemore and Sikkink, "International Norm Dynamics and Political Change."

27. I discuss the decision by developed democracies to invite international observers below.

Because by definition the ideal type of true democrat never cheats, they do not have to pay the costs of manipulating the election and are never caught cheating. I assume that election monitoring is not entirely cost-less for true democrats, who must pay a small sovereignty cost if they invite observers. The sovereignty cost is in part determined by the reaction of domestic audiences to the government's decision to invite observers. Domestic audiences do not necessarily support the decision to invite observers. The sovereignty cost can vary by country because of variation in domestic support for the decision to invite international observers. For example, some domestic actors view international election observers as an unnecessary form of foreign meddling, and in such cases the sovereignty costs associated with inviting observers would be greater. However, as election observation becomes more widely accepted among domestic audiences, the sovereignty cost decreases.[28]

Leaders committing large-scale fraud or who are less willing to risk a negative report must exert more effort to conceal election manipulation, such as by moving election manipulation to the pre-election period, by engaging in indirect rather than direct forms of manipulation (e.g., media bias rather than vote theft), and by training polling officials to disguise election fraud as administrative incompetence. They may also have to increase the rate of cheating in front of observers in order to overcome any fraud deterrence caused by the observation.

In this model, elections represent a gamble with a probabilistic outcome.[29] Across all leaders, the base probability of victory without fraud is assumed to be the same. Incumbents who do not win the election gain nothing, even if they invite observers. Those who win through election manipulation in the presence of observers must also pay the associated cost of election manipulation, although election manipulation makes victory more likely. Figure 1.1 illustrates the basic relationship between the probability of victory and the level of manipulation with and without international observers. The probability of victory for true democrats is labeled in the figure as p. Note that election fraud increases the probability of victory for pseudo-democrats (denoted as q), but this increased probability of victory comes at a price and is marginally more costly when observers are present. Benefits of winning the election

---

28. In the empirically unusual case that the domestic audience increases support for the incumbent because the incumbent invited observers, the sovereignty cost can be modeled as a benefit in the formal model and would increase the likelihood that observers are invited.

29. Cox, "Authoritarian Elections and Leadership Succession, 1975–2000."

come from both domestic and international sources. Domestic benefits associated with winning the election include salary and domestic prestige, which are available to both types of leaders. Following an election victory, the incumbent expects to receive some amount of international benefits based on the total value of their country's characteristics and the updated postelection beliefs among democracy promoters about their type.

When significant fraud is detected, observers issue a negative report, but if cheating is not detected, observers issue a positive report. Given that an incumbent is cheating, the probability that observers issue a negative report is influenced by the level and form of cheating committed. If the incumbent is a true democrat, cheating is never revealed to international observers and negative reports are never issued. For pseudo-democrats who engage in election manipulation, a negative report is possible but not certain and is determined by their success at manipulating the election in a manner that observers are unlikely to criticize. At the conclusion of the game, democracy promoters update their prior beliefs about whether the

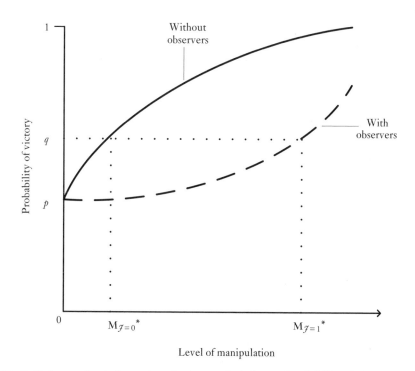

Figure 1.1. International observation, election manipulation, and probability of victory

incumbent leader is a true democrat or a pseudo-democrat and condition their support accordingly.

Although opposition parties are sometimes found to be guilty of election fraud, they do not determine whether observers are invited in the first place; therefore, this possibility is not modeled in my explanation of the decision to invite observers. Additionally, in investigating all negative reports from observers, I have found no cases in which international observers criticized an election when only opposition parties committed election fraud.

Signaling and the Dynamics of Norm Diffusion

Logically, if democracy-promoting actors believe that all true democrats invite international observers, any incumbent government that does not invite observers is assumed to be a pseudo-democrat. In the language of game theory, the norm of election monitoring is defined as the shared expectation among democracy promoters that all true democrats invite observers and receive their endorsement. The international norm of election observation therefore means that if democracy promoters observe that a government (of uncertain type) has refused to invite observers, or they observe that a government has received a negative report from observers, they update their postelection beliefs and assume that the leader is a pseudo-democrat. Using this conceptualization, explaining the creation of the norm is equivalent to explaining how this shared expectation that true democrats invite observers was generated.

Signaling behaviors are common in international relations. Generally, they are most useful when they allow other actors to distinguish between types of governments. If there are two types of governments, and only one type of actor is willing or able to send a specified signal, it is called a "separating equilibrium." In a separating equilibrium, a government can credibly signal its type to the intended recipient of the signal. A "pooling equilibrium" occurs when both types of governments are motivated to send the signal, but in this case the signal does not serve as a credible signal of a government's type. Also possible in many signaling games are semiseparating or semipooling equilibria in which one or more types send the signal some of the time. Under such scenarios, the recipients of the signal can infer some information about the incumbent's type based on whether or not the incumbent attempts to signal, but the signal does not allow other actors to clearly distinguish between types of governments.

I use this general model and the basic concepts underlying signaling games to explain the initiation and diffusion of election observation over time and to outline the motivations for changing behavior among leaders and democracy promoters. As with many signaling games, there are a number of possible equilibrium strategies, which are discussed in appendix A. In order to describe the causal dynamics of norm formation and diffusion over time and the relationship of my theory to signaling behaviors, I discuss various equilibria of the signaling game as they apply to specific periods in the overtime development of the norm of election observation.

In the period preceding the introduction of international election monitoring, states "pooled" on the decision not to invite observers. Neither true democrats nor pseudo-democrats invited observers, and neither type was expected to do so. Given the assumptions in the model, if there are no democracy promoters, or if the incumbent believes that democracy promoters will not recognize and reward the signal of inviting election monitors, whether a government invites observers is not a factor in postelection beliefs about the government's type, and there is therefore no incentive for governments to invite observers.

The equilibrium in which no incumbents choose to invite observers represents the world before election monitoring was initiated. This equilibrium changes if the true democrat believes that inviting election observers may be recognized as a signal of his or her type and there are potential rewards associated with such signaling. Rewards are possible when the democracy-contingent benefits outweigh the sovereignty costs associated with inviting observers and when inviting observers is assumed to be more costly for pseudo-democrats than for true democrats. Because gaining a positive report from observers is relatively easy for true democrats, who never commit election fraud, there is little risk to true democrats associated with inviting observers. As mentioned above, as more actors adopt the view that election observation is consistent with sovereignty and self-determination, sovereignty costs diminish. The growing number of well-respected democracies that have invited international observers since 2002 in part reflects the reduction in sovereignty costs associated with the normalization of election observation. This reduction is a consequence rather than a cause of the international norm.

For pseudo-democrats, the decision to invite observers is more complicated. Like true democrats, they consider the size of the potential democracy premium and sovereignty costs of inviting observers. In weighing the decision to invite observers, they also consider their ideal level of election manipulation, the probability that they will win given this level of election manipulation, the probability that they will receive a positive report from observers, the direct costs of cheating in front of election observers (such as fraud deterrence), and the effort devoted to cheating in front of observers. All else equal, if the democracy premium is large enough to outweigh the risks associated with inviting observers, pseudo-democrats have the incentive to do so. Under these conditions, however, if the democracy premium is large enough to outweigh these risks for pseudo-democrats, they should also outweigh the costs for true democrats. If any pseudo-democrats invite observers, then democracy promoters can reasonably believe that all true democrats invite observers. If true democrats have the incentive to invite election monitors, it should lead to the belief among democracy promoters that all true democrats invite observers, and that all noninviting states are necessarily pseudo-democrats. If such a belief develops, and if there is some possibility that pseudo-democrats can fool observers and receive a positive report, pseudo-democrats have the incentive to invite observers as well. Under such conditions, pseudo-democrats risk receiving a negative report when they invite observers, but failing to invite observers signals their type with certainty. If pro-democracy actors believe that all true democrats invite observers, the only condition under which the pseudo-democrat prefers not to invite observers is when there is no chance of fooling observers and gaining a positive report given their anticipated level and type of election fraud.

If democracy promoters exist, they seek to support true democrats and withhold benefits from pseudo-democrats, and the potential value of the democracy premium changes substantially over time. For both true democrats and pseudo-democrats to invite observers, the anticipated democracy premium must be large enough to outweigh the costs and risks associated with cheating in front of observers. Inviting observers can be the expected strategy for both types of incumbents when the democracy premium is sufficiently high and when pseudo-democrats can potentially gain a positive report from observers. Pseudo-democrats who invite observers must successfully hide or minimize election manipulation: if they do not, democracy promoters update their beliefs accordingly, and the incumbent faces the costs of having signaled that their government is an electoral autocracy.

The pool of countries expected to play the game is not necessarily uniform over time. It is possible that true democrats can graduate from the norm of election observation when there is no longer any uncertainty about their type. It is also possible that unambiguously autocratic governments can work to change their reputation by engaging in credible political liberalization. They can, for example, introduce elections, multiparty competition, and other democratic reforms, such as liberalization of the media.

Because refusing observers became a de facto admission of guilt by pseudo-democrats, however, the incentives faced by governments made it more likely that both types invited observers. The only governments refusing to invite observers became those holding the most blatantly rigged elections, such as Laos, North Korea, and Vietnam; those receiving foreign support for strategic reasons, such as Egypt; and those willing to go without Western support (perhaps because of high sovereignty costs imposed by anti-Western domestic audiences), such as Iran and Malaysia. Reduced sovereignty costs are also evidenced by the fact that even powerful democracy-promoting states began to invite international election observers, in part to avoid charges of hypocrisy from governments such as Belarus and Russia.

Thus, the norm in which all true democrats are expected to invite international observation of their elections leads to an equilibrium in which all true democrats invite observers and many pseudo-democrats attempt to invite observers. All noninviting countries are perceived to be pseudo-democracies or autocracies. Not all pseudo-democrats who invite observers are able to successfully imitate the signal, and some are documented as pseudo-democrats by international observers. Attempting to fake the signal imposes additional costs upon pseudo-democrats.

Explaining the norm of election monitoring requires that this model of individual decision making—in which each government makes a choice about whether observers should be invited—be extended to explain the global diffusion of election monitoring. The model described above and formalized in the appendices focuses on individual decision making but generates empirical predictions about how groups of leaders with specific characteristics should behave. In the early period of election monitoring, inviting observers was initiated by leaders who sought to increase their share of international benefits. The only internationally imposed cost was for leaders caught manipulating elections. In the second period, an exogenous increase in democracy-contingent benefits associated with the end of the Cold War gave nearly all true democrats the incentive to invite observers. As a result of this change in behavior, democracy-promoting actors developed the belief that all true democrats invite observers, which triggered the third stage of election monitoring, its rapid diffusion, and the establishment of international election observation as an international norm. Because the practice was initiated by state leaders seeking observers, and these leaders continued to invite observers, concerns among international actors about violating sovereignty were sidestepped. Predictably, leaders who refused observers after the norm developed justified their decision by arguing that observers violate state sovereignty. Additionally, the link between election observation and democracy, which was created and strengthened by leaders who invited observers in order to boost their democratic credentials, made it possible for international actors to accept election observation as a method of democracy promotion. This link was not obvious when election observation was initiated, but it has become so widely accepted that it now seems self-evident. Election observation is now a central component of democracy promotion, and the reports of observers are overtly linked to a variety of international benefits.

Costly Signals and Domestic Consequences

Because international observers may improve the quality of elections in countries with a history of election manipulation, election monitoring is an important tool of democracy promotion. The domestic consequences of election monitoring are also essential to evaluating my theory. For the signal of inviting international observers to be meaningful, it must be more costly for pseudo-democrats than for true democrats. True democrats should have nothing to hide, so inviting observers carries little risk, except for the sovereignty costs outlined above. When pseudo-democrats invite observers, they face a dilemma. They can hold a clean election and hope that they will win outright but plan to falsify or nullify the results if they lose. Or, they can manipulate the election, betting that efforts to conceal manipulation are successful and the level of observable manipulation is not sufficient to generate a negative report.

Pseudo-democrats may hold clean elections when they believe they are popular enough to win outright, but this does not eliminate potential costs associated with inviting observers. For these leaders, the uncertainty lies in their evaluation of their own popularity. Particularly in the first elections held after a period of nondemocratic rule, leaders are sometimes surprised to lose elections. Huntington calls these "stunning" elections, in which "authoritarian rulers sponsored elections and lost or did much worse than they and others anticipated."[30] Following an unexpected loss, the quintessential pseudo-democrat refuses to accept the result, such as in the 2008 elections in Zimbabwe. In these cases, the presence of observers can make it more difficult for leaders to cancel the election on trumped-up grounds, as Man-

---

30. Huntington, *The Third Wave*, 174–78.

uel Noriega learned in Panama in 1989. Observers draw disproportionate media attention and, as an impartial third-party, their judgment of the rightful victor has more credibility. Additionally, methods such as the parallel vote tabulation (also called the quick count) have made it relatively easy to prove that manipulation has taken place in the vote tabulation process.[31]

It is also possible that leaders may be so skilled at manipulation that observers fail to catch government-orchestrated election fraud. A direct test of this proposition is impossible, but improvements in election observation should mean that undetectable manipulation is increasingly expensive and rare. Observers have expanded the scope of their mission to include virtually all portions of the electoral process and to coordinate with domestic election observers and other domestic actors. Therefore, for perfectly concealed electoral manipulation to succeed it would have to be hidden not just from international observers but from all other actors, many of whom would have a vested interest in exposing efforts to manipulate the election. In theory, the forms of election manipulation that are less detectable should be more difficult, more costly, or more risky to carry out. Changing vote totals takes only the stroke of a pen. Covert election manipulation requires the capacity to manipulate effectively and unobtrusively and the use of only effective and concealed tools of election manipulation. For example, the now notorious pre-election poisoning of presidential candidate Viktor Yushchenko in the Ukraine was never traced and could be an example of well-concealed and indirect election manipulation.[32] Even in this case, however, because of other problems with the election, Ukraine received a strongly negative report from the OSCE/ODIHR. Manipulation of the electoral rules or gerrymandering are indirect and often legal, but even these forms of manipulation can provoke criticism from observers.[33]

When pseudo-democrats choose the second option and invite observers while manipulating the election, observers can have a variety of effects, including directly reducing election fraud, motivating pseudo-democrats to choose less effective or more expensive forms of manipulation, or condemning an election as fraudulent and therefore making international

---

31. Garber and Cowan, "The Virtues of Parallel Vote Tabulations"; Estok, Nevitte, and Cowan, *The Quick Count and Election Observation*; Bjornlund, *Beyond Free and Fair.*

32. Interestingly, both sides claim the Yushchenko poisoning was an effort to manipulate the election covertly: Yushchenko's opponents claim he did it to himself in a bid for sympathy and to discredit his opponent, and Yushchenko's party claims it was a deliberate effort to prevent him from winning.

33. Calingaert, "Election Rigging and How to Fight It"; Schedler, "The Nested Game of Democratization by Elections"; Birch, "Electoral Systems and Electoral Misconduct."

or domestic consequences more likely. Concealed forms of election manipulation may be more or less effective than ballot box stuffing or stealing vote totals, but the expanding scope of election monitoring should constrain the "menu of manipulation" available to pseudo-democrats.[34]

Empirical Implications

State Leaders and the Decision to Invite Observers

There is no single conclusive test of my argument. Rather, the dynamics outlined above generate a number of empirical implications about the diffusion of international election monitoring and the domestic consequences of observed elections. If my theory is true, the empirical evidence should be consistent with the implications outlined below. To be most convincing, I must also demonstrate a lack of support for alternative explanations, and this is considered separately in the relevant empirical chapters. The following twelve empirical implications follow directly from my theory and are presented in the order that they are evaluated in the remainder of the book.

First, because of the manner in which international benefits are allocated, Cold War alliances should dictate patterns of observation before 1989. The only governments likely to benefit from signaling a commitment to democracy during the Cold War should have been those that were already anti-communist. After the Cold War, the value of anti-communism decreased relative to democracy, and formerly communist or nonaligned states became eligible for democracy-contingent benefits.

1. Before 1989, only U.S. and Western allies should be eligible for democracy-contingent benefits. After 1989, all benefit-seeking governments should compete for democracy-contingent benefits. Therefore, only U.S. allies should invite observers during the Cold War, and U.S. and non-U.S. allies should invite observers after the Cold War.

The diffusion of election monitoring should also exhibit observable empirical patterns over time and space. My theory predicts that early inviters of international monitors should be different from those who invited them in the latter period of election monitoring. On average, they should be more democratic and hold cleaner elections in the early period

---

34. Schedler, "The Menu of Manipulation."

of election observation. As cheating pseudo-democrats began to mimic the signal of true democrats, the average level of democracy among inviting countries should decrease. Eventually, as election monitoring became an international norm and nearly all benefit-seeking governments had the incentive to invite observers, inviting countries should converge toward the average level of democracy throughout the developing world.

2. Initially, leaders who invite observers are likely to be more democratic than the average. Over time, there should be convergence between the average level of democracy in developing countries and the average level of democracy among governments that invite observers.

The third empirical implication stems in part from the observation that leaders with highly uncertain government types should have the most to gain by signaling their commitment to democracy. This tendency was recognized in the early 1990s by Samuel Huntington and Thomas Franck, two prominent scholars of democracy in political science and international law, respectively, who separately noted that international observers were expected at virtually all transitional elections.[35] Governments without experience with democracy should be the most likely to invite observers, such as those holding the first multiparty elections, governments holding elections after a nondemocratic alteration in power such as a coup, or those holding the first elections following independence.

3. Governments with highly uncertain regime types should be more likely to invite observers, including those holding the country's first multiparty elections, transitional governments holding elections following a period of nondemocratic rule, and elections held after previous elections had been suspended.

Conversely, governments with certain regime types, including unambiguously democratic and unambiguously autocratic governments, should be less likely to invite observers. Governments that successfully establish a reputation as fully democratic can graduate from the expectation that they should invite international observers. Two implications follow.

4. Countries that hold elections but that do not allow electoral competition should be unlikely to invite election observers.

35. Huntington, *The Third Wave*; Franck, "The Emerging Right to Democratic Governance."

5. Countries that are widely considered consolidated democracies or that become widely perceived as such after having invited observers should be unlikely to invite observers.

Similarly, increases in the probability that elections are observed should follow increases in the available democracy-contingent benefits, the existence of which may also vary by region.

6. The rate of election monitoring should increase with increases in available democracy-contingent benefits.

States receiving high levels of foreign support for other reasons should be less likely to invite observers, especially those states that are strategically important to the United States.

7. States that are strategically important to the United States for reasons unrelated to their regime type should be less likely to invite observers.

Democracy-Contingent Benefits and International Pressure

From the supply side of election monitoring, my theory suggests several patterns of behavior among democracy promoters. Changes in the provision of democracy-contingent benefits are modeled as an exogenous shock in my argument. Democracy promoters must have changed their behavior in order to generate such a shock and must have provided democracy-contingent benefits. Therefore, during the period in which election monitoring was initiated, some democracy-contingent benefits must exist and incumbents must be aware that they exist. Democracy promoters should link democracy-contingent benefits to election monitoring only after they believe that all true democrats invite observation. This generates an over-time prediction representing a corollary to (6) above.

8. Before election monitoring is initiated, there should be evidence of an increased link between democracy and international benefits. As election monitoring spreads, democracy promoters should marginally increase benefits to democratizing states but should link democracy-contingent benefits overtly to election monitoring only after the norm is generated or after they believe that all true democrats invite observers.

After election observation is accepted among democracy promoters as a valid signal, if pseudo-democrats are caught manipulating the election and observers issue a strongly negative report, pseudo-democrats should face various consequences. Leaders should forgo international benefits but may also face domestic protest and other costs for being internationally criticized for election fraud. International election observers are rarely the only voice criticizing a fraudulent election: domestic election observers, opposition political parties, and other governments also comment on election quality. It appears to be easier, however, for motivated regimes to discredit domestic actors as biased or as sore losers. Unlike domestic observers and opposition parties, international observers are relatively risk-free in their criticism, so when reputable observers do issue an overtly negative report, it is more likely to be viewed as credible. Additionally, their reputations are formed internationally, and when leaders attempt to discredit the reports of internationally reputable observers as biased, they are usually unsuccessful. Nevertheless, an important implication of the theory is that if a negative report is issued, the sanctioned government should face reduced or forgone international benefits.

9. Governments that invite observers and receive a negative report should receive reduced international benefits.

Similarly, as the norm took hold and democracy promoters developed the belief that all true democrats invite observers, those governments that refuse observers should be treated as pseudo-democracies by democracy-promoting actors.

10. After the norm developed, few governments should refuse observers, and there should be consequences for not inviting observers. Countries that do not invite observers should be perceived as pseudo-democrats.

Domestic Consequences of Election Observation

In addition to international reaction to negative reports, observers can potentially influence election fraud in a variety of ways. If observers reduce election fraud directly, they make it more difficult for leaders to steal votes on election day and effectively lower the vote share for cheating parties. Direct deterrence of manipulation may also take place in other periods of the electoral process. Leaders may be less likely to abuse state control of the media or shut down certain TV stations if international observers are monitoring the media and issuing regular reports on the amount of air time devoted to each candidate. Nevertheless, I focus primarily on the possibility that observers have a direct effect on election day behavior.

11. Election monitoring should be more costly to pseudo-democrats than true democrats. If observers reduce election fraud, pseudo-democrats should perform worse in the presence of observers.

My theory also predicts an evolving game of strategy between pseudo-democrats and international observers. Because observers prefer to be accurate, as more pseudo-democrats invite observers, election observers and democracy promoters have the incentive to develop better fraud-detection technology. As observers get better at catching fraud, pseudo-democrats should work to reduce the chances they will be criticized. The scope of monitoring and the ability of incumbents to conceal their cheating should therefore escalate jointly. It is not only international observers who benefit from higher-quality monitoring. As international actors accepted election observation as an international norm, it was used to distinguish between true democrats and pseudo-democrats. True democrats, international observers, and democracy promoters wish to increase the accuracy of the signal by making it more costly for pseudo-democrats to invite observers and get away with election manipulation.

12. Forms of manipulation and observation should change over time, with observers expanding their focus and manipulation becoming less direct as the quality of election monitoring improves.

Toward a Theory of Signaling Norms

Within the field of democratization, international pressure for democracy has made a number of other characteristics of democratic elections widespread, such as independent election commissions, nationally centralized voter registers, the publication of election results at polling stations, and the use of transparent ballot boxes, uniform ballots, and indelible ink. Although there are advocates for some of these practices, I would argue that the reason they have diffused is not because norm entrepreneurs campaigned for indelible ink to safeguard against multiple voting, for example, but rather because using indelible ink (and the iconic election day photos of smiling voters proudly displaying their purple fingers) has become a widely shared behavioral expectation and internationally recognized signal for governments holding elections in developing countries.

In much of the existing work on international norm formation, some actors have the incentive to promote the global diffusion of the new international norm. In the case of election observation, if I assume that democracy-contingent benefits are finite, it would not necessarily be in any actor's interest for the norm to develop, particularly when the practice was initiated and began to spread rapidly. Notably, the norm of election observation was actually generated in part by the actors who are most hurt by the normalization of the practice. In this case, true democrats face little cost if election observation becomes a widely accepted international norm, although they may face increased competition over scarce international benefits. Increasingly constrained pseudo-democrats, in contrast, would be better off if the norm did not exist.

This theory has the potential to explain a subset of international norms that have not attracted the support of committed activists, are not imposed by powerful states, and do not necessarily help facilitate international co-operation. Because of this, signaling norms may seem more benign or less interesting at first glance, but I argue that they are just as consequential as those that arise through other causal mechanisms, if not more so. They are the unintended result of strategic interaction, but they become an important part of the rules and norms governing international politics.

2

SOVEREIGN LEADERS
AND THE DECISION TO
INVITE OBSERVERS

The Costa Rican elections of February 1962 are widely cited as the first internationally observed election in a sovereign state, but they were not the first elections for which a government had sought international observers.[1] Four years earlier, the democratizing government of Costa Rica and the threatened Cuban dictatorship each attempted to invite international observers, foreshadowing the trajectory of international observation in which both true and pseudo-democrats invite foreign election monitors. These invitations were issued amid heated debates within the Americas about the relationship between democracy, anti-communism, and U.S. support for dictators in the Western Hemisphere. Costa Rica invited observers from the UN and the Organization of American States (OAS) to the 1958 elections for the purpose of making the election, in the words of President José Figueres, "an example to the Americas."[2] The *New York Times* coverage describes the extensive efforts undertaken by the Costa Rican government to identify a credible signal of the quality of their democratic institutions:

> Dr. Alberto F. Canas, representative of Costa Rica at the United Nations, said today that the presidential election in his country next February would be the first to be conducted in Latin America with neutral observers

---

1. See Slater, *The OAS and United States Foreign Policy;* Beigbeder, *International Monitoring of Plebiscites, Referenda and National Elections;* Santa-Cruz, "Constitutional Structures, Sovereignty, and the Emergence of Norms"; McCoy, "Monitoring and Mediating Elections during Latin American Democratization"; Middlebrook, *Electoral Observation and Democratic Transitions in Latin America;* Legler, Lean, and Boniface, *Promoting Democracy in the Americas;* Organization of American States, "Supporting the Electoral Process."

2. Special to the *New York Times,* "Costa Rica Inviting Election Observers," *New York Times,* January 16, 1958.

present under the auspices of an international organization. The initiative came from the Costa Rican Government and was a voluntary move, he added....President José Figueres asked Secretary General Dag Hammarskjöld to submit a list of individuals from democratic countries around the world, as potential observers of the balloting. On Sunday Dr. Canas will fly to San José with the confidential list delivered to him today.[3]

President Figueres' reputation as the country's "father of democracy"[4] and his vehement opposition to other dictatorships in the region made him one of the hemisphere's leaders in lobbying the U.S. and other governments to adopt more explicitly pro-democracy foreign policies. Despite his efforts to attract foreign observers, the UN and the OAS denied the government's request to provide official observers for the 1958 Costa Rican elections, and no record of a formal observation mission has been uncovered.[5]

Several months later, the Cuban government also attempted to invite international election observers. Facing threat from Fidel Castro, an arms embargo, and pressure from the United States "to curtail repression and hold honest elections without his own participation,"[6] Batista scheduled multiparty elections, allowed opposition candidates to run, and released a number of political prisoners.[7] In November of 1958, following demands from the opposition parties, Batista invited international observers from the OAS and the UN to monitor the elections.[8] Both organizations refused to send observers, but the invitation stands out as an early example of a government with few democratic credentials attempting to demonstrate its new—and likely false—commitment to democratic elections following heavy international and domestic pressure for political liberalization.

Although the central question of this book is ultimately why inviting foreign observers became an international norm, the first question to ask is why leaders invite observers at all. This chapter evaluates why leaders began inviting election monitoring and why election observation spread throughout the world by using a variety of empirical evidence, including

3. Special to the *New York Times*, "Vote Will Be Observed: U.N. Hands Costa Rica List of Individuals She Requested," *New York Times*, December 14, 1957.

4. United Press International, "José Figueres, Father of Costa Rican Democracy, Dies," *UPI*, June 8, 1990.

5. It is possible that the three observers suggested by the United Nations were present for the 1958 Costa Rican elections.

6. Aguila, *Cuba*, 36.

7. Braddock, "1958 Elections."

8. Special to the *New York Times*, "Cuba Will Accept Voting Observers," *New York Times*, October 18, 1958.

government rhetoric about the decision to invite observers and cross-national data from 1960 to 2006 documenting when and where election monitoring diffused. The evidence in this chapter evaluates and lends support to the first seven empirical implications outlined in chapter 1, all of which focus on explaining the decision by governments to invite election monitors. I conclude the chapter by discussing the normalization of election monitoring, including its nearly universal spread, even among the long-term developed democracies.

Early Inviters and the Diffusion of Election Observation

The early history of election observation shows a majority of cases in which leaders were attempting to demonstrate that they were leading genuine transitions to democracy, and a few cases, such as in the Dominican Republic in 1966, Bolivia in 1978, and Nicaragua in 1963, in which electoral autocrats attempted to bring some undeserved democratic legitimacy to their continued rule by holding elections and allowing a managed transition to a puppet president. International election monitoring had previously taken place only in nonsovereign or trust territories, most commonly for plebiscites on territorial issues.[9]

Although these first cases are notable for initiating the practice of international election monitoring in sovereign states, such as those in Costa Rica and the Dominican Republic in the 1960s, they are distinct. The rate of observed elections continued at less than five per year until the early 1970s. With several exceptions, these early missions sent only one or two observers to the capital city on election day and rarely criticized elections.[10] No elections were observed between 1973 and 1976, with the practice picking up again in the late 1970s.[11]

As election observation spread, observers were particularly likely to be invited to high-profile elections following transitions from authoritarian rule in which the government's commitment to democracy was uncertain. For example, the 1984 Guatemalan elections were observed by the OAS following a 1983 coup. The Efraín Ríos Montt government, remembered

---

9. Wambaugh, *Plebiscites since the World War*; Wambaugh, *A Monograph on Plebiscites*; Joseph Coy Green Papers, *Report of the Allied Mission to Observe the Greek Elections*.

10. Reports from the 1962 and 1966 Dominican elections suggest that foreign observers were willing to criticize elections, but they simply chose not to do so based on their observations of the quality of the election.

11. Legler, Lean, and Boniface, *Promoting Democracy in the Americas*.

for the worst human rights abuses in Guatemala's history, was deposed in a coup led by Oscar Mejías.[12] Although Mejías came to power through blatantly undemocratic means, he attempted to manage a return to democracy in Guatemala. He lifted the state of siege, put forth electoral laws, allowed political activity that had been banned under Ríos Montt, and did not permit his government to support any parties or candidates. Concluding his role in the transition, he did not run for office and allowed another individual to be elected president.[13]

In El Salvador, the OAS observed the 1982 elections to the constituent assembly that were conducted in an attempted return to democracy. In 1984 presidential elections were held amid widespread violence.[14] The OAS also sent observers to these elections, and pro-United States and anti-communist candidate José Duarte was elected. Other notable elections include Grenada in 1984 following the 1983 U.S. invasion; the 1978 general elections in the Dominican Republic, in which Joaquín Balaguer (Trujillo's former puppet president) was voted out of office; and the 1978 national assembly elections in Panama in which there was a peaceful transfer of power.

Leaders of sovereign states outside Latin America also began to invite observers in the 1980s. After having observed elections for independence in several nonsovereign states such as Rhodesia in 1979, the Commonwealth began observing elections in newly sovereign states in Africa with observation missions in Zimbabwe and Uganda in 1980.[15]

By the mid-1980s, increasingly blatant pseudo-democrats began to seek international observers. The growing strength of the link between democracy and internationally observed elections meant that pro-democracy advocates—both domestically and internationally—began to pressure for observers. Government rhetoric displays the reluctance of these pseudo-democrats to invite observers as well as their attempts to manipulate them. Before the 1986 "snap" elections in the Philippines, the foreign minister was quoted as saying that "[t]he Republic of the Philippines is a sovereign and independent state, with the supreme authority to conduct its electoral processes any way it sees fit" and that Marcos was under "no obligation"

12. Sanford, *Buried Secrets: Truth and Human Rights in Guatemala.*
13. McCleary, "Guatemala's Postwar Prospects."
14. Montgomery, *Revolution in El Salvador.*
15. The Commonwealth is an international organization based in London, with fifty four member states as of 2010. It was formalized as an organization when the British Empire dissolved, and many member states are former British colonies. The Commonwealth also observed elections in the nonsovereign countries of British Guiana (1964), Mauritius (1967), and Gibraltar (1967).

to invite observers but did so as "a gesture of the good faith" and to prove that "we are a government of laws."[16] President Ferdinand Marcos announced his decision to invite international observers on a television program that was broadcast in the United States and the Philippines:

> You're all invited to come and we will invite the members of the American Congress to please come and see what is happening here. All this talk about fraud—that's sour grapes [from] all these poor losers.[17]

After twenty-six years of single-party rule, President Kenneth Kaunda of Zambia agreed in July of 1990 to allow a national referendum on one-party rule. He proposed the referendum following an attempted coup and during widespread unrest over increases in the price of food. Kaunda was also facing serious international pressure, having defaulted on a $23 million payment to the World Bank. In response to the proposed referendum, opposition groups and trade unions demanded the end to a nearly three-decade-long state of emergency, the legalization of opposition parties, and the presence of international observers. By September 1990, Kaunda scrapped plans for the referendum in favor of multiparty elections, and by February 1991, he had agreed to invite foreign observers, including the Commonwealth, the Carter Center, and the National Democratic Institute, which helped organize and fund a broad-based domestic election monitoring network.

Displaying tactics that have become common among pseudo-democrats, in the year before the elections Kaunda's government "arrested political opponents, banned opposition gatherings, fired critics from within the ruling party and unleashed riot police on protesters…fired the chief editors of the country's two daily newspapers" and prohibited the government printing press from producing an independent weekly paper.[18] The government also attempted to manipulate and discredit international observers after they had issued somewhat critical statements about the government's preparations for elections and its misuse of state resources. Kaunda's campaign ran a full-page newspaper advertisement alleging that the international observers were biased and that they were in conspiracy

---

16. Quote and paraphrase from R. Gregory Nokes, "Administration Studying Aid Use in Philippines," The Associated Press, January 22, 1986.

17. Fernando del Mundo. Newswire report. United Press International, November 3, 1985.

18. Melinda Ham, "Kaunda Manipulates Media in Struggle for Political Survival," Associated Press, January 2, 1991.

to overthrow him.[19] Yet despite these efforts Kaunda lost to Frederick Chiluba and, surprising many witnesses to the event, peacefully stepped down and respected the results of the country's first multiparty elections.

Pro-democracy domestic actors also began pressuring for observers in some countries. Some pseudo-democrats also came under pressure from domestic constituencies with an interest in signaling the country's commitment to democracy and potentially exposing the country's leadership as less than democratic. In inviting observers from the Commonwealth Secretariat to the 1990 elections, Malaysian Prime Minister Mahathir Mohamed explained his decision, saying that "we suspect certain groups are already plotting to smear the image of the country in the next election" and that "it is vital that we get outside people with no interest to witness and observe our election."[20]

Although individual leaders invite international observers for diverse reasons, early election monitoring is notable for its signaling character. The rhetorical justifications used by leaders to explain their decision to invite observers suggest that they were primarily interested in finding a way to signal the quality of their elections to international and domestic audiences. Arguing for international observers for the 1997 elections in Jamaica, the president of the Jamaica Manufacturers' Association said that inviting observers "would send a signal to the international community that our democratic process is open." Jamaican Prime Minister Percival Patterson initially refused international observers, complaining that "it would be a travesty to the legacy of our democratic reputation were we now to suggest that we are incapable, as a country, to administer our electoral or other affairs."[21] Patterson later relented, inviting an official delegation from the Carter Center.

That inviting international election observers became a widely accepted signal of democratic elections is perhaps an historical accident I document in greater detail in chapter 3. However, election monitoring became a credible signal of a government's commitment to democratic elections because observers made it more difficult for pseudo-democrats to cheat and get away with it and because attempts by pseudo-democrats to discredit election monitoring as unwanted foreign intervention were undermined

19. Obinna Anyadike, "Zambia: Commonwealth Observers Demand an Apology from Kaunda," IPS-Inter Press Service, October 28, 1991.

20. "Malaysia to Invite Observers for General Elections," Xinhua Genera News Service, June 21, 1990.

21. Lloyd Williams, "Jamaican Leader: International Elections Observers Not Necessary," Associated Press Worldstream, April 7, 1997.

by the increasing numbers of countries seeking international monitors. As the reputation of observers began to spread and it became clear that they were willing to criticize fraudulent elections, as more countries began holding elections in which the intentions of the government were uncertain, and as election monitors criticized several high-profile elections, pro-democracy domestic groups began to voice their support for inviting observers. Domestic support for observers was far from universal, however, with some arguing that they "sprinkled holy water on a rigged process."[22] Nevertheless, the incentive for leaders to find a signal of their commitment to democratization led them to invite observers, even when (or perhaps because) doing so would increase the risk that election fraud would be caught and condemned. I now turn to a cross-national quantitative evaluation of the spread of election monitoring and more explicit evaluation of the first seven empirical implications outlined in chapter 1.

Global Data on Elections and Election Observation

Much of the quantitative evidence in this chapter is drawn from an original dataset on national election events in the developing world. When beginning research for this project, existing data on elections were inadequate or incomplete, particularly for elections held in nondemocratic regimes. Because part of the puzzle is why leaders invite international monitors to undemocratic elections, including even the worst elections in the analysis is particularly important. My dataset includes all national elections from 1960 to 2006 in countries with a population greater than 500,000. Appendix B provides a more detailed codebook, lists the primary sources, and lists all countries included and excluded from the analysis.

Coding National Elections

Each observation in the dataset is a separate election in an independent state. If multiple offices are elected on the same day (or during one consecutive multiday election period), the election is treated as one observation. Elections on separate days, even when held in the same country in the same year, are treated as separate observations (for example, a legislative election in June and a presidential election in December are counted as separate observations). Although data were collected on multiround elections, the statistical analysis examines only first-round elections because

---

22. Beigbeder, *International Monitoring of Plebiscites, Referenda and National Elections*, 297.

the decision to invite observers in the second round is completely determined by first-round invitations. National referenda on constitutional or other substantive issues were excluded because they represent different strategic decisions made by the incumbent leader. In some isolated cases, incumbents held referenda on their own continued rule. Referenda on the continued rule of the executive are equivalent to elections with only one candidate, and both are included.

Defining Internationally Observed Elections

For every election event, I also code whether the election was internationally observed. International election observers are official delegations of foreigners who observe and report on the electoral process. In nearly all cases, international observers were formally invited by the host government. There are some minor exceptions to this rule, discussed below. Sometimes the incumbent government delegates the decision to invite observers to an agent, such as the central election commission. However, because international observers must be allowed access to the electoral process in order to do their job (which includes entering polling stations on election day and observing the vote tabulation process), it is difficult for them to observe without official credentials from the host government. Even in cases in which observers are issued a formal invitation by a government agent, the central government retains the residual ability to prevent them from entering the country to observe on election day. In 2005, the rule that observers must be invited was institutionalized in the *Declaration of Principles for International Election Observation*. The document, signed by more than twenty of the largest and most respected organizations that sponsor observation missions, states that an international observation mission should not be recognized as such unless the election-holding country, "issues an invitation or otherwise indicates its willingness to accept international election observation missions."[23]

Data were collected from election observation missions whose quality varied, including observers whose reputation suggests that they always approve elections regardless of their quality. No organizations sending official delegations of foreign observers were excluded from the data, although I explore varying quality of observers in chapter 5. Election monitoring data were collected in two ways. First, information was collected

---

23. UN, *Declaration of Principles for International Election Observation and Code of Conduct for International Election Observers.*

directly from organizations that sponsor election observation missions. Because some reports have been lost or were never made public, and because some organizations do not keep comprehensive documentation of all observer missions, for each election after 1978 newswire reports for dates surrounding elections were also searched for mention of international observers.[24] In this manner, the record of whether an election was monitored was checked by organization and by election. Additional information from case studies and scholarly articles supplemented these sources.[25]

There are four types of borderline cases in coding observed elections. In a handful of elections, observers were invited and deployed, but because the conditions were judged to be so poor that a democratic election was impossible, the missions withdrew before election day. In these cases, when the observer mission issues a report on the quality of the election but suspends the mission before election day, I coded the election as observed.

As election observation began to spread throughout Latin America in the late 1970s, there was some debate about which domestic actors had the authority to invite international observers. In some cases, the agreed upon standard was that if all political parties requested observers, they considered themselves invited. Additionally, in several isolated cases between 1978 and 1984, domestic human rights organizations, such as the Guyana Human Rights Association, extended invitations to international election observers directly, and observers from international human rights organizations such as the International Human Rights Law Group or the British Parliamentary Human Rights Group accepted. These elections are coded as internationally observed.

There are also several cases in which autocratic regimes "invited" observers via press release on the newswire, but the invitation was not perceived as credible and no observers were willing or able to accept the invitation. For example, Saddam Hussein's regime officially announced that they had invited 10,000 foreign observers to the 1995 Iraqi elections in which he was the only candidate. No specific organizations were invited, no official delegations were deployed to the country, and no reports were issued. This election and several others like it were not coded as internationally observed even though an invitation to observers was technically issued.

---

24. The terms "international," "foreign," "monitor," and "observer" were used in Lexis-Nexis searches.

25. Legler, Lean, and Boniface, *Promoting Democracy in the Americas.*

Finally, there are some reports of "international observers" that are, in fact, direct representatives of individual governments and that observe the election only for internal purposes. These delegations are usually not invited, and they typically do not issue public reports on the quality of the election. They are also more likely to be viewed as biased toward one candidate or party. In general, I do not code these delegations as international observers because they do not issue public reports on election quality and are frequently indistinguishable from foreign embassy staff, which have long paid close attention to election day proceedings in the countries in which they are stationed. There are, however, cases in which these country-sponsored delegations joined with official observer missions from intergovernmental organizations (IGOs) or international nongovernmental organizations (INGOs), or combined with representatives of other countries under "coordination and support" by the UN. These missions are coded as official international observers despite the involvement of embassy staff.

Therefore, for each election (each observation in the dataset), there is an indication of whether it was observed and by whom. Many elections are observed by multiple groups, and both international NGOs and IGOs are recorded as sponsors of observation missions.[26]

26. The majority of election-monitoring missions were carried out by the following organizations: NGOs include the Asian Network for Free Elections, Carter Center, Electoral Institute of Southern Africa, International Foundation for Electoral Systems, International Human Rights Law Group, International Republican Institute for International Affairs, National Democratic Institute, and the Washington Office on Latin America. IGOs include the African Union (formerly Organization of African Unity), Caribbean Community and Common Market, Commonwealth Secretariat, Commonwealth of Independent States, Council of Europe, Economic Community of East African States, European Union, Organization of American States, Organisation Internationale de La Francophonie, Organization for Security and Cooperation in Europe's Office of Democratic Institutions and Human Rights, Parliamentary Assembly Council of Europe, Southern African Development Community, and the United Nations. Other organizations recorded in the dataset as having deployed one or more international observer missions include the Andean Parliament, Andean Community, Arab Centre for the Independence of the Judiciary and Legal Professions, Arab League, Arab Maghreb Union, Association of Asian Election Authorities, Association of Central and East European Election Officials, Association of European Parliamentarians for Africa, British Helsinki Human Rights Group, Canadian Association of Former Parliamentarians, Center for Exchange and Solidarity, Common Market for Eastern and Southern Africa, Community of Portuguese Speaking Countries (CPLP), Community of Sahel-Saharan States, East African Community, Economic Community of Central African States, European Elections Observatory, European Federation of Liberian Associations, European Network of Election Monitoring Organizations, Freedom House, Global Exchange, Helsinki Committee of Norway, Indian Ocean Commission, International Mission for Iraqi Elections,

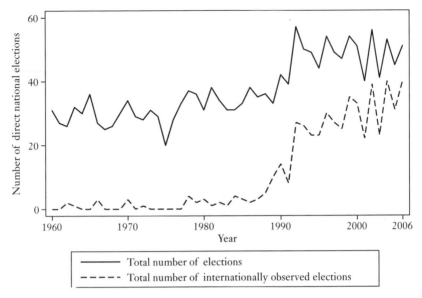

Figure 2.1. Total number of elections per year, 1960–2006
Source: Author
Note: Includes 1,759 elections in 157 independent states.

Trends in International Election Monitoring

Earlier I presented the puzzle of election observation in part by showing the rate of internationally observed elections over time, as well as the percentage of those elections that received negative reports (see introduction, figure I.1). As illustrated in greater detail in figure 2.1, the total number of elections, as well as the rate of observed elections, increased substantially between the 1980s and 1990s, when the number of states in the international system also grew.[27]

International Mission for Monitoring Haitian Elections, Islamic Conference Organization, Jewish Institute for National Security Affairs, Latin American Studies Association, NATO Parliamentary Assembly, Pacific Islands Forum Secretariat, Parliamentary Confederation of the Americas (COPA), Research Group on the Democratic, Economic and Social Development of Africa (GERDDES-Africa), Shanghai Cooperation Organization, South American Common Market (MERCOSUR), South African Association for Regional Cooperation, South Asian Association for Regional Cooperation, United Kingdom Parliamentary Human Rights Group, West Africa Civil Society Forum, and the West African Economic and Monetary Union (UEMOA).

27. Fazal, "State Death in the International System"; Lake and O'Mahony, "The Incredible Shrinking State."

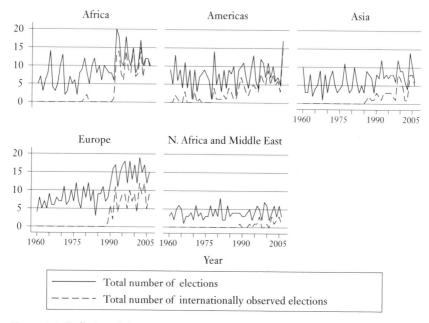

Figure 2.2. Diffusion of elections and election observation by region

These trends also exhibit strong regional dynamics, as shown in figure 2.2. Election observation was initiated and spread first in Latin America.[28] Europe and Africa display similar patterns, with a dramatic increase in both elections and election monitoring in 1990. In Asia, election observation began in the mid-1980s but increased only gradually in the 1990s. Finally, in North Africa and the Middle East, elections are not as frequent, and it remains the region with the lowest rate of election monitoring.

Cold War Politics and Patterns of Diffusion

The end of the Cold War brought with it a dramatic change in the types of countries that could seek democracy-contingent benefits. During the Cold War, U.S. and allied preferences for supporting anti-communist countries meant that this variable outweighed any preference for democracy

---

28. Lean, "External Validation and Democratic Accountability"; Santa-Cruz, "Constitutional Structures, Sovereignty, and the Emergence of Norms."

Table 2.1. Observed elections and Cold War alliances, 1962–1988

Alliance	Country
Allied with USSR	Nicaragua (1963, 1972, 1984)
Nonaligned (residual category)	Guyana (1980); Uganda (1980); Zimbabwe (1979, 1980)
Allied with United States	Argentina (1983); Bolivia (1966, 1978, 1979); Chile (1988); Costa Rica (1962, 1966, 1970, 1978, 1982); Dominican Republic (1962, 1966, 1970, 1978); Ecuador (1968); El Salvador (1982, 1984, 1985, 1988); Guatemala (1970, 1984, 1985); Haiti (1987, 1988); Honduras (1981, 1985); Pakistan (1988); Paraguay (1988); Panama (1978); Philippines (1986, 1987); South Korea (1987); Trinidad and Tobago (1986); Uruguay (1984)

Notes: Cold War alliance patterns coded from Walt (1987). State membership and dates of independence from Gleditsch and Ward (1999).

in countries that were not recognized as anti-communist. The diminished importance of anti-communism as a state-level characteristic was most visible in Africa, where many governments during the Cold War sought international benefits by engaging the United States or the USSR in a bidding war for their allegiance. After the few cases of Commonwealth observation in Africa in the early 1980s, no elections were observed in sovereign African states until the 1991 elections in Zambia.

The first empirical implication outlined in chapter 1 specified that democracy-contingent benefits should be available only to a subset of states during the Cold War, and that before 1989, only anti-communist Western allies should have invited international observers. As shown in table 2.1, the pattern of observed elections in the early period of election observation closely correlates with Cold War alliance patterns: the only Soviet ally to invite international observers before 1989 was Nicaragua (whose alliance switched during the Cold War), and only three nonaligned countries invited observers, all of which are former British colonies.

Alliance patterns also roughly illustrate which countries were positioned to benefit the most from inviting observers at the end of the Cold War. Table 2.2 shows the breakdown of observed elections during this transition by Cold War alliance patterns from 1989 to 1994, with the addition of a category for states that became independent in 1989 or later. Election observation was no longer confined to U.S. allies, and the rates of election observation among former Soviet allies and nonaligned states increased substantially.

Table 2.2. Observed elections and Cold War alliance patterns, 1989–1994

Alliance	Country
Allied with USSR	Albania (1992); Angola (1992); Bulgaria (1990, 1991, 1994); Burundi (1993); Congo (1992, 1993); Czechoslovakia (1990, 1992); East Germany (1990); Estonia (1992); Ethiopia (1994); Guinea (1993); Hungary (1990, 1994); Madagascar (1992, 1993); Mali (1992); Mongolia (1990, 1992, 1993); Mozambique (1994); Nicaragua (1990); Poland (1991); Romania (1990, 1992); Russia (1989, 1990, 1993); Yugoslavia (1992); Zambia (1991)
Nonaligned (residual category)	Bangladesh (1991); Cambodia (1993); Cameroon (1992); Central African Republic (1992, 1993); Djibouti (1992, 1993); Gabon (1993); Ghana (1992); Guinea-Bissau (1994); Guyana (1992); Lesotho (1993); Malawi (1994); Nepal (1991, 1994); Niger (1993); Peru (1992); South Africa (1994); Sri Lanka (1989); Togo (1993, 1994); Uganda (1994)
Allied with United States	Bolivia (1989, 1993); Chile (1989); Colombia (1994); Costa Rica (1990); Dominican Republic (1990, 1994); El Salvador (1989, 1991, 1994); Guatemala (1990); Haiti (1990); Honduras (1989, 1993); Kenya (1992); Malaysia (1990); Mexico (1994); Morocco (1993); Pakistan (1990, 1993); Panama (1989, 1991, 1994); Paraguay (1989, 1991, 1993); Senegal (1993); Tunisia (1989); Uruguay (1989); Venezuela (1993)
Newly independent states (post-1988)	Azerbaijan (1992, 1993); Belarus (1994); Croatia (1992, 1993); Georgia (1992); Kazakhstan (1994); Latvia (1993); Lithuania (1992); Macedonia (1994); Moldova (1994); Namibia (1994); Slovenia (1992); Ukraine (1994); Uzbekistan (1994)

Notes: Cold War alliance patterns coded from Walt (1987). State membership and dates of independence from Gleditsch and Ward (1999).

Pre- and post-Cold War trends should also be visible in the existing level of democracy in countries that invite foreign observers. The second empirical implication outlined in chapter 1 described the types of governments likely to initiate election monitoring. Early inviters should be more democratic than average until the norm is established. As pseudo-democrats mimic the signal of true democrats and all true democrats continue inviting, the average level of democracy in inviting countries should converge with the global average. Figure 2.3 presents a visual representation of the types of countries likely to invite observers by plotting the average *POLITY* scores among countries that invited observers (using a locally weighted regression line) against the average *POLITY*

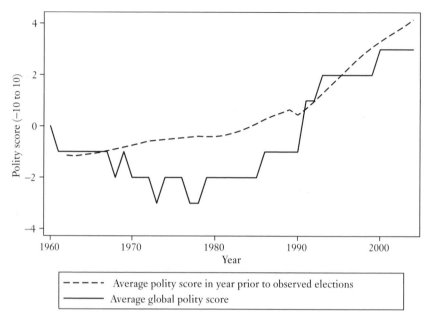

Figure 2.3. Regime type in observed elections vs. global average

score across all countries in the world. All scores for observed elections lag by one year to exclude changes caused by the observed elections. Note that the average *POLITY* scores in the first observed elections in the 1960s were close to the global mean. From 1970 to 1990, observers were more likely to be invited to elections in countries with more democratic political institutions than the global average, which is consistent with the idea that relatively more democratic countries initiated the trend of election observation. From 1990 to the present, the means converge as elections and election observation spread widely.

To look at this trend of decreasing quality of observed elections from another angle, I also examine the over-time changes in election monitoring based on whether there were domestic pre-election concerns about election fraud (see appendix B). This indicator provides an alternative measure of the average characteristics of elections to which observers were invited. As shown in figure 2.4, although the rate of elections with pre-election concerns about fraud is relatively constant over time, averaging about 40% of elections in the developing world, the percentage of these elections that were observed approached 100% by 2006.

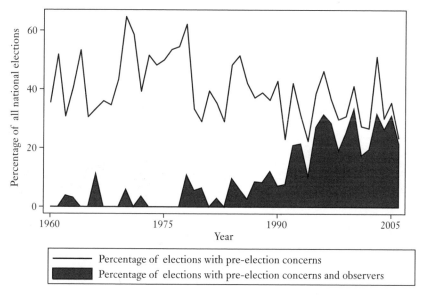

Figure 2.4. Elections with pre-election concerns about fraud
Sources: Author and NELDA
Note: Includes 1,759 elections in 157 independent states.

The third implication of the model outlined in chapter 1 relates to *ex ante* uncertainty among other international actors about a government's "type." Governments of widely known type should not invite observers, whereas governments of more uncertain types should converge quickly toward inviting observers during periods in which it is clear that democracy-contingent benefits exist. I examine three likely election-specific indicators of uncertainty about a government's commitment to democracy: elections held by transitional governments following a period of nondemocratic rule, elections held after previous elections had been suspended, and governments holding the country's first multiparty elections. All of these trends fluctuate significantly over the period under study. Nevertheless, as figures 2.5–2.7 show, "uncertain" types of governments became highly likely to invite international observers by the early 1990s. For example, before 1988, 23% of elections were observed if they were run by a transitional government tasked with holding elections. After 1988, 85% of these elections were internationally monitored, and after 1995, 100% were internationally observed. Similar trends are shown for a country's first multiparty elections and elections held after elections were suspended, with invitations to observers at all three types of elections approaching 100% by the mid-1990s.

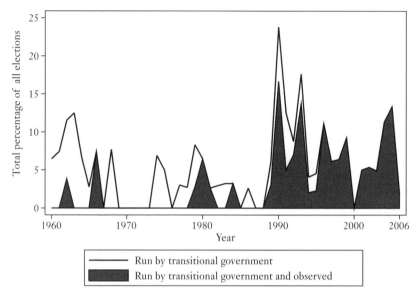

Figure 2.5. Elections held by transitional government
Sources: Author and NELDA
Note: Includes 1,759 elections in 157 independent states.

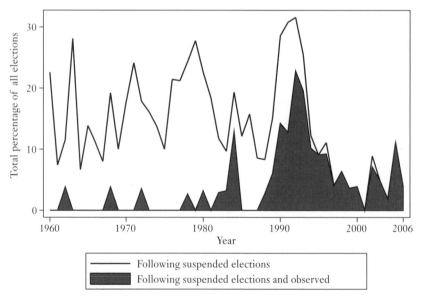

Figure 2.6. Elections held following suspended elections
Sources: Author and NELDA
Note: Includes 1,759 elections in 157 independent states.

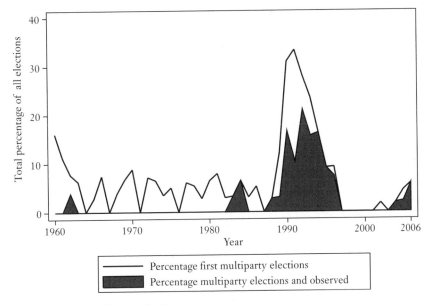

Figure 2.7. First multiparty elections
Sources: Author and NELDA
Note: Includes 1,759 elections in 157 independent states.

Cross-National Analysis

Building on these descriptive statistics, I now turn to a more comprehensive evaluation of the correlates of observed elections. I argue that leaders began inviting international scrutiny of their elections in part because they believed that they would be better off by signaling their commitment to democratization. For leaders committed to holding democratic elections, the decision to invite observers is determined by their likely share of international benefits and the uncertainty among democracy promoters about their commitment to democracy. For pseudo-democrats, their decision to invite observers is based on the potential benefits from democracy promoters relative to the possibility that they will be caught committing election fraud. In addition to providing graphical documentation of the relevant trends over time, I use regression analysis to show that the cross-national evidence is consistent with my argument. Because of the clear break in the rate of election monitoring at the end of the Cold War and the complexity of modeling such time trends in data that are not traditional time-series cross-sectional, I focus the analysis only on the 1991–2005 period. Additionally, election monitoring before 1991 is a relatively rare event, and data on several important variables of interest, such as democracy-contingent benefits, are not available.

In my theory, focusing on the 1991–2005 period in which election monitoring is known to exist and be available in all regions of the world, two general sets of variables are important in explaining a given state's decision to invite observers. The first set of variables pertains to whether there is existing pre-election uncertainty about a given government's type. There are several ways to think about uncertainty in this context. First, there are some types of governments for which little ambiguity exists about their status as a democracy. Governments that never hold national elections, such as China and Saudi Arabia, are clearly perceived as nondemocracies. In order to be part of the relevant universe of cases included in this study, a government must hold elections. However, if the government holds elections in which opposition electoral competition is banned, there is little chance that they will be able to mimic the signal of true democrats, even if they invite election observers. I therefore include a measure of whether opposition parties are allowed to participate in elections, a variable called *Opposition Competition*. This is a dichotomous indicator that is equal to one if all of the following three conditions hold: opposition parties are legal, opposition parties are allowed (even minimally), and there is a choice of candidates on the ballot. If any of these conditions do not hold, or if there is any uncertainty or ambiguity about whether these conditions hold, the variable is coded as zero. *Opposition Competition* should be positively associated with the probability that observers are present at an election.

Similarly, if a country is already a consolidated democracy, or becomes widely viewed as a consolidated democracy, it should be less likely to invite observers during the 1991–2005 time period. Note that this has begun to change, especially since 2006, as all OSCE members, including countries such as Belgium, France, the UK, and the United States, have recently invited observers. The spread of election observation to developed democracies is further evidence of the normalization of election observation and is discussed in greater detail at the end of this chapter. Nevertheless, between 1990 and 2006 there is little evidence that the democratic credentials in the long-term developed democracies of Western Europe and North America were questioned, nor were Japan, Australia, or New Zealand.[29] After 1989, countries that were successful in

---

29. The long-term developed democracies are those countries that have been continuously democratic for forty years or more, as coded by Lijphart ("Patterns of Democracy") and that were also OECD members in 1960. These twenty-three countries are Australia, Austria, Belgium, Canada, Denmark, Finland, France, Germany, Greece, Iceland, Ireland,

joining the European Union are also coded as consolidated democracies beginning in the year that they formally became members of the organization. I code Israel and India as consolidated democracies, although the results are not sensitive to the classification of these two states. Additionally, several countries initially invited international observers but became widely perceived as democracies and were told as much by international monitoring organizations. These countries included Chile after 1992 and the Czech Republic after 2003. Therefore, I code *Consolidated Democracy* as one if the country is one of the long-term developed democracies, is a member of the European Union, or was told explicitly and publically by a well-respected international monitoring group that it no longer needed to invite international observers because their elections were now considered democratic.

Uncertainty about the quality of the process should also influence whether leaders invite observers. Elections held following an interruption of democratic rule are highly uncertain and can lead to democratization or further entrenchment of autocracy. Given my argument, elections with high levels of uncertainty should be more likely to be observed. I therefore include measures of whether the election is the first multiparty election (*First Multiparty*), whether previous elections had been suspended (*Suspended Elections*), and whether the election was run by transitional leadership tasked with holding elections (*Transitional Leadership*). As I argued above, all three variables imply uncertainty about the government's commitment to democratization and represent situations in which existing information about the government's commitment to democracy is frequently low. I include them as individual variables in a model and then create an aggregate variable called *Uncertain Type* that is equal to one if the elections are the first multiparty elections, if previous elections had been suspended, or if the elections were held by transitional leadership.

In my theory, leaders are aware of their potential share of international benefits before they choose to invite observers. Leaders vary, however, in their preferred types of such benefits and may seek a reward such as international legitimacy, which is not easily quantifiable. Recall that leaders should be responding to a change in the weight given to democracy relative to other characteristics valued by powerful international actors. The ideal cross-national measure of international benefits would be an evaluation of what each state leader expected to receive as a result of inviting

---

Italy, Japan, Luxembourg, Netherlands, New Zealand, Norway, Portugal, Spain, Sweden, Switzerland, United Kingdom, and United States. International system membership data are from Gleditsch and Ward (1999).

observers and gaining a positive report. Unfortunately, this is impractical for many reasons, and such data are not systematically available.

I instead use a variable intended to serve as a proxy for year-to-year fluctuations in the relative level of international support for democracy in each country. Official development assistance is one observable indicator that can be disaggregated by sector, including foreign aid targeted toward democracy and governance, and such assistance is a reasonable measure of relative international interest in promoting democracy. Note that this variable is not intended to measure the "democracy premium" directly but should be highly correlated with the availability of democracy-contingent benefits. Data on democracy assistance were compiled by a team of researchers who, in cooperation with USAID, study the impact of U.S. democracy assistance on governance. They made data available for the U.S. and non-U.S. OECD donors from 1990 to 2005.[30] I use the percentage of all official development assistance (ODA) devoted to democracy and governance in the previous year, called *Democracy and Governance/ODA*. This measure is based on the assumption that the rate of aid spent on democracy and governance in a country should be an observable pre-election indicator of the degree to which influential international actors support democratization in that country. To ensure that the amount of democracy and governance assistance is in fact observable before the election, it is lagged by one year. Finally, I argued in chapter 1 that countries that are otherwise strategically important, such as Israel, Egypt, and more recently, Iraq and Afghanistan, are likely to gain high levels of foreign assistance for other reasons. Therefore, to account for this strategic importance I also include a variable indicating the percentage of U.S. military assistance received by the country in the previous year. Countries receiving a higher percentage of U.S. military aid should be less likely to invite observers.

To account for the possibility that a country's decision to invite observers is related to the size of the economy or the country's economic development, I include measures of GDP (logged) and GDP per capita (logged). GDP data are from the World Development Indicators.[31]

Time trends are clearly important, although I sidestep some of the biggest problems by limiting the analysis in this section to 1991–2005. In part to account for remaining unexplained temporal variation, a year variable is included in all models. Elections are not annual events and therefore do not follow traditional cross-sectional time-series structure. The average number of elections held by a given country in the 1991–2006 time period

---

30. Finkel et al., "Effects of U.S. Foreign Assistance on Democracy Building."

31. World Bank, *World Development Indicators*.

Table 2.3. Binary logit, observed elections

Variables	(Model 1) 1991–2005	(Model 2) 1991–2005	(Model 3) 1991–2005	(Model 4) 1991–2005
Previously Observed	2.819**	3.157**	3.180**	3.061**
	(0.341)	(0.317)	(0.315)	(0.313)
Opposition Competition	1.550**	1.379**	1.375**	1.438**
	(0.417)	(0.445)	(0.400)	(0.415)
Consolidated Democracy	−1.624*	−1.821**	−1.817*	−1.650*
	(0.675)	(0.726)	(0.756)	(0.812)
Previous Elections Suspended		1.453**		
		(0.348)		
First Multiparty		0.730		
		(0.478)		
Transitional Government		0.937		
		(0.550)		
Uncertain Type			1.933**	1.908**
			(0.326)	(0.321)
Democracy and Governance / ODA$_{t-1}$				2.852*
				(1.424)
U.S. Military Assistance (Current USD)$_{t-1}$				−0.188*
				(0.086)
GDP (logged)	−0.085	−0.046	−0.054	0.009
	(0.093)	(0.100)	(0.103)	(0.101)
GDP per capita (logged)	−0.477**	−0.326*	−0.324*	−0.406**
	(0.130)	(0.148)	(0.145)	(0.144)
Year	0.042	0.093**	0.099**	0.087*
	(0.035)	(0.036)	(0.038)	(0.038)
Constant	−79.894	−185.630**	−197.187**	−174.607*
	(69.255)	(71.424)	(75.520)	(75.612)
Wald X^2	178.50	249.94	230.29	217.11
Prob > X^2	0.000	0.000	0.000	0.000
Pseudo-R^2	0.4919	0.5283	0.5284	0.5397
Observations	710	710	710	710
Number of countries	146	146	146	146

Notes: Robust standard errors in parentheses are clustered by country. *Significant at 5%; **Significant at 1%.

is nine, but numbers range from one election to eleven elections (and twenty-seven in the full 1960–2006 sample). Although they are pooled by country, the variation in the number of temporal observations for each country means that many statistical tools for binary time-series cross-sectional analyses are not appropriate.[32] Because the decision to invite

32. Statement made based on information in Beck, Katz, and Tucker, "Taking Time Seriously." Because the number of time points (*T*) is not "reasonably large" for all units, their

observers in the current time period is not likely to be independent from the decision to invite observers in previous time periods, I include an indicator of whether any previous election in the country was internationally monitored. All models use robust standard errors clustered by country.

Including all independent states holding national elections with a population greater than 500,000, the full dataset consists of 1,759 individual first-round elections held between 1960 and 2006. In the models presented below, which are limited to the 1991–2005 period, there are 714 observations of elections in 146 countries.

Discussion of Results

Models 1–4 include two sets of variables: those associated with uncertainty over a state's commitment to democracy and those associated with a state's need for and potential access to international benefits tied to democracy. Governments should be mostly likely to invite observers when they need to signal their type or when they believe they can gain democracy-contingent benefits.

The specification of the baseline logit model (Model 1) is:

$$Pr(\text{observed election} \mid x_i) = 1 / (1 + e^{-x_i\beta}),$$

Where $x_i\beta = \beta_0 + \beta_1$ *Previously Observed* $+ \beta_2$ *Opposition Competition* $+ \beta_3$ *Consolidated Democracy* $+ \beta_4$ *Uncertain Type* $+ \beta_5$ *GDP (logged)* $+ \beta_5$ *GDP per Capita (logged)* $+ \beta_6$ *Year*.

As shown in table 2.3, Model 1, consistent with expectations, a country's previous invitation to observers is a strong predictor of whether a given election will be observed. Also consistent with the empirical implications derived from my theory, elections in which competition is allowed are significantly more likely to be observed than elections in which competition is not allowed. However, until 2006, if a country was considered a consolidated democracy, either because it was long considered fully democratic or it had recently become regarded as such, it should be less likely to invite election monitors.

In Model 2, several characteristics of election-holding countries that should correspond to external uncertainty about their type are introduced: *Suspended Elections, First Multiparty,* and *Transitional Government.*

---

recommended method for binary TSCS data is not appropriate. Some countries in the dataset have as few as one election.

As expected, all three are associated with a positive probability that a given election will be observed, although *Transitional Government* and *First Multiparty* is just short of traditional levels of statistical significance. Because each of these events is relatively rare, and because I expect them to be associated with uncertainty about a government's type in the same manner, I combine them into one measure in Model 3. *Uncertain Type* is equal to one if the election is characterized by any of the three events, and the aggregated variable is associated with significantly greater probability that an election will be observed.

On the international benefit side of the decision to invite observers, the percentage of aid devoted to democracy and governance in the country in the previous year is a significant predictor of invitations to international monitors, as shown in Model 4. Model 4 also includes a measure of U.S. military aid, which helps account for the fact that countries that are strategically very important to the United States are unlikely to seek democracy-contingent benefits. As expected, countries receiving more U.S. military assistance are less likely to invite observers, although this result is sensitive to the inclusion of Egypt and Israel.

When all variables in Model 3 are set at median values, the probability that an election will be observed is 27%. Because the substantive interpretation of the size of logit coefficients presented in table 2.3 is not clear, table 2.4 provides simulated first differences for six substantively interesting independent variables included in Models 3 and 4. When all other variables are held at their median values, a previous invitation to observers increases the probability that a given election will be observed by about 62%, from 27% to 89%. This large substantive effect illustrates that once countries begin inviting observers, they are highly likely to continue doing so. Similarly, countries that have never invited observers during this time period are not likely to start, a result that accounts for temporal dependence in a country's decision to invite observers. Supporting my argument, holding elections when the country's regime type is uncertain increases the probability that an election will be observed by 43%. Being a consolidated democracy decreases the likelihood that an election will be observed by about 20%. All else being equal at median values, holding competitive elections increased the probability that observers will be invited by 18%.

The magnitude of the effect of democracy-contingent benefits is relatively small, but it is positive and statistically significant despite the imperfect nature of the proxy measure. It is also instructive to examine how the predicted probabilities of *Observed* change with respect to democracy-contingent benefits in a few illustrative cases, rather than only when other

Table 2.4. Effects of country characteristics on the probability of inviting observers

When this variable . . .	Shifts from . . . to . . .	Change in probability of observed election (%) (95% confidence interval)
Previously Observed	zero to one	62
		(52 to 70)
Competitive	zero to one	18
		(8 to 27)
Democratic	zero to one	–20
		(–33 to –5)
Uncertain Type	zero to one	43
		(29 to 54)
Percentage ODA to	25th to 75th percentile	4
Democracy and Governance		(0.3 to 9)
U.S. Military Assistance	25th to 75th percentile	–0.1
		(–0.2 to –0.01)

Notes: Estimations are based on a logit model estimated in Stata 10.0, with first differences drawn from 1,000 simulations performed by CLARIFY (Tomz, Wittenberg, and King 2003). The first four estimates are based on Model 3. The final two estimates are based on Model 4.

variables are held at median values. Assume a country is holding elections in which competition is allowed, but it is not a consolidated democracy and has never invited observers. This hypothetical government is assumed not to be an "uncertain" type per the definition above, and it receives no U.S. military aid. In this case, increasing the amount of democracy and governance aid from the 25th percentile (.3%) to the 90th percentile (23%), which is a huge assumed increase in democracy-contingent benefits, increases the probability that an election will be observed from 23% to 38%.[33] If this country is assumed to be an uncertain type and all other variables are the same, the same increase in democracy-contingent benefits changes the probability that an election will be observed by 14%, from 69% to 82%.

For regions with other characteristics that make them unlikely to invite election monitors, increasing democracy-contingent benefits results in a smaller increase in the probability that the election will be observed. For example, consider a hypothetical country that has never invited observers, does not hold competitive elections, is not democratic, does not have an "uncertain" type, receives about 1% of total U.S. military assistance,

33. The 95% confidence interval of the 14% simulated first difference ranges from 2.7% to 28%.

and receives only a small percentage of development assistance targeted to democracy and governance. The probability that a country with these characteristics will invite observers is about 8%. All else being equal, changing the percentage of development assistance devoted to democracy and governance increases the probability that an election will be observed by about 6%, from 8% to 14%.[34]

Robustness and Alternative Explanations

Thus far the empirical results in this chapter have focused primarily on variables derived from my theory to explain internationally monitored elections. As discussed in the introduction, there are alternative explanations suggested by the existing literature on election monitoring and the international diffusion of policies between states. Judith Kelley argues that a country's level of democracy is an important variable in determining who invites observers. This is similar to my argument about whether there is uncertainty regarding a government's commitment to democracy, but her explanation is more general and does not detail a testable causal mechanism. Following Kelley's treatment of election observation, I include a measure of a government's regime type with the *POLITY2* measure from the *POLITY IV* data,[35] as well as the same measure squared. The twenty-one-point *POLITY2* scale ranges from −10 to 10, or from most autocratic to most democratic. The squared term is included in order to account for Kelley's finding that countries in the middle of the *POLITY* scale are most likely to invite observers.[36]

The literature on policy diffusion suggests a second alternative explanation for the spread of election monitoring. Although my theory explicitly involves mimicry of election monitoring by states, I account for this empirically by specifying the characteristics of individual regimes that are most likely to invite observers. The diffusion literature does not explain election monitoring, but related arguments would suggest that a country would be more likely to invite international observers if that country's neighboring states also invited observers. Therefore, to evaluate the explanatory power of a more general diffusion argument, I include a variable that measures the percentage of all elections that were internationally monitored in a given region in the previous year. *Regional Percent Observed*

---

34. The 95% confidence interval of the 7% simulated first difference ranges from 1% to 15%.

35. Marshall and Jaggers, *Polity IV Project*.

36. Kelley, "Supply and Demand of Election Monitoring."

excludes elections that took place in a country in the previous year, so it is not necessarily equal across all region-years.[37]

Because using the *POLITY* data introduces new sources of missing data and reduces the number of observations from 714 to 650, I first replicate Model 4 without the observations for which *POLITY* scores are not available, shown in table 2.5, Model 5. The loss of observations due to missing *POLITY* data does not substantially change the results presented in table 2.3, Model 4. Model 6 adds the three variables outlined above, *POLITY, POLITY Squared,* and *Regional Percent Observed.* For 1991–2005, none of these variables are statistically significant, although the signs are in the predicted direction.

These results suggest that the election and regime-specific variables derived from my theory are better predictors of internationally monitored elections than the more general measures of regime type and regional diffusion of election monitoring suggested by the existing literature. These findings support the empirical implications outlined in chapter 1 and lend general support to my theory relative to the two central alternative explanations that can be evaluated in this framework. Note that the alternative explanations presented in table 2.5 are sufficiently general that they are also broadly consistent with my argument. Nevertheless, the cross-national empirical evidence presented in this chapter provides strong support for the first seven empirical implications presented in chapter 1 and shows that variables associated with my argument are more strongly correlated with observed elections than two of the leading alternative explanations.

Note that two other alternative explanations were introduced in the introduction but are not tested in table 2.3. The argument that the norm of election monitoring was generated through advocacy or pressure from powerful states is addressed more thoroughly in the next chapter with detailed evidence about the behavior of democracy promoters. I demonstrate that their role was primarily to make benefits available to states that were recognized as democratizing and that overt advocacy of election monitoring by external actors did not occur until well after the norm was initiated and spread widely. The fourth alternative explanation outlined in the introduction is that election monitoring is costless for pseudo-democrats and they invite observers because election monitoring is inconsequential.

---

37. Note that in related work on this subject, I had also included *POLITY* and *Regional Percent Observed* as central independent variables explaining internationally monitored elections (Beaulieu and Hyde, "In the Shadow of Democracy Promotion.").

Table 2.5. Alternative explanations

Variables	Model 5 1991–2005	Model 6 1991–2005
Previously Observed	3.121**	3.083**
	(0.329)	(0.328)
Opposition Competition	1.485**	1.417*
	(0.438)	(0.523)
Consolidated Democracy	–1.624*	–1.561
	(0.794)	(0.847)
Uncertain Type	1.993**	1.995**
	(0.339)	(0.335)
Democracy and Governance / ODA	3.605*	3.638*
(computed from 2-year mean)	(1.487)	(1.455)
U.S. Military Assistance (Current USD)$_{t-1}$	–0.094	–0.088
	(0.063)	(0.062)
GDP (logged)	0.021	0.026
	(0.105)	(0.103)
GDP per capita (logged)	–0.402**	–0.360*
	(0.154)	(0.177)
Year	0.083	0.074
	(0.041)	(0.043)
POLITY		0.001
		(0.032)
POLITY Squared		–0.004
		(0.005)
Regional Percent Observed$_{t-1}$		0.503
		(0.631)
Constant	–166.954*	–149.339
	(82.221)	(84.838)
Wald X^2	193.15	198.27
Prob > X^2	0.000	0.000
Pseudo-R^2	0.536	0.537
Observations	653	653
Number of countries	143	143

Notes: Robust standard errors in parentheses are clustered by country. *Significant at 5%; **Significant at 1%. For both alternative explanations the null hypothesis that the coefficient is equal to zero cannot be rejected (not reported).

This alternative, addressed in chapters 3–5, demonstrates three ways that election monitoring is consequential to pseudo-democrats.

The Normalization of International Election Observation

Thus far, the empirical analysis has focused on the question of why leaders invite observers, including why election observation diffused widely, and has sidestepped the question of when election monitoring became an international norm. When did international expectations change? When did it become a widely shared expectation among influential international actors that leaders of democratizing countries would invite international election monitors? Pinpointing the exact moment when election observation changed from an entirely voluntary, state-initiated behavior to a behavior expected and enforced by international actors is difficult. However, it is still possible to provide evidence related to how and when the change took place.

As recognized by a number of prominent scholars, one observable characteristic of norm development is a change in rhetoric surrounding the new behavior and new norm.[38] When election observation was initiated, both the leaders who invited observers and the organizations that sponsored them routinely explained and justified their behavior in public forums. As the connection between election observation and democracy grew stronger in the 1990s, leaders began to cite invitations to election monitors as evidence that the elections would be democratic. For example, in the pre-norm period, Georgian President Eduard Shevardnadze discussed preparations for the 1992 elections:

> [Reform] can only be done by a democratically elected government and only such a government can get the support and solidarity of the rest of the world.... We realise this and, at any price, will hold elections.... They will be free elections and we will invite observers from other countries and international organisations.[39]

For the most part, in the mid 1990s leaders ceased explaining the decision to invite observers. Instead, leaders of noninviting countries began to publicly justify their behavior, explaining why they chose not to invite observers. Rather than emphasizing the novelty of international observers, international media reports on elections began to note when observers were not invited, and governments under such indirect pressure began to pre-emptively defend their decisions, often relying on nationalist sentiment or arguing that observers violate sovereignty. For example, in the 1999 Algerian presidential elections, all but the military-backed candidate dropped out of the race ahead of the election due to alleged fraud. A representative of the incumbent party who was also the lone candidate and

38. Payne, "Persuasion, Frames and Norm Construction"; Finnemore and Sikkink, "International Norm Dynamics and Political Change"; Checkel, "International Norms and Domestic Politics."

39. Seamus Martin, "Shevardnadze one hundred days into toughest mission," Herald (Glasgow), June 15, 1992.

eventual winner of the contest, Abdelaziz Bouteflika was asked in a press conference about the absence of international observers and responded as follows. "I don't think elections are more transparent because there are a few UN, OAU (Organization of African Unity) or Arab League observers....I won't accept, now or in the future, any foreign interference in my country."[40] The United States had previously put pressure on the Algerian government to invite international observers, but none were invited to the one-candidate election.[41]

In 2000 Ethiopian Prime Minister Meles Zenawi made an official statement that Ethiopia would not invite international observers to the May 14 parliamentary election.

> We are people capable of managing ourselves and our affairs. We have to be able to conduct our elections on our own, as part of our right to exercise self-determination. If there is the assumption that the election is not democratic unless foreign observers monitored the process, this is a distorted outlook.[42]

The 2000 elections were not observed, but five years later the same prime minister agreed to opposition party demands and invited international observers. The Carter Center and the European Union observed the election.

Egypt has held elections for decades but has yet to invite international observers. Prior to the 2005 presidential election, domestic groups and the U.S. government joined in attempting to pressure the government of President Hosni Mubarak to invite international observers. Although President Mubarak initially appeared to consider the idea, even going so far as to send a foreign minister on a television speaking tour in the United States in which the minister suggested the government's interest in impartial observers, Mubarak ultimately banned their presence. In a press conference just a few weeks before the election, he was quoted as saying, "We are not a trust country to allow our elections to be subjected to international supervision. We can alone organize our elections and ensure their

40. "Algeria in Crisis as Six Presidential Contenders Withdraw on Poll Eve," Agence Free Press, April 14, 1999.

41. "We urge both the government of Algeria and the parties to invite international observers to the elections," said Martin Indyk, Assistant Secretary of State for Middle East Affairs, Agence Free Press, February 24, 1999.

42. Quoted in Yemisrach Benalfew, "Politics—Ethiopia: No Foreign Election Observers Needed," IPS-Inter Press Service, September 17, 1999.

success."[43] This statement was in contrast to earlier demands by Egyptian human rights groups who called for the opening of the process to international observers. "It is not true that [election observation] constitutes an infringement on sovereignty or interference in internal affairs," said Hafez Abu Seda, head of the Egyptian Organization for Human Rights.[44] The support for election observation from pro-democracy actors at the domestic and international level is an implication of the normalization of election monitoring.

Also reflecting the global norm of election observation was a trend for leaders in less-democratic countries to call for international election observers at the 2004 U.S. general elections. In an overt public attempt to highlight the paternalistic nature of election observation and U.S. democracy promotion, a leader of the Iranian militia asked UN Secretary General Kofi Annan to appoint observers, saying that "the presence of observers from the Islamic republic of Iran, one of the most democratic regimes in the world, is necessary to guarantee fairness in the U.S. presidential election."[45] Similar claims demanding international observers for the U.S. elections were made in Malaysian and Cuban newspapers. Ultimately, in part to enhance the credibility of international election monitoring, the United States invited, and the OSCE sent, a delegation of observers to the 2004 U.S. presidential elections.

After 2004, and perhaps in response to growing criticism of democracy promotion as Western imperialism, many developed democracies also began to change their behavior and began to invite international election observers. Invitations from countries such as Austria, Belgium, France, Switzerland, and the United Kingdom are not signals of governments' commitment to holding democratic elections. In these cases, invitations to observers—and their subsequent reports—reveal little information about the country's commitment to democracy. International actors view these countries as democratic before they invite observers, and the invitation and the observers' report do little to update this belief. Rather, invitations from stable democracies to international election observers represent a confirmation of their compliance with the norm of international election monitoring and is a further sign that only non-democratic governments refuse to invite observers. For example, in announcing the United States' invitation

43. "Egypt Insists Refusal of International Election Monitors," *Financial Times Information,* August 31, 2005.

44. "Rights Group Calls for International Monitoring of Egypt Polls," Agence Free Press, June 13, 2005.

45. "USA: Iranian Militia Wants Observers at Presidential Election," ANSA English Media Service, October 18, 2004.

to OSCE observers for the 2006 congressional elections, the U.S. ambassador to the OSCE explained why the United States invited observers by saying that "the United States supports fully the OSCE's important work, in particular its election observation efforts in promoting free and fair elections throughout the OSCE community."[46] Underscoring the widespread acceptance of the norm of election monitoring, in response to a question about why Austria's 2010 elections were going to be observed by the OSCE, the head of the government's election commission responded that "observing elections in western Europe has become a routine act."[47] This change occurred relatively quickly. In 2000, it was still rare for long-term consolidated democracies to invite international observers and even more unusual for an organization to agree to send them. By 2010, many of the widely accepted democratic countries began inviting and receiving observers, including Canada, France, Italy, the Netherlands, Spain, the United Kingdom, and the United States. The trend continues to expand throughout Europe, and it remains to be seen whether other democracies, such as Chile and India, will follow the trend and seek international observers.

The normalization of election observation is also reflected in domestic public opinion. A 2009 survey conducted in seventeen nations by the University of Maryland's Program on International Policy Attitudes confirmed widespread support for observers in both developed and developing countries:

> Asked whether "when there are concerns about fairness of elections," nations should be willing to have international observers monitor their elections, on average, across all nations polled, 64 percent say that they should. In no nation do most people oppose the idea, though views are divided in Turkey and India. Most of the nations favoring election monitors do so by solid majorities, often two-to-one. The highest levels of support are found in Azerbaijan (83%), Kenya (82%) and Britain (81%)....Perhaps most striking, most publics also say that their nation would "benefit from having international observers monitor elections here." The most enthusiastic are Kenya (85%) and Nigeria (74%). In no country do more than 51 percent oppose the idea.[48]

The diffusion of the norm led even developed democracies to accept election observation. Returning to the model outlined in chapter 1, the

46. Marissa Eubanks, "U.S. Invites OSCE to Observe Congressional Elections in November; Election Observation Promotes Free and Fair Elections, Says U.S. Official." *State Department Documents and Publications*, June 30, 2006.

47. "OSCE election observation 'a routine act'." *Austrian Independent*, March 31, 2010.

48. Program on International Policy Attitudes, "World Publics Strongly Favor International Observers for Elections, Including Their Own," news release, September 8, 2009.

norm reduces any sovereignty costs associated with inviting observers, and domestic support for observers may even make these costs positive for some leaders.

To be clear, it was governments that lacked clear reputations as democracies that initiated the practice of election monitoring, eventually causing it to become an international norm. The norm of election monitoring, in turn, has now led many stable democracies to invite international observers. The spread of election observation to even the consolidated democracies further increases the number of elections that are internationally observed and creates an even shorter list of governments that refuse to invite observers.

Explaining the Diffusion of Election Observation

In this chapter I evaluated why leaders invite international election monitors, focusing on qualitative evidence about early inviters, rhetoric from powerful states about democracy and democracy promotion, and a cross-national examination of whether trends in elections and the types of states that invited election monitors are consistent with my theory. The decision to invite observers was made independently by many state leaders but ultimately contributed to the creation of a norm of international election observation. Although the determinants of the decision to invite observers have changed over time, most notably due to the creation of the norm, there is qualitative and quantitative evidence that leaders were motivated to invite observers, in part because it provided a credible signal of their intent to hold democratic elections and because they could gain more benefits from democracy promoters as a result. Election monitoring became an effective signal because it provides valuable information to international actors and it was more costly for pseudo-democrats to imitate. In subsequent chapters, I examine election monitoring from the perspective of democracy promoters, explaining why they were initially reluctant to send election monitors and how their views changed over time. I also explore the consequences of international election observation within countries to which they are invited. I show that international observers can reduce election fraud directly, therefore making it more difficult for leaders to cheat; that they have changed the form of manipulation, leading pseudo-democrats to engage in more strategic forms of election manipulation; and that if leaders are caught and criticized by international observers, they can face serious consequences.

3

DEMOCRACY-CONTINGENT BENEFITS

As of January 2005, Ethiopia received nearly a third of its total budget from the United States and European Union member states. It was one of the leading aid recipients in Africa, and prior to parliamentary elections in 2005, the country was considered a darling of the donor community on the African continent, setting an example of relative stability, economic growth, and political liberalization. Although he had refused to invite international observers in 2000, Ethiopian Prime Minister Meles Zenawi's government invited and accredited more than three hundred monitors for the May 2005 general elections, including delegations from the African Union, the Arab League, the Carter Center, and the European Union. As the *Economist* reported, the election was supposed to "mark the safe passage of Ethiopia from blood-soaked Marxist rule to multiparty democracy."[1] Prior to the election, Meles was praised for allowing open debate, the relative lack of violence in campaigning, and overall movement toward democracy.

Instead of fulfilling expectations and holding democratic elections, however, the Meles government engaged in carefully orchestrated manipulation. Initially, international observers found the process to be relatively clean, without significant evidence of fraud on election day or in the pre-election period, and the election gained widespread international approval. The EU called it "the most genuinely competitive elections the country has experienced," and the Carter Center reported that "Ethiopia has made tremendous strides toward democracy."[2]

Almost immediately following the close of polls, however, concerns began to surface. The government announced election results before official

---

1. "Hoping That a Star Won't Fizzle," August 11, 2005, *Economist*.
2. "Ethiopia's Governing Party Claims a Victory," May 18, 2005, *New York Times*.

results were compiled, asserting a landslide victory for the government. Several hours after the election, Meles decreed a ban on all public protest and demonstrations. International observers began to issue warnings to the Meles government, citizens protested despite the ban, and thirty-six protesters were killed in the week after the election. Almost before the ink was dry on their statements praising the election, the European Union warned that the postelection behavior by the government was "seriously undermining the transparency and fairness of the elections" and that their actions "increase[d] the scope for manipulation...and put in doubt public confidence in the process."[3] Dozens of additional deaths, thousands of arrests, and the intimidation of journalists continued in subsequent months, provoking further international condemnation. Continuing to play the part of a democratic leader, Meles attempted to distance himself from the government violence against protesters, expressing shock at the deaths and ordering an independent investigation. The Carter Center was more circumspect than the EU in their criticism of the election, a fact exploited by Meles's government in an attempt to discredit EU criticism.[4] Additionally, because Ethiopia was a U.S. ally in the "war on terror," the U.S. reaction was mixed.

Even in these ambiguous circumstances, international actors responded to the reports of fraud, criticism from international observers, and politically targeted postelection violence, seeking to punish the Meles government: the UK immediately froze more than $30 million in aid, and other donors followed suit, particularly after opposition and journalist-targeted violence continued in November. By January 2006, donors had halted more than $375 million in budgetary support initially intended for direct disbursement to the Ethiopian government. Pre-election recommendations by donors to double aid to Ethiopia vanished from discussion. The *New York Times* headline on the election was "Mr. Good Governance Goes Bad," the paper's editorial writers complained that "Mr. Meles is in favor of democracy only when people are voting for him" and recommended a series of actions aimed at punishing his government.[5] Concern about humanitarian conditions led those donors who did not suspend aid entirely to channel it through private organizations in an effort to sanction the government without causing further humanitarian suffering.

---

3. "Post-election Developments Undermining Confidence in Ethiopian Vote: EU," May 25, 2005, Agence France Presse.

4. "Minister Points out Glaring Differences in EU-EOM, Carter Centre Reports. September 23, 2005, *The Ethiopian Herald.*

5. "Mr. Good Governance Goes Bad," November 27, 2005, *New York Times.*

In short, Meles's attempts to hold internationally certified elections ultimately failed, provoking serious international consequences. His sterling reputation as a democratic leader was tarnished, democracy-promoting states reduced and rechanneled foreign aid, and the pre-election discussions by donors of debt relief for the country dissipated. Meles ultimately stayed in power, although one can imagine that he would have fared better if he had not been under international pressure to comply with the norm of election observation and if international observers had not criticized the election. Had he managed to invite international observers and evade their criticism, it is likely he and his government would have received the promised aid increases and other benefits that would have accompanied recognition as one of Africa's leading democracies.

By 2005, the norm of election monitoring was well established, and the leaders of Ethiopia and other similar countries were well aware of the links between democracy promotion, internationally certified elections, and international benefits. In the early period of election observation, democracy-promoting organizations played a crucial role in motivating governments to invite observers, but their role was not to advocate the practice of election observation. Rather, democracy promoters succeeded in making a greater share of international benefits conditioned on a government's regime type. Thus, the existence of democracy-contingent benefits gave some leaders the incentive to signal their commitment to democratization. When democracy promoters recognized election monitoring as a signal of a government's commitment to democracy, other leaders also had the incentive to invite election monitors, even in the absence of overt advocacy for election monitoring. Again, the norm of election monitoring was generated by the new belief among democracy promoters that all true democrats invite international observers to judge their elections, particularly if their "type" is not already well-established.

This change in the expectations of democracy promoters and their recognition that election monitoring signaled valuable information about a government's commitment to democracy was not inevitable. As discussed in previous chapters, the first invitations from governments in sovereign states to foreign observers were refused. Although the OAS began to provide observers in 1962, the UN continued to refuse such invitations from sovereign states until 1990, with debate playing out for years within the General Assembly.[6] Election monitoring was also a contentious issue

---

6. Kelley, "Assessing the Complex Evolution of Norms."

within other international organizations. Over time, however, as governments continued to invite election monitors, the practice became more widely accepted, and democracy-promoting actors developed the shared belief that all true democrats invite election monitors.

This chapter documents the indirect role that pro-democracy actors played in generating the norm of election monitoring. The dramatic increase in support for democracy across a diverse set of international actors underscores the idea that international benefits tied to democracy exist; that the relative importance of democracy promotion has fluctuated over time, growing considerably with the end of the Cold War; and that leaders of benefit-seeking states were aware of the existence of such benefits and their relative importance.

I first summarize changes in democracy promotion during the Cold War, including increases in democracy-contingent benefits available to a subset of states for which election monitoring was initiated. I also document the initial reluctance of international actors to provide election monitors and the reactions within international organizations to the first governments that attempted to invite observers. I show that observers do, in fact, issue negative reports and demonstrate that such reports influence perceptions of a country's commitment to democracy, including the most widely referenced indicators of a country's regime type. I then present evidence of increased post–Cold War democracy promotion by a growing number of international actors and document that democracy promoters used the reports of observers when allocating international benefits.

According to my argument, the strengthening of the link between international benefits and the reports of international observers generates several empirical implications (outlined in chapter 1), including the conditioning of international benefits on internationally certified elections and increases in internationally imposed costs for those governments exposed as pseudo-democrats. As more international actors grew willing to send election monitors, and as an invitation to international election monitors and their endorsement began to be recognized as a signal of a government's commitment to democracy, there should be evidence that democracy-promoting actors used the reports of election monitors to update their beliefs about governments' types. To the extent that their beliefs change regarding a government's commitment to democracy, the allocation of international benefits should also change.

The types of international benefits sought by states are diverse and fungible, creating a variety of challenges in measuring international benefits and evaluating my argument cross-nationally. Although my theory suggests a strengthening link between election-monitoring reports and international benefits, I do not necessarily expect a positive cross-national relationship between international benefits and positive reports from international observers. If pseudo-democrats believe that democracy promoters will react to the reports of observers, they should adjust their behavior accordingly. The counterfactual—or what would have happened if each election-monitoring report were different—is unobservable, and the evidence provided so far should make clear that there is an obvious selection bias in the countries that are most likely to invite observers. Governments that are caught holding fraudulent elections or that refuse to invite observers at all may already be pariah states from the perspective of Western democracies and therefore have few international benefits that can be withdrawn if their reputation worsens. Similarly, many governments are already perceived as democratizing and continue to invite observers and receive positive reports. If a government with a reputation as an electoral autocrat held surprisingly good elections, the country would increase its share of international benefits. Likewise, if a government that was believed to be committed to democratization held surprisingly bad elections, such as the Meles government in Ethiopia, international benefits would decrease. However, most countries behave in a manner that is consistent with their existing reputation. In addition, governments that democratize typically also require less foreign aid, creating a complicated situation in which positive reports can be correlated with the perception that a government is a fully developed democracy no longer in need of democracy-contingent benefits. In cases of successful democratization, a country may decrease its share of easily measurable international benefits, such as foreign aid, while increasing intangible benefits, such as reputational benefits associated with joining the exclusive club of long-term stable democracies.

Nevertheless, democracy-contingent benefits should respond to the reports of election monitors, particularly when their reports are contrary to the pre-election perception of a given government's commitment to democracy. Reactions should include reduced benefits for states receiving (unanticipated) negative reports and increased benefits for those receiving (unanticipated) positive reports, as well as updated evaluations of a country's level of democracy. As the norm becomes widely shared, my theory also suggests that democracy promoters should begin to view governments that do not invite international observers as governments that are necessarily holding fraudulent elections. For clarity, these predicted changes in the behavior and beliefs of democracy-promoting actors are mapped on a timeline in figure 3.1.

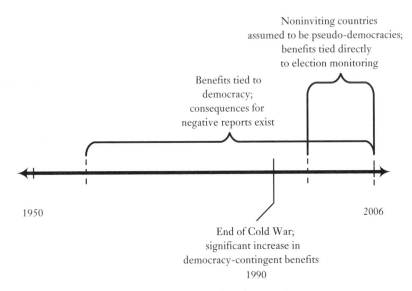

Figure 3.1. Changes in democracy-contingent benefits over time

In the remainder of this chapter, I document changes in democracy promotion and the supply of election monitoring over time. I also show that the initiation of election observation coincided with increases in democracy promotion before 1989 and that the rapid increase in election monitoring beginning in the late 1980s coincided with a dramatic increase in democracy-contingent benefits brought about by the end of the Cold War. I then present evidence from several detailed cases of elections in which reports from international observers were linked to international benefits. Finally, I document and explain cases in which governments refused observers after 2000, showing that democracy promoters perceive these governments as nondemocracies, despite the fact that they hold national elections.

Democracy Promotion during the Cold War

Democracy promotion began long before the Cold War and includes efforts by the United States and the United Kingdom, support for German political party foundations (beginning in 1925), and, notably, efforts by Woodrow Wilson and the League of Nations. Following World War II, the 1948 charter of the Organization of American States (OAS) proclaimed that the "solidarity of the American States and the high aims which are sought through it require the political organization of those

States on the basis of the effective exercise of representative democracy."[7] The 1948 Universal Declaration of Human Rights contains provisions for democracy, including Article 21, calling for "periodic and genuine elections...by universal and equal suffrage and...secret vote or...equivalent free voting procedures."[8] The Yalta Declaration on Liberated Europe specifically called for Britain, Russia, and the United States to help liberated nations "form interim governmental authorities broadly representative of all democratic elements in the population and pledged to the earliest possible establishment through free elections of governments responsive to the will of the people; and to facilitate where necessary the holding of such elections."[9] The post–World War II Marshall Plan included provisions for fostering democracy in Europe and Japan.

By the late 1940s, support of these commitments through foreign policy was, in most cases, soon outweighed by Cold War politics. As historian Tony Smith writes, "with the tensions of the Cold War intensifying in 1947, American interest in gambling on democratic forces abroad steadily diminished."[10] By the mid-1950s, foreign support for democracy was limited. Some partisan U.S. allies continued to receive covert aid channeled through the Central Intelligence Agency. Germany restarted a tradition of supporting political party foundations or *Stiftungen*, which gave aid directly to political parties during the Cold War, notably in Portugal, Spain, and several other countries that later started the "third wave" of democratization.[11] U.S. rhetoric about democracy continued, but anti-communism dominated U.S. foreign policy and the policies of its allies until the late 1950s, when democracy reemerged as an important variable in foreign policy debates, in part due to questions raised by Latin American leaders about whether repressive dictatorships created favorable conditions for communist revolution.

International monitoring of elections in sovereign states is rooted in this debate about how to best promote security and economic growth in the Americas while continuing to limit the spread of communism. The fall of the reliably anti-communist Cuban president Fulgencio Batista and the beginning of Fidel Castro's presidency in 1959 raised the profile of this debate within the OAS and the United States regarding whether supporting anti-communist dictatorships was the best Cold War strategy. Throughout much

---

7. *Charter of the Organization of American States*, Chapter II, Article 3.
8. *Universal Declaration of Human Rights*, Article 21, 3.
9. Stalin, Roosevelt, and Churchill, *Yalta (Crimea) Conference*, Section II.
10. Smith, *America's Mission*, 182.
11. Huntington, *The Third Wave*.

of the Cold War, the United States had relied on support from dictators such as Cuba's Batista, Haiti's François Duvalier, and the Dominican Republic's Rafael Trujillo. In the late 1950s and early 1960s, Batista's defeat and the Cuban revolution increased the influence of pro-democracy forces who argued that repressive dictators created conditions favorable to communist revolution. A coalition of pro-democracy states within the OAS began to argue for more explicit support of democratic governments, and the organization reaffirmed its commitment to supporting democracy and human rights in the Declaration of Santiago at the August 1959 OAS Meeting of Foreign Ministers. Among other commitments, the declaration stated that

> harmony among the American republics can be effective only insofar as human rights and fundamental freedoms and the exercise of representative democracy are a reality within each one of them, since experience has demonstrated that the lack of respect for such principles is a source of widespread disturbance and gives rise to emigrations that cause frequent and grave political tensions between the state that they leave and the states that receive them.[12]

Several democratic governments were under more direct threats from other dictatorships in the region. Two of the most vocal pro-democracy leaders—President Figueres of Costa Rica and President Rómulo Betancourt of Venezuela—had survived plotted or attempted assassinations and coups sponsored by their dictatorial neighbors. These leaders argued that the United States had "foolishly fostered extremism by supporting right-wing dictators" and advocated for a policy emphasizing support for democratically elected governments.[13]

Within the United States, although the Eisenhower administration had allied with many anti-communist regimes regardless of their commitment to democracy, policies toward the most repressive dictators were being questioned. In the first months of 1960, the United States suspended diplomatic relations and imposed economic sanctions on Cuba and the Dominican Republic. By the beginning of the Kennedy administration, providing support to democratic governments and pressuring anti-communist dictatorships had become an explicit part of U.S. foreign policy. Kennedy continued the policies of Eisenhower toward the Dominican Republic and increased pressure on François Duvalier, the Haitian dictator.[14] Although

---

12. Organization of American States, "Fifth Meeting of Consultation of Ministers of Foreign Affairs," 538.
13. Rabe, *The Most Dangerous Area in the World*, 28.
14. Rabe, *The Most Dangerous Area in the World*.

it now stands as a brief experiment, at the time Kennedy's *Alliance for Progress* represented the most ambitious effort to promote democracy in Latin America, involving the distribution of $22.3 billion between 1961 and 1965.[15]

The promises of aid for democratic states gave some Latin American leaders the impression that they could count on U.S. support as long as they were democratically elected. However, renewed support for democracy by the United States during the Cold War did not trump other foreign policy interests; preventing the spread of communism continued to be the central priority of the Kennedy administration, even if it meant denying support to democratically elected leaders who failed to be sufficiently anti-communist, such President Arturo Frondizi of Argentina.[16] As Kennedy summarized this sentiment in describing his administration's policy on the possibility of continuing support for the Trujillo dictatorship,

> there are three possibilities in descending order of preference: a decent democratic regime, a continuation of the Trujillo regime, or a Castro regime. We ought to aim for the first, but we really can't renounce the second until we are sure that we can avoid the third.[17]

Democracy reemerged on the U.S. foreign policy agenda of the early 1960s, and a coalition of states within the Americas continued to argue that the United States and the OAS should condition their foreign policy on democratic governance. At the January 1962 meeting of the Council of Foreign Ministers, the United States successfully pushed for Cuba's suspension from the OAS. At the same meeting, the council reaffirmed the OAS's commitment to democracy, proclaiming that member governments should "organize themselves on the basis of free elections that express, without restriction, the will of the people."[18] Detailing this policy, they "recommended that nondemocratic governments hold free elections 'as the most effective means of consulting the sovereign will of their peoples, to guarantee the restoration of a legal order based on the authority of the law and respect for the rights of the individual.'"[19]

Creating an opening for the provision of international election monitors when invited by member states, the council also came to agreement

15. Smith, *America's Mission*, 214.
16. Rabe, *The Most Dangerous Area in the World*.
17. Ibid., 41.
18. Ball, *The OAS in Transition*, 495.
19. Ibid.

on a crucial question: how to reconcile respect for nonintervention with requests from member states to act on OAS commitments to support democracy within member states. In a resolution passed at the January 1962 meeting, after the organization had denied several requests to provide international election monitors, the member states agreed that "formation by free elections" is

> the surest guarantee for the peace of the hemisphere and the security and political independence of each and every one of the nations that comprise it; and [f]reedom to contract obligations is an inseparable part of the principle of the self-determination of nations, and consequently a request by one or more countries that such obligations be complied with does not signify intervention.[20]

This statement endorsed the position that a government-requested "intervention" was acceptable if it supported the existing obligations of member states, including the commitments made by OAS members to support democracy.[21]

Before the 1962 meeting and the suspension of Cuba from the OAS, previous proposals within the organization that international monitoring be provided were rejected. Following the 1962 meeting, "[g]overnments began to take up the idea of technical assistance in electoral matters and observers at elections almost at once."[22] Costa Rica again requested that the OAS send monitors to their 1962 elections, and the OAS secretary general decided to send a small delegation to observe the Costa Rican elections without asking for approval from the governing body. It was billed as a technical assistance mission, with the mission's report on the elections first delivered directly to the Costa Rican government. The three-member delegation reported favorably on the election and on the practice of election monitoring more generally:

> The Mission suggests that, to provide the nations of the hemisphere with adequate information, and to ensure honest, proper elections everywhere, other countries that so request should be given the opportunity to receive technical assistance by OAS observers as provided on this occasion.[23]

---

20. Organization of American States, "Eighth Meeting of Consultation of Ministers of Foreign Affairs," 608.

21. Ball, *The OAS in Transition*, 494.

22. Ibid., 495.

23. Pan American Union, *Report of the Technical Assistance Mission of the Organization of American States on the Presidential Elections in the Republic of Costa Rica*, 14.

This trend continued, and by 1980 the OAS had provided international observer missions to elections in Bolivia (1966), Costa Rica (1966, 1970), Dominican Republic (1962, 1966, 1970), Ecuador (1968), Guatemala (1970), and Nicaragua (1963, 1972).

As Jennifer McCoy writes, the OAS's purpose at these early missions was "less to monitor the electoral process per se than to show moral support for democratic elections."[24] Early OAS acceptance of election observation did not spread outside the hemisphere, and concerns about violations of sovereignty and unnecessary intervention in the domestic affairs of sovereign states continued to be an issue. Several international nongovernmental organizations (INGOs), including the International Human Rights Law Group (established in 1978) and the Washington Office on Latin America (established in 1974), sent early election observation missions but initially did so in order to "take advantage of the openness provided by an election period to investigate specific cases involving allegations of human rights violations" rather than out of enthusiasm for the practice of election observation per se.[25] In the late 1970s, several governments that were reluctant to allow human rights monitors were actively seeking international election observers. Human rights INGOs realized they could exploit government interest in international election monitors in order to gather information about human rights abuses in countries or regions where they would not otherwise be allowed access.[26] The 1980 elections in Guyana, for example, were observed by the OAS and by the British Parliamentary Human Rights Group. Guyanese President Forbes Burnham announced on the radio that foreign observers would be welcome to observe the election, and the Guyana Human Rights Association then invited the British group directly. Notably, they condemned the elections, with the mission's leader arguing that it was "fraudulent in every possible respect."[27] It quickly became clear, however, that international observers were able to successfully observe elections only when they were invited and credentialed by the host government. Without some formal arrangement between the host government and international observers, governments could deny access, restrict which observers were allowed entry into the country, and otherwise undermine the work of foreign observers. Even

24. McCoy, "Monitoring and Mediating Elections during Latin American Democratization," 57.

25. Garber, *Guidelines for International Election Observing*, 6–7.

26. Garber, *Guidelines for International Election Observing*.

27. "Guyana Vote a Fraud, Foreign Observers Say," *Globe and Mail*, December 20, 1980.

with invitations from leaders of sovereign states, some international organizations continued to find the prospect of sending international election observers to be incompatible with their organization's other objectives.

Most notably, the UN began receiving invitations to observe elections from sovereign states as early as 1957, but they did not consent to send observers until thirty-three years later, for the 1990 Nicaraguan elections. Although they continued to receive requests to observe elections, the UN followed a general guideline of organizing observation missions only when self-determination of a nonindependent territory was at stake. In the post–World War II period, and during the early Cold War, the UN and its members were concerned with territorial sovereignty and were willing to send observers to occupied regions only when elections were held and only to elections or plebiscites concerning other territorial issues. This policy began to change in the late 1980s when pro-democracy member states argued for a change in policy.[28] In response to the successive UN resolutions between 1988 and 1992 on the principle of periodic and genuine elections, UN Secretary General Boutros Boutros-Ghali argued that UN policy in the area of electoral assistance "emerged in response to the rising tide of interest in democratization and requests for United Nations support."[29] Yet at the end of the 1990s, the UN remained a reluctant and occasional player in election monitoring, offering technical assistance to support democratic elections far more frequently than the organization consented to provide election observers to sovereign states, even when they were invited.

Democracy Promotion and International Benefits

The actions of democracy promoters during the Cold War, including their initial reluctance to send election monitors and the absence of evidence that norm entrepreneurs or powerful states pressured governments to invite observers, represents additional support for my argument. However, the work of advocates for democracy promotion (rather than advocates for election monitoring) provides a clear link between my theory and the leading theories of norm development outlined in previous chapters. Although I have argued that neither norm entrepreneurs nor powerful states were central in generating the norm of election monitoring,

---

28. Kelley, "Assessing the Complex Evolution of Norms."
29. Boutros-Ghali, *An Agenda for Democratization*, 15–16; Kelley, "Assessing the Complex Evolution of Norms," 240.

advocates for democracy and the institutionalization of support for it within international organizations led to the development of democracy as an international norm and were central in increasing support for its promotion in the late 1980s.

Within Europe and the former Soviet sphere, election observation was virtually nonexistent before 1989 but became quickly institutionalized within the Conference on Security and Cooperation in Europe (CSCE, later the OSCE) and eventually within the European Community/European Union. The initial proposals within the CSCE focused on supporting democracy and democratic elections. Between 1989 and 1990, the United States, the United Kingdom, and other Western governments began to pressure for more overt forms of support for elections and democracy within the Soviet sphere of influence. At the 1989 meeting of the CSCE in Paris, the U.S. representatives introduced a proposal "calling for free elections and the establishment of multiple political parties within all the signatory countries," which they said "represents a long-term Western goal for democracy in the Soviet Union and Eastern Europe."[30] At the time, the proposal was not considered realistic. Just a year later, however, after the fall of the Berlin Wall, the proposal was adopted by the organization in the 1990 Copenhagen agreement. In part based on the demand for observers from the CSCE for several elections in late 1989 and early 1990, this document also explicitly called for CSCE member states to invite international and domestic observation of their elections, setting the stage for the organization's future provision of international election observers to member states.[31] Signatories to the 1990 Copenhagen Document agreed to abide by a variety of democratic commitments, invite international election observers, endorse the general principle that "the will of the people, freely and fairly expressed through periodic and genuine elections, is the basis of the authority and legitimacy of government."[32] The OSCE/ODIHR now refers to the 1990–1994 period as the "free and fair years," before the organization sought to make its observation more comprehensive and systematic.[33]

Also in the early 1990s, a number of organizations began sending observation missions to sub-Saharan Africa, including U.S.-based NGOs

30. CSCE, *Implementation of the Helsinki Accords: Hearing before the Commission on Security and Cooperation in Europe*, 1–2.

31. OSCE, *Document of the Copenhagen Meeting of the Conference on the Human Dimension of the CSCE*.

32. Ibid., Article 6.

33. OSCE/ODIHR, *A Decade of Monitoring Elections: The People and the Practice*.

such as the Carter Center, the National Democratic Institute (NDI), and the International Republican Institute (IRI), as well as the Organization for African Unity, the Commonwealth Secretariat, and the International Organization of La Francophonie.[34] The European Commission began by observing several high-profile elections, including Russia's first multi-party parliamentary elections in 1993 and the first postapartheid election in South Africa in 1994. Since 2000 the European Commission has officially considered election observation "part of the mandate of the EU, whose Treaty considers the protection and promotion of human rights as well as support for democratisation as cornerstones of EU foreign policy and EU development co-operation."[35]

A number of scholars recognized the post–Cold War strengthening of the link between democracy and international benefits. As Kristian Gleditsch and Michael Ward argue, "after the Cold War, when the strategic importance of allies in the developing world [had] declined…many long-standing autocratic rulers who had enjoyed international support found themselves increasingly isolated."[36] Similarly, Judith Kelley emphasizes the legitimacy of democratic governance after the Cold War, in that "running an illegitimate government became increasingly costly as international actors moved toward more democratic conditionality and exerted greater pressure on governments to be seen as legitimate."[37]

Since the end of the Cold War democracy has become more widely accepted by citizens, states, and political leaders than at any point in history. Strikingly, even among nondemocracies, there are few leaders willing to admit that their country is not moving toward democracy. As Michael McFaul points out, "they either claim that their regimes are already democratic even if they are not (Russia) or that their political leaders are moving their countries 'step by step' toward democracy (China)."[38] No institutional alternative to democracy has gained popularity, and for nearly all states in the international system since the 1990s, democratic institutions are already in place or democracy has been outlined as the stated goal. Francis Fukuyama articulated the most extreme form of this argument, arguing that Western liberal democracy would be the "final" form

34. Anglin, "International Election Monitoring"; Sives, "A Review of Commonwealth Election Observation."

35. European Commission, "Communication from the Commission on EU Election Assistance and Observation," 3.

36. Gleditsch and Ward, "Diffusion and the Spread of Democratic Institutions," 278.

37. Kelley, "Assessing the Complex Evolution of Norms," 246.

38. McFaul, "Democracy Promotion as a World Value," 148.

of government.[39] Although there are exceptions and other priorities that often trump democracy, it is clear that a large increase in international pressure for democracy took place during the 1990s.

Underscoring the magnitude of this change, the economist and Nobel Prize winner Amartya Sen pointed to "the emergence of democracy as the preeminently acceptable form of governance" as "the single most important event of the twentieth century."[40] John Ikenberry calls democracy promotion the "hidden grand strategy" of American foreign policy, representing a remarkably consistent yet not necessarily coordinated agreement among a variety of policy actors that promoting democracy is in the best interest of the United States.[41] Rhetorically, support for democracy and democracy promotion has become a mainstay of the U.S. presidency, and is relatively consistent across Democratic and Republican administrations. Many U.S. presidents since 1960, including John Kennedy, Jimmy Carter, Ronald Reagan, George H.W. Bush, Bill Clinton, George W. Bush, and Barack Obama, incorporated democracy promotion explicitly into U.S. foreign policy priorities. In a March 1961 speech, Kennedy said that "democracy is the destiny of humanity" and it is the United States' obligation is to "serve as the single largest counter to the adversaries of freedom."[42] Carter, in 1977, said that "because we are free, we can never be indifferent to the fate of freedom elsewhere."[43] Reagan, in a widely cited address to the British Parliament, said that "we must be staunch in our conviction that freedom is not the sole prerogative of a lucky few, but the inalienable and universal right of all human beings," and "it would be cultural condescension, or worse, to say that any people prefer dictatorship to democracy."[44] Beginning with George H.W. Bush, the link between U.S. security and democracy promotion became more overt, with Bush arguing that "the community of democratic nations is more robust than ever, and it will gain strength as it grows...abandonment of the worldwide democratic revolution could be disastrous for American security."[45] Clinton continued with this argument, in 1993 stating that the United States' "overriding purpose must be to expand and strengthen the world's community of market-based democracies."[46] George W. Bush in 2005 said that "it is the policy of the

---

39. Fukuyama, *The End of History and the Last Man*, 137.
40. Sen, "Democracy as a Universal Value," 4.
41. Ikenberry, "Why Export Democracy?," 56.
42. March 22, 1961. Quoted in Smith, *America's Mission*, 214.
43. Ibid., 241.
44. June 8, 1982. Address to British Parliament.
45. December 15, 1992. Quoted in Smith, *America's Mission*, 311.
46. September 27, 1993, speech before the United Nations General Assembly.

United States to seek and support the growth of democratic movements and institutions in every nation and culture, with the ultimate goal of ending tyranny in our world."[47] Addressing an audience in Cairo, Obama said that even the controversy over democracy promotion generated by the Iraq War "does not lessen my commitment...to governments that reflect the will of the people..." and that such governments are "ultimately more stable, more successful, and more secure."[48]

As Mark Peceny argues in reference to U.S. decisions to promote democracy following military interventions, although "realist" security concerns sometimes override U.S. interest in democracy promotion, "the promotion of democracy is one of the most important tools American leaders use to transcend the potential contradictions involved in being a liberal great power."[49] Although democracy promotion has consistently been part of U.S. foreign policy, it should not be mistaken for an entirely U.S.-driven mission. Many other states and international actors promote democracy, sometimes in spite of U.S. involvement. I have already mentioned democracy promotion by the German political party foundations, or *Stiftung*, and their role in some of the early "third-wave" democratic transitions.[50] Democracy promotion outside the United States increased with the end of the Cold War. French Presidents François Mitterrand (first in 1990) and Jacques Chirac (first in 1995) each laid out democracy promotion as part of their administrations' foreign policies, with Chirac stating that "the requirement of democracy and the respect for human rights have to figure among the main criteria of our international action."[51] In 1997, Tony Blair's first foreign secretary, Robin Cook, pledged that the British government would "work through international forums and bilateral relationships to spread the values of human rights, civil liberties, and democracy, which we demand for ourselves."[52]

The controversy surrounding the Iraq War caused some leaders to justify their support for democracy promotion in spite of growing domestic sentiment against the United States. Defending Danish democracy promotion efforts against domestic charges of U.S. imperialism, Prime Minister Anders Fogh Rasmussen said that "In the fight between democracy

---

47. Bush, January 20, 2005, Second Inaugural Address.
48. Obama, June 4, 2009, "Remarks by the President on a New Beginning."
49. Peceny, *Democracy at the Point of Bayonets*, 4.
50. Pinto-Duschinsky, "Foreign Political Aid."
51. Quoted in Daguzan, "France, Democratization and North Africa," 136.
52. Quoted in Youngs, *The European Union and the Promotion of Democracy*, 210.

and dictatorship one cannot act neutrally. One must take a firm stand in favour of democracy, and against dictatorship."[53]

Even in states in which the 2003 U.S. invasion of Iraq and subsequent rhetoric about democracy promotion were highly unpopular among the voting public, the reaction of governments was not to reject democracy promotion out of hand but to object to the Bush administration's methods of democracy promotion. Thus, following the 2004 Spanish election in which the winning party had committed to withdrawing Spanish troops from Iraq, democracy promotion policy was not eliminated. Instead, the Spanish turned to emphasizing an alternative "dialog-based" approach to democracy promotion, and the country's efforts to promote democracy continued.[54]

Intergovernmental organizations that have made democracy a membership condition include the Organization of American States, the Council of Europe, the Commonwealth, the African Union (formerly the OAS), the Pacific Islands Forum, La Francophonie, and the European Union.[55] In 2004, the UN commissioned a document detailing relevant policies and agreements published by intergovernmental organizations pertaining to the promotion of democracy, a document that totaled nearly five hundred pages and included agreements from IGOs throughout the world, many of them with relatively few Western democratic members. Additionally, dozens of prominent states and international organizations have detailed provisions for democracy promotion and standards for democratic elections, many of which have been compiled by the European Commission for ease of enforcement by their election-monitoring delegations.[56] Avery Davis-Roberts and David Carroll published an overview of existing international legal obligations that states have made to hold democratic elections.[57] Considerations for democracy are woven into other policy areas such as poverty alleviation, postconflict economic recovery, anticorruption campaigns, trading relationships, and even military assistance.[58]

---

53. Ibid., 33.
54. Ibid., 130–31.
55. Rich, "Bringing Democracy into International Law."
56. European Union, *Compendium of International Standards for Elections.*
57. Davis-Roberts and Carroll, "Using International Law to Assess Elections."
58. Institute for Democracy and Electoral Assistance, "Focus: Democracy Forum 2000, Attacking poverty by supporting democracy"; Gillespie and Youngs, "Themes in European Democracy Promotion"; Committee on International Relations and Committee on Foreign Relations, "Legislation on Foreign Relations Through 2002"; Dimitrova and Pridham, "International Actors and Democracy Promotion in Central and Eastern Europe."

Thus, the rhetorical record of increased support for democracy is difficult to dispute. For my argument to be supported, however, benefit-seeking states must believe that democracy-contingent benefits exist. Even without advocating for election observation per say, democracy promoters play an important role in my argument by increasing the "democracy premium" and therefore giving benefit-maximizing states the incentive to signal their commitment to democratic elections.

If it were not for growing international acceptance of democracy and increasing rewards attached to a country's status as a democratizing state, international election observation would not have become an international norm. In my argument, the decision to invite international observers is conditioned on leaders perceiving some level of international benefits tied to democracy. This argument does not specify why other actors tie international benefits to democracy, or whether democracy promoters are motivated by normative, self-interested, or other reasons. Democracy promoters' motivations are less important in this context. So long as democracy-contingent benefits (or autocracy-contingent costs) exist, they should affect the behavior of benefit-seeking states in a similar manner regardless of the motivations of pro-democracy actors. As European Union policy on the subject has been summarized,

> democracy and protection of human rights are universal values to be pursued in their own right; they are also seen as integral to effective work on poverty alleviation...as vital tools for conflict prevention and resolution, and as the indispensable framework for combating terrorism. Democratic processes of accountability are also key to ensuring government transparency and combating corruption.[59]

Thus, from the perspective of benefit-seeking leaders, it is only necessary that some desired international benefits are tied to democracy or democratization. The composition of anticipated international benefits varies by recipient country. Links between democracy and international benefits may be implicit or explicit and include the following: direct democracy assistance, provisions within bilateral and multilateral agreements, membership conditionality in international organizations, articulation of preferences for trading with democracies, emphasis on democracy by foreign investors, diplomatic pressure, and normative or legal appeals, such as those articulated by Thomas Franck as the "emerging

---

59. European Commission, "Programming Guide for Strategy Papers: Democracy and Human Rights."

right to democratic governance."[60] Other scholars have explored this topic in much greater detail and point to demonstration or contagion effects stemming from developed democracies, in addition to more overt forms of pressure for democracy.[61]

In promoting democracy overtly, dozens of countries and international organizations fund democracy assistance, place democratic conditions on foreign aid, and even support intervention to restore democracy following the overthrow of democratically elected leaders. One of the remarkable features of the post–Cold War era is the fact that democracy promotion is a policy adopted by so many international actors other than the United States.[62]

Measuring the precise amount of benefits tied to democracy is difficult, for the reasons outlined above and in chapter 2. Nevertheless, measures of democracy assistance illustrate the over-time changes in international support for promoting democracy. Figure 3.2 shows the annual amount of bilateral foreign aid from OECD donors to government and civil society, a category that includes overt democracy assistance. Similarly, figure 3.3 shows the percentage of U.S. and foreign official development assistance devoted to democracy and governance, as reported by Finkel et al. and used as a variable in chapter 2's empirical analysis.[63] Neither indicator presents comprehensive data on available democracy-contingent benefits, but both show that such benefits exist and that they have increased considerably over time in parallel with patterns in the global diffusion of election observation.

The diversity in support for democracy, both in terms of the number of states and international organizations that reward it and the great variety of methods of democracy promotion, combine to underscore the idea that international benefits tied to democracy exist, that leaders of benefit-seeking states are aware that they exist, and that the relative importance

---

60. Franck, "The Emerging Right to Democratic Governance."

61. Beigbeder, *International Monitoring of Plebiscites, Referenda and National Elections;* Burnell, "From Evaluating Democracy Assistance to Appraising Democracy Promotion"; Carothers, *Critical Mission;* Ikenberry, "Why Export Democracy?"; Cox, Ikenberry, and Inoguchi, *American Democracy Promotion;* Knack, "Does Foreign Aid Promote Democracy?"; Levitsky and Way, "International Linkage and Democratization"; McFaul, "Democracy Promotion as a World Value"; Monten, "The Roots of the Bush Doctrine"; Schraeder, "The State of the Art in International Democracy Promotion"; Simmons and Elkins, "The Globalization of Liberalization"; Simmons, Dobbin, and Garrett, *The Global Diffusion of Markets and Democracy;* Youngs, *The European Union and the Promotion of Democracy;* Simmons and Elkins, "The Globalization of Liberalization"; Simmons, Dobbin, and Garrett, *The Global Diffusion of Markets and Democracy;* Whitehead, *The International Dimensions of Democratization.*

62. Kelley, "Assessing the Complex Evolution of Norms."

63. Finkel et al., "Effects of U.S. Foreign Assistance on Democracy Building."

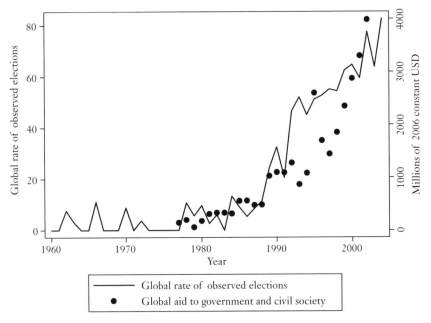

Figure 3.2. Trends in observed elections and foreign aid to government and civil society

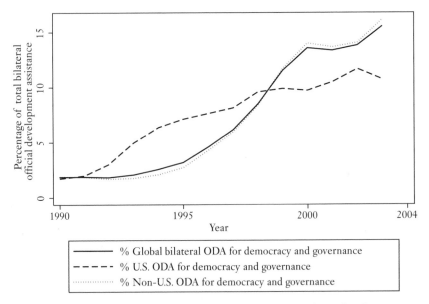

Figure 3.3. Percentage of bilateral official development assistance devoted to democracy assistance

Source: Calculated from Finkel et al. (2007) from two-year mean in millions of 2000 USD

of democracy promotion has fluctuated over time, growing considerably with the end of the Cold War.

In addition to supporting democracy more generally, democracy promoters accepted internationally certified elections as a meaningful signal that a government was committed to democratization. This dynamic created the belief among democracy promoters that governments that refuse to invite observers or that receive negative reports are pseudo-democrats. In the next sections, I examine how international actors react to negative reports from international observers, show that negative reports lead to reductions in several widely used measures of a country's level of democracy, and document and explain the few governments that refuse observers after the norm developed.

Democracy Promoters vs. Pseudo-Democrats

It is surprising to many political scientists that leaders who invite international election observers are caught committing election fraud. Inviting observers, cheating, and getting caught is not an expected strategy for any type of leader, particularly before the norm of election monitoring developed. In the model presented in chapter 1, pseudo-democrats should attempt to manipulate the election enough to win while minimizing the risk that they will be caught. They are motivated to conceal election fraud from observers because they can gain international benefits if they are recognized as a democratizing country and because they will face consequences if they are caught stealing the election. The empirical record shows, however, that leaders do not always successfully employ such strategic manipulation. Democracy promoters have attempted to increase the quality of election monitoring (as I document further in chapter 5), and leaders are periodically caught and condemned for election manipulation.

Negative reports in the early period of election observation were rare because true democrats were driving the trend, and investment in the quality of observation missions was just beginning. As more pseudo-democrats had the incentive to invite observers, and as the quality of observation increased, negative reports became more likely. For example, following the fraudulent 1986 elections in the Philippines, internationally observed elections in Panama (1989) and Pakistan (1990) were also strongly criticized, as were the 1992 elections in Cameroon, Kenya, Romania, and Yugoslavia. All else held equal, the increased willingness of observers to criticize fraudulent elections could be expected to slow the spread of observed elections among pseudo-democrats. Yet the increased willingness of observers to criticize elections coincided with the dramatic increase in democracy-contingent benefits at the end of the Cold War. Rather than avoid observers entirely, many pseudo-democrats instead had the incentive to invite observers and attempt to avoid being caught.

Defining Negative Reports

It is an inherently subjective exercise to evaluate whether a given report from international observers is negative. In general, when I refer to negative reports, I mean that foreign observers seriously questioned the winner of the election or the legitimacy of the process. Some groups use diplomatic language, and other organizations are blunt. The more professionalized observer groups—including those most likely to criticize election manipulation where it exists—issue numerous interim statements throughout the election period, providing feedback to the election authorities and sometimes pressuring governments to remedy problems such as incomplete voter registration lists before election day. In these cases, high-quality election monitors may interact with the government during the pre-election period in a manner that actually prevents negative reports because observers pressure governments to improve election quality.

Nevertheless, most missions issue a postelection statement detailing preliminary findings, which the international news media cite most widely. Reputable organizations also issue a comprehensive final report several months after the election and include reports of their monitoring of the postelection period, certification of results, and resolution of any postelection disputes.

In order to gather a more systematic picture of negative reports over time, I collected the summary statements from the official final reports or from the widely cited postelection press releases. When neither of these was available, I also coded the evaluation of observers from news reports following the election. Comparing observer reports on an objective scale may not be possible, and judging whether an individual report is more or less negative than any other report is difficult. However, several features of statements from observers provide clear indications that an election was judged to be fraudulent or otherwise received serious condemnation from international observers.

The strongest possible international observer criticism of elections occurs when observers are invited but refuse to send a mission or withdraw an already deployed mission because they judge that credible elections are highly unlikely. This is a relatively rare occurrence, but when it does happen, it sends a strong message that pre-election conditions are so bad that a democratic election is virtually impossible. When observers cancel a planned mission before election day, their decision and criticism of the election is widely reported in international news coverage of the election.

Many negative reports from international observers are strongly worded and are clearly intended to cast doubt upon the legitimacy of the process, but they stop short of arguing that the winner would have been different in a more democratic election. Thus, when observers do assert that the "wrong" party won, it is a strong condemnation and draws more negative attention to the election as being "stolen." Reports that question the integrity or the legitimacy of the process are also interpreted as serious condemnation, even if they suggest that the outcome would have been the same in a free and fair process. This type of summary judgment is most likely when the margin of victory is quite large, yet the process is obviously flawed, as in Belarus.

Following the 2003 Georgian parliamentary elections, the head of the OSCE observer mission said that the observed irregularities caused the process to be "spectacularly flawed." Following the 1995 elections in Niger, NDI condemned the elections, stating that the irregularities they observed "represent a willful effort to subvert the process in order to achieve predetermined results."[64] In Zambia in 2001, the EU summary judgment was that "in view of the administrative failures on polling day, the serious flaws in the counting tabulation procedures, together with the close outcome of the elections, we are not confident that the declared results represent the wishes of the Zambian electors on polling day."[65] Summary statements from the OSCE/ODIHR tend to focus on whether the elections met the country's commitments as an OSCE member state. For example, the 1998 report on the Armenian elections concluded that they did not "meet the OSCE standards to which Armenia has committed itself in the Copenhagen Document of 1990."[66]

Even when observer reports are critical, most are written in diplomatic language and emphasize positive components of even the worst elections, such as praising voters for their patience, enthusiasm, willingness to stand in long lines at polling stations, and their support for the democratic process. This praise, when it was presented along serious criticism, was not

---

64. National Democratic Institute, "Statement by the National Democratic Institute on the July 7 and 8 Presidential Election in Niger," news release, July 19, 1996.

65. European Union Election Observation Mission, "Final Statement on the Zambia Elections 2001," news release, May 2, 2002.

66. OSCE/ODIHR, "Republic of Armenia Presidential Election March 16 and 30, 1998, Final Report," 3.

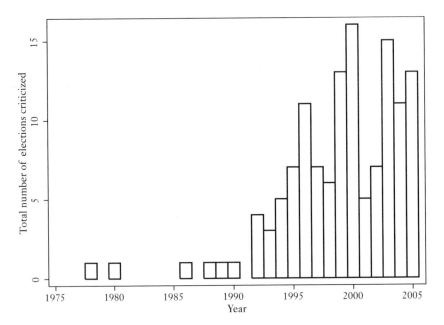

Figure 3.4. Negative reports, 1975–2005

interpreted as an endorsement of the election in my coding, because some positive comments are present in nearly all observer reports.

Figure 3.4 presents the frequency of negative reports over time. Election monitoring reports were coded as negative if they questioned the winner of the election or seriously questioned the legitimacy of the process.[67] If an election receives a negative report from more than one monitoring group, it is only counted once in figure 3.4. Out of all observed elections between 1995 and 2005, about 35% were criticized by one or more international observer groups.

Building on the theory outlined in chapter 1, if pseudo-democrats vary in their ability and willingness to conceal election manipulation, leaders are most likely to be caught stealing elections in two circumstances. Some pseudo-democrats have little to lose from international condemnation, or the risks of political liberalization may be too great to allow plausibly democratic elections. As electoral autocrats, they are willing to

---

67. Summary statements from observers were coded a second time by a research assistant in the absence of any identifying information about the elections, and the limited disagreements in coding were resolved by carefully rereading each case and considering how observer reports were interpreted in the international news media.

invite observers in order to avoid pariah status, as in the Armenian case described in chapter 4, but nevertheless engage in massive election fraud. Similarly, as I discuss below, if a leader is aware that their country's other characteristics outweigh any attention given to democracy, or if they do not need international benefits, they may be willing to refuse observers entirely, such as in Iran, Egypt, and Malaysia. In some countries, leaders may enjoy domestic support for taking anti-Western positions and therefore the domestically imposed "sovereignty costs" associated with inviting observers are greater.

A subset of pseudo-democrats are heavily dependent on international benefits, and when these leaders get caught manipulating the election, it is frequently because they lack the resources, skill, or support from other government officials to conceal their efforts at manipulation. It is these leaders that are most likely to face serious consequences when they are condemned for election fraud. Thus, my expectations about international responses to negative reports are nuanced. Leaders who have little to lose if they are caught stealing elections or who are unwilling to give up authoritarian control are less motivated to conceal election manipulation, correspondingly more likely to get caught and criticized, and may work to discredit the negative reports of international observers rather than prevent them. It is a sign of the norm's strength that these leaders continue to invite observers who condemn them, rather than simply refusing them entirely.

More interesting from a substantive perspective are those benefit-seeking leaders who lack the resources or skill to engage in successful strategic manipulation. These leaders tend to be more heavily dependent on international support and may have weaker domestic authority, making it difficult for them to marshal the resources to carry out covert election manipulation. Because of their reliance on international support, these leaders are unlikely to refuse international observers, particularly after election monitoring became an international norm.

International Consequences of Observer Criticism

When elections are criticized by international observers, what are the international consequences? This is a difficult empirical question for a variety of reasons: international benefits cannot be comprehensively measured, leaders are both rewarded and punished for their elections, and governments that successfully develop economically and democratize receive less foreign aid because they no longer need it, not because they are being penalized. Additionally, given my argument, if commitments by democracy promoters to support democratizing states are credible, observable shifts in international support for countries based on whether they signal their commitment to democracy should follow changes in the postelection beliefs among democracy promoters about a government's commitment to democracy.

International reaction to the reports from observers should depend on previous perceptions of leaders' types and the levels of international support the government already receives. Following an election, pro-democracy actors update their belief about the incumbent's "type." There are many reasons why the perceptions of a government's commitment to democracy change, as well as why foreign support of a given government changes. Many foreign aid donors are particularly reluctant to withdraw aid from the poorest countries or from strategic allies, even if they hold relatively poor elections.

Nevertheless, several empirical implications are clear. Other scholars have demonstrated that relatively more democratic institutions—as measured by various indices of democracy and regime type—are correlated with a variety of other international benefits, such as foreign direct investment[68] and international trade.[69] When a government receives a negative report from international election observers, its perceived level of democracy should decrease. International actors turn to a variety of sources when evaluating a country's level of democratization. It is worth noting that several widely used measures, including the Freedom House measures of political rights and civil liberties (a source widely used in policy circles) and the Polity measure of regime type, now explicitly incorporate the reports of international observers into their coding. The coding checklist for political rights asks whether "established and reputable national and/or international election monitoring organizations judge the most recent elections for head of government to be free and fair?"[70] Similarly, several of Polity IV component variables explicitly code the reports of "international and domestic election observers" in determining the quality of the election and in turn, the country's level of democracy.[71] Given this information, it is unsurprising that both indices change systematically based on whether observers are invited and whether they issue a negative report.

68. Jensen, "Political Risk, Democratic Institutions, and Foreign Direct Investment"; Jensen, "Democratic Governance and Multinational Corporations."

69. Mansfield, Milner, and Rosendorff, "Free to Trade"; Milner and Kubota, "Why the Move to Free Trade?"

70. Freedom House, "Freedom House: Methodology."

71. Marshall and Jaggers, *Polity IV Project*, 58.

To demonstrate this correlation between the reports of observers and widely referenced annual measures of country's level of democracy, I estimate several statistical models with three measures of regime type as the dependent variables.[72] Inviting observers is associated with a statistically significant increase in a country's Polity2 score of 1.7 points, and inviting observers and receiving a negative report is associated with a reduction of almost 1 point.[73]

Freedom House data are arguably more widely used by policymakers. From 1973 to 2006 (all available data), inviting observers is associated with a statistically significant 0.4 point improvement in a country's political rights score, whereas receiving a negative report from observers is associated with a 0.5 point decline in the civil liberties score.[74] Other measures of democracy are similarly sensitive. Even the *International Country Risk Guide's* measure of political risk, an indicator marketed to foreign investors, is likely to increase when observers are invited.[75]

Overtime Variation in International Benefits within Countries

As stated previously, leaders already receiving some level of international benefits should experience reductions in international benefits following internationally criticized elections, and leaders without significant existing international support should not gain additional benefits. These consequences are in addition to any domestic costs caused by reported election fraud, such as increased support for postelection protests and the

---

72. The reported estimates are from the following model, $y_{it} = y_{it-1} + \beta_1 Election_{it} + \beta_2 Observed_{it} + \beta_3 Negative_{it} + \alpha_i + \varepsilon_{it},$ where y is a variable representing country i's democracy score at time t, and α_i represents country fixed-effects.

73. The *Polity2* variable ranges from -10 to 10, with higher values representing more democratic political institutions. The coefficient on *Observed* is 1.70 with a standard error of 0.12. The coefficient on *Negative* is -0.87 with a standard error of 0.21. The coefficient on *Election* is 0.11 with a standard error of 0.06.

74. Freedom House political rights and civil liberties indices range from 1 to 7, with 1 representing the highest levels of political rights and civil liberties. The coefficient on *Observed* is -0.40, with a standard error of 0.04. The coefficient on *Negative* is 0.50 with a standard error of 0.07. The coefficient on *Election* is -0.13 with a standard error of 0.02.

75. *Political Risk* theoretically ranges from 0 to 100. The coefficient on *Observed* is 1.12 with a standard error of 0.5. The reported estimates are from the following model, $y_{it} = y_{it-1} + \beta_1 Election_{it-1} + \beta_2 Observed_{it-1} + \beta_3 Negative_{it-1} + \alpha_i + \varepsilon_{it},$ where y is a variable representing country i's Political Risk score average over the current year t, and α_i represents country fixed effects. Independent variables are lagged by one year to ensure that the monthly political risk score incorporates months following the election but excluding the developed democracies, *Observed* has a coefficient of 0.40 and a standard error of 0.12. *Negative* is not statistically significant.

increased potential for an electoral revolution, as in Yugoslavia, Georgia, and Ukraine. Empirical predictions about the consequences of negative reports must consider whether the country expects to gain new international benefits or avoid losing existing benefits by inviting observers. For countries already receiving low levels of international benefits, either because they have previously committed blatant anti-democratic actions and/or human rights abuses or because they have never been recognized as a democratizing country, internationally approved elections may be required for international benefits to increase or resume. If such states receive negative reports from election monitors, international benefits may not change, but the negative report causes these governments to forgo benefits that would have followed internationally certified elections.

When elections are criticized in countries that were previously perceived as democratizing, existing levels of international benefits should be noticeably reduced. However, for the poorest and most aid-dependent countries, donors cut off international support only reluctantly. International reaction to Haitian elections reveals both the reluctance of pro-democracy actors to punish very poor countries and their willingness to do so following blatant violations of democratic norms. The United States and other Western donors to Haiti had high hopes for Jean-Bertrand Aristide, first elected to the presidency in 1990 in what was widely regarded as the country's first democratic election. Aristide was soon deposed in a coup, but reinstalled as president by the U.S. military in 1994. Aristide's government received massive but short-lived increases in aid, especially from the United States and the European Community, a condition of which was a promise to leave office at the end of his constitutionally allowed term.[76] Although he technically kept his promise, rather than allowing open competition for the presidency, he engineered the 1995 victory of his chosen successor, René Préval. Reportedly ruling from behind the scenes until he could run for reelection, Aristide's democratic luster began to fade. Rigged legislative by-elections in 1997 provoked further international condemnation and, combined with the 1999 disbandment of parliament and the lack of a legitimate government, led to the suspension of most foreign aid to the country.[77]

76. Marilyn Greene, "Haiti to Get Infusion of Cash/Nations Plan More Than $1 Billion," *USA Today*, October 6, 1994.

77. Michael Norton, "United Nations Suspends Election Aid in Haiti," Associated Press, August 22, 1997; Ives Marie Chanel, "Haiti: Political Crisis Undermines Foreign Aid," Inter Press Service, December 27, 1999.

Aid resumption and other forms of international support were conditioned on new, democratic, and internationally certified legislative elections, which were postponed four times before they were held in May 2000. The elections were preceded by "a wave of murders of opposition leaders and candidates."[78] Aristide was reelected president in November 2000 with 92% of the vote in an election boycotted by all major opposition parties. Observers judged the 2000 elections to be "fundamentally flawed," and aid was suspended or channeled through private organizations. Aristide's attempts to reassure donors and restore aid were not successful, and in February of 2004, he left office under disputed circumstances and was replaced by an interim leader.[79] His ouster and the country's near-crisis conditions—exacerbated by a devastating hurricane in 2004—led major donors to begin releasing foreign aid and other forms of support in order to "help the country promote democracy and economic recovery."[80] Figure 3.5 illustrates trends in bilateral aid from the country's biggest donors over time, although note that foreign aid was not the only international benefit that was withdrawn from Haiti during this period. Aid is, however, more easily quantifiable than other international benefits.

When some governments invite observers, they do so because they have already developed reputations as pseudo-democracies or electoral authoritarian regimes. These countries may have experienced military coups, already held blatantly fraudulent elections, or have never held elections at all. For example, the period leading up to Peru's 2000 presidential elections was characterized by rapid democratic reversal. Incumbent President Alberto Fujimori's 1992 *autogolpe* brought significant international attention to these threats to Peruvian democracy, but the 2000 elections were viewed as the point of no return. International election observers were invited by Fujimori, who was eager to put concerns about his authoritarian tendencies to rest. Failing to invite observers to the 2000 elections would have been a sure sign they were blatantly fraudulent. Inviting observers allowed Fujimori some additional scope for manipulation but also increased the possibility that he would be caught and internationally condemned for election fraud.

---

78. "The Inevitable President," *Economist*, November 16, 2000.

79. Whether or not Aristide was forced to resign or did so willingly is the subject of debate, but it is not disputed that he was escorted out of Haiti on a U.S. military jet to the Central African Republic on February 28, 2004.

80. Nicolas Brulliard, "Donors Pledge $1 Billion in Aid to Haiti," United Press International, July 20, 2004.

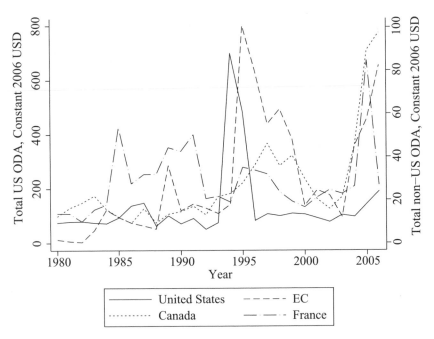

Figure 3.5. Bilateral foreign aid to Haiti

Following the first round of the 2000 elections in Peru, Fujimori was found to have engaged in widespread efforts to manipulate the election, and various observer organizations levied stinging criticism. The OAS head of mission said that "something sinister is happening here," and the mission issued a statement that "the Peruvian electoral process is far from one that could be considered free and fair."[81] The joint NDI/Carter Center report called the process "irreparably damaged," and the final report similarly left little room for interpretation:

> The 2000 election process in Peru failed dramatically to meet minimum international standards for a genuine, democratic election. As a result, the people of Peru were denied the opportunity to exercise their right to democratic elections, and the government that emerged from the elections lacks a legitimate mandate based on the will of the electorate.[82]

81. Clifford Krauss, "Peruvian's Lead in Vote Prompts Charge of Fraud," *New York Times*, April 10, 2000.

82. National Democratic Institute and The Carter Center, *Peru Elections 2000: Final Report of the National Democratic Institute/Carter Center Joint Election Monitoring Project*, 35.

After the clearly fraudulent first round, the Carter Center, NDI, the European Union, the OAS, and thousands of domestic observers withdrew their official delegations in protest. Announcing their withdrawal from the second round, the EU said that "the elections could not take place in a credible manner and in accordance with international standards."[83] As evidence of the unquestionably large-scale fraud, in the second round, official government tallies initially reported that the number of votes cast exceeded the number of registered voters by 1.4 million.[84] Not surprisingly, the negative reports by election observers were enough to discredit Fujimori as a democratically elected leader, although the international reaction to the fraudulent elections was not fully realized; discovery of videotapes proved that his office had engaged in widespread bribery of government officials and he subsequently resigned.[85] As Arturo Santa-Cruz writes,

> What was important in the Peruvian case was not just that the Andean country was perceived as undemocratic, but that this fact endowed the international community with the right to advance claims on Fujimori's government, just as it also endowed the Peruvian people with the right to advance claims on the international community.[86]

By the 1990s it became common for states and international organizations to suspend support for regimes that had committed blatant violations of democracy or human rights.[87] Many pro-democracy states made overt commitments to support democratic states and made provisions for such support an explicit part of their foreign policy. For example, an amendment to the 1986 U.S. Foreign Assistance Act prohibited U.S. aid to "any country whose duly elected head of government is deposed by decree or military coup."[88] Following such a suspension, the resumption of bilateral foreign aid and normal diplomatic relations with many developed democracies became increasingly conditioned on the holding of free and fair elections.

The case of Togo clearly demonstrates this dynamic. Amid widespread pressure on African governments to hold multiparty elections in the early

83. European Union, "Peru Presidential and Congressional Elections—EU Observation," news release, April 6, 2001.

84. Taylor, "Patterns of Electoral Corruption in Peru."

85. Cooper and Legler, *Intervention Without Intervening?*

86. Santa-Cruz, "Monitoring Elections, Redefining Sovereignty," 767.

87. Donno, "Defending Democratic Norms: Regional Intergovernmental Organizations, Domestic Opposition and Democratic Change."

88. Committee on International Relations and Committee on Foreign Relations, "Legislation on Foreign Relations Through 2002."

1990s, the Togolese government's failure to hold plausibly democratic elections led to a near-total suspension in nonhumanitarian foreign aid for more than a decade. General Gnassingbe Eyadema, who came to power in a 1967 coup d'état, came under increasing international pressure in the early 1990s to hold multiparty elections (he allowed noncompetitive presidential elections in 1979 and in 1986). In early 1993, major donors, including the United States, France, Germany, and other members of the European Commission suspended foreign aid to Togo over the "worsening political situation" and the president's "unwillingness to create conditions for a peaceful transition to democracy."[89] Following the suspension, Eyadema agreed to multiparty elections but allowed only forty-five days of preparation and campaigning. International observers from the Carter Center, NDI, the Organization for African Unity, La Francophonie, and several smaller NGOs deployed missions to the country.

After elections were scheduled and international observers arrived, conditions deteriorated, ultimately leading all major international observers except La Francophonie and the OAU to suspend their missions. Following ten months of observation, and after the government refused to delay the elections, the joint Carter Center and NDI statement said that the "minimum conditions did not exist to conduct meaningful elections."[90] The problems cited in their statement included the refusal of all major opposition candidates to participate and the resulting lack of real competition; the election commission's own concern about their preparations for the election; out-of-date, manipulated, and inflated voter registration lists; the election commission's failure to distribute electoral identification cards to voters; the government's refusal to accredit nonpartisan domestic election observers; the printing of many more voter identification cards than registered voters; unbalanced media time; the distribution of faulty indelible ink; misuse of state resources for campaigning; and the overt partisanship of election officials.[91] As reported in the international news media the day after the election, the decision by international monitors to withdraw was a "fatal blow to the elections' credibility."[92]

89. "Aid to Togo halted," *Globe and Mail*, Reuters News Service, February 12, 1993.

90. National Democratic Institute, "National Democratic Institute / Carter Center Joint Post-Election Statement on Withdrawal from 1993 Togolese Elections," news release, September 1, 1993.

91. Ibid.

92. Karl Maier, "Poll Deemed to Lack Credibility," *Irish Times*, London Independent Service, August 26, 1993.

Even the leader of the delegation from La Francophonie, an organization that rarely criticizes election fraud, was quoted as saying that the election was "meaningless."[93] Their twenty-member delegation stayed to observe election day proceedings and found that the election scarcely took place.

> Nearly one-third of the polling stations were either closed or did not exist. The second third of the polling stations opened, but no one came to vote [and] the remaining third of polling stations functioned more or less correctly, but with a voter turnout of only five to fifteen percent.[94]

In 1998 Eyadema again held presidential elections and invited international observers. The EU and The Carter Center again found the electoral process to fall far short of international standards, and aid was not resumed from the EU and other bilateral donors. Virtually the same process was repeated in 2003 and again in 2005, following the death of Eyadema. In 2006, after the Togolese government complied with a series of mandated democratic reforms, the EU released 40 million Euros in foreign aid. When Togo held its first credible elections in October 2007, the EU and other donors resumed full development cooperation. Figure 3.6 illustrates the trend of aid from the European Community to Togo.

The relationship between internationally certified elections and foreign support for governments is not always clear-cut, and there remains room for pseudo-democrats to engage in strategic manipulation or try to discredit the reports of observers. However, the perception of a connection between international benefits and internationally certified elections is widespread. Governments that are already facing cuts in international support because of previous anti-democratic actions must hold internationally certified elections in order to resume international benefits. Consistent with the norm of election monitoring, the vast majority of countries now invite international election observers. I now explore those few governments that do not.

Refusing to Invite International Observers

By 2000, few countries were violating the norm and not inviting international observers. One interesting feature of the evolving game between international observers and pseudo-democrats is how rarely leaders

---

93. "Presidential Election in Togo: This Election Was Meaningless!" *Le Figaro*, August 29, 1993.
94. Ibid.

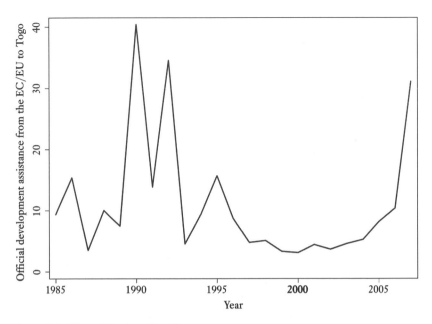

Figure 3.6. Bilateral foreign aid to Togo

simply refuse to invite international observers. Outside of the exclusive club of wealthy and stable democracies, a small subset of countries refused observers even after the norm became widely accepted. As mentioned in previous chapters, some countries stopped inviting observers because they became widely regarded as democracies, such as the Czech Republic and Chile, and were no longer expected to have their elections observed. Other countries, such as Cuba, North Korea, Oman, Vietnam, and Turkmenistan, held elections in which multiparty competition was impossible and therefore stood no chance of holding plausibly democratic elections.

Figure 3.7 summarizes patterns of election monitoring for all countries that did not invite observers to at least one national election between 2000 and 2006. I have excluded noninviting countries that are long-term consolidated democracies, members of the European Union, or countries that are considered to have very democratic political institutions (with a *Polity2* score of 8 or higher). The fourteen countries that never invited observers during this period are Bahrain, Cuba, Egypt, Guinea, Iran, Jordan, Kuwait, Laos, Malaysia, North Korea, Oman, Syria, Turkmenistan, and Vietnam. As indicated in figure 3.7, some of these elections lacked any real multiparty competition, as in Cuba, North Korea, or Oman. The puzzle in these cases is not why they refuse international election monitors, but why they hold elections at all.

Equatorial Guinea, Ethiopia, Iraq, and Singapore invited election monitors to some but not all of their elections in this period. Malaysia and Gabon are two of the very few countries that invited international observers in the 1990s and then stopped after the norm had developed. Guinea invited observers from the European Union to elections in 2002, but the EU declined to send a mission.

Benin is considered one of the more democratic countries in Africa but does not meet the conditions that I have used to exclude democracies from figure 3.7. The country invited international observers to all but the 2003 national assembly elections. Madagascar similarly invited observers to most elections since 1990 and resumed inviting observers after the disputed 2002 presidential elections.

Other countries (such as Iran and Malaysia) do not rely heavily on international assistance from the West or would otherwise suffer little for

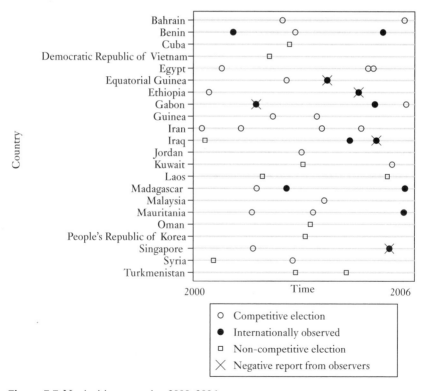

Figure 3.7. Noninviting countries, 2000–2006

violating the norm (such as Egypt). As referenced previously, Egypt is heavily dependent on international support but receives aid despite its political institutions and because of its strategic importance to the United States in the Middle East. Yet even Egypt has responded to the norm of election monitoring. Before the 2005 elections, heated debate took place within the Egyptian government about whether to invite international observers, with President Mubarak's son Jamal unsuccessfully arguing in favor of international observers in response to U.S. pressure on the country to hold democratic elections.[95] The decision in part sparked widespread editorializing about "Egypt's Imitation Elections," including the following condemnation, reprinted in the *International Herald Tribune:*

> Here are some simple ways to identify a real democratic election. The ruling party should not be allowed to shape the election arrangements and intimidate voters. The candidates should be able to compete on a reasonably level playing field. Impartial observers should be welcome and given time to deploy themselves at polling places nationwide. Not one of these defining features was evident in last week's Egyptian presidential voting.[96]

Despite the fact that opposition parties were allowed to compete for the first time in the presidential elections, the Egyptian elections were widely viewed as a charade. Overall, the vast majority of governments invite observers, and the majority of governments that do not comply with the norm are unambiguous autocrats or unambiguous democrats.

Evidence of the Democracy-Contingent Benefits

In this chapter I have provided evidence in support of three of the empirical implications outlined in chapter 1 and documented the role of democracy promoters in contributing to the norm of election monitoring. Democracy promoters play a fundamental role in explaining the diffusion of international election monitoring by increasing democracy-contingent benefits, but they did not advocate for the norm. Rather, by increasing support available to governments that were committed to democratization, and eventually by recognizing internationally endorsed elections as a signal sent by all true democrats, they gave governments the incentive

---

95. "US Presses Egypt to Allow in Election Monitors," Agence France Press, August 29, 2005. Q & A: Egypt's Election Issues. November 15, 2005.

96. "Egypt's Imitation Election," *New York Times*, September 11, 2005.

to initiate international election monitoring and increased the constraints on pseudo-democrats. By the late 1990s, choosing not to invite observers signaled with certainty that a government was a pseudo-democracy not interested in internationally recognized elections. By inviting observers, pseudo-democrats risked a negative report and a reduction in international benefits. However, for governments already perceived to be pseudo-democracies, gaining a positive report from international observers was the path back to full international support, as demonstrated by Togo. Inviting observers and receiving a negative report is not an expected strategy for any type of leader. By showing that some governments are punished for failing to hold internationally certified elections, I have demonstrated that a plausible connection between election monitoring and democracy-contingent benefits exists and that this connection is observable to other governments that decide whether to invite observers. The threat of reduced international benefits is only one of several ways in which inviting monitors can be costly to pseudo-democrats. In the next chapter, I document how election monitors can have a direct effect on election day behavior and present causal evidence that observers can decrease vote share for pseudo-democrats but that observers do not necessarily have the same effect for true democrats.

4

DOES ELECTION
MONITORING MATTER?

Are international election monitors more costly to pseudo-democrats than to true democrats? In this chapter, I continue investigating the consequences of internationally monitored elections as they relate to norm formation and show that the presence of international observers correlates with several types of costs to incumbent leaders. I also use experimental evidence involving the randomization of short-term election observers to demonstrate that international observers can have a direct deterrent effect on election day fraud. By causing a reduction in vote share through fraud deterrence, at the very minimum election monitors make it more difficult for pseudo-democrats to steal elections, a cost that must exist for election monitoring to be a credible signal of a government's commitment to democratic elections. I also show that for true democrats, the same cost does not exist and present evidence that observers can have unintended consequences that help incumbent true democrats. Chapter 5 continues this investigation by exploring the evolving game of strategy between international observers and pseudo-democrats. Here I provide a detailed examination of whether international observers have both direct and micro-level effects on election day behavior in two elections, either by deterring fraud or making it more likely that polling officials follow the rules.

An important empirical implication of my theory is that election observation must be more costly to pseudo-democrats than to true democrats. Supporters of election observation argue that observers improve the quality of elections and make it more likely that election fraud will be uncovered. Cross-nationally, the presence of international observers is correlated with a variety of outcomes that are costly to the incumbent governments that invite them. These correlations suggest that, on average, observed elections are more competitive, and the incumbent government is more likely to lose such elections. I present these cross-national descriptive statistics to support my argument and to contrast them with the experimental evidence provided later in this chapter. Although it is true that incumbents are more likely to lose elections when monitors are present, such evidence cannot demonstrate a causal relationship between observers and increased costs to pseudo-democrats, unlike the natural and field experimental evidence shown in this chapter.

Incumbent Turnover and the Correlates of Observed Elections

In chapter 1, I argued that pseudo-democrats, all else equal, should perform worse when international monitors are present. The descriptive statistics below provide some support for this claim, but establishing causality is difficult. Critics of international election monitoring have been especially vocal in arguing that the central raison d'être of observers is to legitimize flawed elections.[1] It is true that observers sometimes legitimize flawed elections. My argument suggests, however, that the possibility that observers will not condemn a manipulated election is a central reason why pseudo-democrats are willing to invite them in the first place. Nevertheless, the fact that pseudo-democrats take this risk should increase the chances that they will lose, either directly, through fraud deterrence, or indirectly, by making election fraud more expensive and diverting resources that could be used elsewhere. Consider the following descriptive statistics for elections held between 1990 and 2006, when international observers were widely available (I exclude the consolidated democracies for ease of interpretation):

- Out of all elections in which the incumbent leader or governing party was replaced, 75% were internationally monitored (161 of 215).[2]
- Out of all elections in which the office of the incumbent executive was contested, and in which the incumbent both ran and was replaced, 68% were internationally observed (45 of 66).[3]

---

1. Abbink and Hesseling, *Election Observation and Democratization in Africa*; Geisler, "Fair?"

2. Data are from the Hyde and Marinov NELDA dataset described in appendix B.

3. Coding of leaders from the Archigos dataset, Goemans, Gleditsch, and Chiozza, "Introducing Archigos." Other data from NELDA data described in appendix B (Hyde and Marinov, "National Elections Across Democracy and Autocracy").

- From 1960 to 1989, observers were present at only 10% of elections in which there were significant concerns before the election that it would not be free and fair. After 1989, this number increases to 69% and to 75% when single-party elections are excluded.
- Out of all elections in which the vote count was considered a "gain for the opposition," observers were present at 70% (258 of 368).

These data suggest that observers are invited by incumbent governments to many elections that are more competitive and that are more likely to result in negative outcomes for the incumbent regime. Yet it is possible that governments were more likely to invite observers in these circumstances. Although they are suggestive, these cross-national data do not demonstrate that observers caused more competitive election outcomes.

An Alternative Micro-level Approach to Testing the Effects of Observers

One persistent alternative argument is that it is costless for leaders to invite international election monitors, and the phenomenon is therefore not interesting as a case of international norm formation. This chapter disputes this alternative explanation by showing that inviting monitors can have several types of direct effects on election day behavior. Using experimental methods involving the randomization of international election observers, I show that in Armenia (2003) the (pseudo-democratic) incumbent president performed much worse in polling stations that were monitored compared with those that were not. In Indonesia (2004), in what was widely considered a democratic election, observer presence actually increased votes cast for the incumbent true democrat, who went on to lose the election and peacefully transfer power.

Natural and field experimental tests are increasingly popular within the social sciences because of their potential to demonstrate cause and effect. The cases included in this chapter are described in greater detail elsewhere and are condensed here in order to link the results from these projects to the international norm of election observation.[4] The distinguishing characteristic of experimental methods versus observational research is that the central independent variable, or "treatment" variable, is randomly assigned. In field experiments such as those conducted recently by Alan

---

4. See Hyde, "The Observer Effect in International Politics"; Hyde, "Experimenting with Democracy Promotion"; Dunning and Hyde, "The Analysis of Experimental Data."

Gerber and Donald Green,[5] Edward Miguel and Michael Kremer,[6] Benjamin Olken,[7] and Leonard Wantchekon,[8] the researcher supervises the random assignment of the treatment variable. In natural experiments, the researcher does not manage the assignment of the treatment variable, but natural experiments can occur when the variable is assigned "as if" the assignment was random.[9] The burden in natural experiments rests on the researcher to provide evidence that the treatment can, in fact, be treated "as if" it had been randomly assigned. Existing natural experiments vary in the degree to which the treatment approaches true randomization.[10]

There are few published natural or field experiments within the discipline of comparative politics and fewer within international relations. Exceptions for comparative politics include the work of Mei Guan and Donald Green;[11] Macartan Humphreys, William Masters and Martin Sandbu;[12] and Wantchekon.[13] Despite the relative scarcity of experimental work, the advantages are well established: properly conducted experimental work is one of the few means by which causal inference can be tested, and as has been noted in the leading political science journal, experiments have an "unrivaled capacity to demonstrate cause and effect."[14]

I evaluate the micro-level effects of observers using evidence from two different natural and field experiments surrounding elections in Armenia in 2003 and Indonesia in 2004. In both cases, I exploit the randomization of international observers during their election day observation in order to test for differences between the areas that were visited and the areas that were not. Due to the randomization (or in the case of Armenia, the "as if" randomization), any differences between the groups can be causally attributed to international election observers. By combining experimental tests of the effects of international observers with cross-national and qualitative evidence, I provide a more complete picture of the effects of election monitoring, provide some hard evidence that election monitors

5. Gerber and Green, "The Effects of Canvassing."

6. Miguel and Kremer, "Worms."

7. Olken, "Monitoring Corruption."

8. Wantchekon, "Clientelism and Voting Behavior."

9. For examples of natural experiments, see Snow, *On the Mode of Communication of Cholera*; Schargrodsky and Galiani, "Property Rights for the Poor."

10. Dunning, "Improving Causal Inference."

11. Guan and Green, "Noncoercive Mobilization in State-Controlled Elections."

12. Humphreys, Masters, and Sandbu, "The Role of Leaders in Democratic Deliberations."

13. Wantchekon, "Clientelism and Voting Behavior."

14. Druckman et al., "The Growth and Development of Experimental Research in Political Science," 627.

are costly to pseudo-democrats, and link my theory of international norm formation with its micro-level implications.

Direct Effects on Election Day Behavior

Although academics remain skeptical that observers can have direct effects on election day behavior, practitioners and proponents of international election observation frequently assert that international observers reduce election fraud and otherwise improve election quality. As referenced above, a cross-national study of this issue cannot demonstrate causality: elections that are clean because they are internationally observed are indistinguishable from elections that are observed but would have been clean without international observers. Although the cross-national data are consistent with the argument that observers reduce election fraud and observed elections are systematically more competitive than unobserved elections, there is no set of "control" variables that could disprove the alternative argument: leaders are more likely to invite observers when they know elections are going to be more competitive.

This chapter illustrates that the effects of international election observers can be measured by exploiting subnational variation in election results. In the most clear-cut case, if observers reduce election fraud directly owing to their presence in polling stations, this effect should be revealed by differences in voting patterns between monitored and unmonitored polling stations.

The typical election observation mission includes teams of observers who, throughout the course of election day, roam within predefined geographic areas. Observers take note of activities in and around polling stations and frequently talk to voters, polling station officials, political party witnesses, domestic nonpartisan observers, and to other international observers.

Observers are also able to observe fraud directly, and observers sometimes express surprise that election fraud is carried out blatantly in front of them. Teams of foreign observers have directly witnessed many forms of outright election day manipulation, including premarked and bundled stacks of ballots clearly visible within transparent ballot boxes; the allocation of multiple ballots to individual voters; theft of ballot boxes and burning of ballots before the count; overt vote-buying schemes; prohibitions on secret voting, including the presence of individuals who "assist" voters by filling out their ballots for them and/or accompanying each voter into the voting booth; illegal disenfranchisement of eligible voters; or widespread voting by children.

Less overt "irregularities" are also commonly witnessed by international observers, and these may or may not be a sign of intentional election manipulation. These more ambiguous irregularities include polling stations that open late or without sufficient materials, a lack of provisions for secret voting, the failure to follow procedures that prevent multiple voting, election day violence and disturbances that reduce voter turnout, extremely long lines, and the presence of unauthorized individuals, police, or military in polling stations.

Although it is clear from the records of election-monitoring missions that election manipulation tactics are frequently carried out in front of observers, observers may reduce election fraud without eliminating it entirely. Similarly, even though international monitors witness irregularities, polling station officials may be more likely to follow rules and regulations when they are being watched by international monitors. The remainder of this chapter tests for an "observer effect" across varying conditions, including in the presence of overt election day fraud (in the case of Armenia) and in relatively democratic elections (in the case of Indonesia). The inclusion of both studies in this chapter demonstrates that, at least in this comparison, observers were more costly to the pseudo-democratic government (in Armenia) than the incumbent government in Indonesia that was revealed to be a true democrat.

There are a few other points about election-observation methodology that are not unique to these countries but that are important to note. First, international observers do not preannounce which polling stations they will observe on election day. Keeping deployment plans confidential is standard practice for reputable international observer groups and is intended to enhance the safety of the observers by making it difficult for potential attackers to anticipate where observers will be. It also makes it difficult for the competing parties to anticipate the arrival of observers and thereby restrict their cheating to polling stations at which international observers are not expected.

Second, international observers are usually mobile, moving from polling station to polling station throughout election day. During the course of one day, an observer team could visit between ten and twenty polling stations or neighborhoods based on the length of the election day and the distance between polling stations. Critics of election observation are fond of pointing out that it would be very difficult to catch any irregularities in such short periods of observation. However, if there are ongoing problems or red flags indicating that there might be problems, observer teams are instructed to stay for as long as they think is useful, which in some cases can be as long as several hours. The questionnaires filled out by international observers include a number of observations related to the structure of the polling station, the available staff and materials, and the order of voting procedures that are immediately obvious. If the seal on the ballot box has been broken, international observers are most likely to see this and other evidence of fraud as soon as they enter a polling station. In addition, the partisan witnesses in each polling station remain there throughout the day and are often able to report irregularities to the international observers.

Elections in Armenia and Indonesia

The 2003 presidential elections in Armenia provide the opportunity for a direct test of whether international observers can reduce election fraud. During these elections, international observers from the Organization for Security and Cooperation in Europe's Office for Democratic Institutions and Human Rights (OSCE/ODIHR) were assigned to polling stations in a way that closely approximates randomization, making this case a natural field experiment. In the 2004 presidential elections in Indonesia, I worked directly with the Carter Center in designing the deployment plans. The Carter Center, founded by former U.S. President Jimmy Carter and Rosalynn Carter and based in Atlanta, GA, is a well-respected international election-monitoring group. The field experiment was generated by randomizing the assignment of international observers within predefined geographic areas.

The case of Armenia demonstrates that when election day fraud occurs, election monitoring can cause a reduction in the vote share of the cheating candidate. The Indonesian case provides an interesting contrast because election day fraud was not widely expected, and the incumbent government was not accused of cheating. Even so, international observers increased the vote share of the incumbent candidate, I argue, by making it more likely that polling station officials followed election day regulations.

By presenting these cases together, I show that international election observers can have important effects on election quality. Particularly when election day fraud is widespread, observers can reduce election day fraud directly, making it more difficult for pseudo-democrats to steal elections. True democrats experience no such costs, and even when elections are widely perceived to be democratic, international observers can have important and sometimes unanticipated effects on election day behavior. In Indonesia, these unanticipated effects actually *increased* the vote share for the incumbent, who went on to lose the election and peacefully transfer power. Overall, the results strongly refute the alternative hypothesis that inviting international observers is costless to pseudo-democrats or is equally costly to both types of leaders.

For both cases, I provide a brief background to the election, an evaluation of the randomization, and a summary of the empirical results and conclusions. I then conclude the chapter by discussing the results of these experiments in relation to my theory.

The 2003 Presidential Elections in Armenia

Of all countries that invite international election monitors, Armenia represents what might be termed a repeat offender. Between independence in 1991 and the 2003 presidential election, Armenia held six elections, none of which were viewed as democratic. Political participation by voters and by most candidates generally complied with democratic standards, but the executive office participated in elections in a manner that has been labeled "flagrantly undemocratic."[15] Following independence, the elected president Levon Ter-Petrossian and his supporters successfully consolidated power within the executive office while other nascent parties were still attempting to gain organizational strength.[16] As a result, the president is generally the controlling force in Armenian politics by virtue of his authority to dissolve parliament, appoint all judges, and declare martial law.[17] Strong political parties did not develop as a challenge to executive power, in part because of Ter-Petrossian's overt efforts to prevent any such opposition party from organizing.[18] As of 2003, there were more than one hundred registered political parties. Because successful election day manipulation requires at least minimal organizational capacity, the political structure in Armenia points to the incumbent executive as the political actor with the preponderant ability to commit widespread fraud.

The two most prominent political figures in the postindependence period are Ter-Petrossian and Robert Kocharian. The former was president until 1998, when he resigned amid wide public dissatisfaction as a result of his failure to increase the standard of living and his willingness to negotiate with Azerbaijan over the territorial conflict in Nagorno-Karabakh.

---

15. Welt and Bremmer, "Armenia's New Autocrats," 78.
16. Welt and Bremmer, "Armenia's New Autocrats."
17. Diamond, *Developing Democracy*, 55.
18. Welt and Bremmer, "Armenia's New Autocrats."

Kocharian, who was elected to replace Ter-Pertrossian in 1998, was the incumbent candidate in the 2003 presidential election.

The 2003 elections were viewed as a potential turning point for Armenian democracy. As an OSCE/ODIHR official report states,

> The election provided an important test of the progress of democratic practices in Armenia, since the previous presidential elections were characterized by serious flaws and generally failed to meet international standards. Issues of concern at the two previous presidential elections...included inaccuracy of voter lists, shortcomings in the election administration, media bias, abuse of State resources, flawed voting by military personnel, the presence of unauthorized persons during polling and counting and discrepancies in the vote count.[19]

The only item on the ballot for the 2003 elections was the presidential race, in which nine candidates ran. The incumbent president Robert Kocharian was the front-runner; he faced a serious challenge from Stepan Demirchian, the son of the late speaker Karin Demirchian, who had been killed in a 1999 attack on parliament.[20] The other notable challenger was Artashes Geghamian, the last Soviet-era mayor of the capital city of Yerevan.

The ongoing conflict with Azerbaijan over the Nagorno-Karabakh region has been the single most important postindependence issue in Armenian politics. Kocharian, a native of Nagorno-Karabakh, was seen as a resolute supporter of its independence. Ter-Petrossian's willingness to negotiate with Azerbaijan over the territory in 1998 was partly responsible for his resignation from the presidency and Kocharian's succession to his post through the 1998 special elections.

Kocharian, who did not have his own political party, officially ran as an independent. He had been supported by a shifting coalition, which in 2003 included the ruling Republican Party of Armenia and the Armenian Revolutionary Federation (also known as *Dashnak*, or the Socialist Party). He also enjoyed the strong support of the military. Although his resolute unwillingness to negotiate on the Nagorno-Karabakh conflict was his most defining characteristic, in 2003 he also campaigned on the promise of economic stability, as did all of the candidates. Thus, the relative homogeneity

---

19. OSCE/ODIHR, *Republic of Armenia Presidential Election 19 February and 5 March 2003*, 3.

20. Armenian politics are characterized by violence, which overshadowed the 2003 elections. Most notably, in 1999 the parliament was attacked by gunmen, and eight prominent politicians were assassinated. The 2003 presidential elections were the first to be held after the attack.

of Armenian politics, the lack of other issues on the ballot, the fact that the incumbent ran without a political party, the presence of a dominant executive, and the central issue of Nagorno-Karabakh provide the background to the 2003 presidential election and the context of the natural experiment, making it a relatively clean setup to evaluate the effects of international observers on election fraud committed by the incumbent government.

The first round of Armenia's 2003 presidential elections took place on February 19, followed by a runoff on March 5. The Armenian constitution requires a second-round runoff if no presidential candidate garners more than 50% of the vote in the first round of the single-district national election. The official first-round vote share for Kocharian was 49.48%, thus triggering a runoff election.

Several months prior to the election, the Armenian Ministry of Foreign Affairs invited the OSCE/ODIHR to sponsor an international election-observation mission. The delegation included members of the Parliamentary Assembly Council of Europe. In the first round of the election, the OSCE deployed 233 observers from thirty-five participating countries. The second round was observed by 193 short-term observers from twenty-one countries.

The Natural Experiment Research Design in Armenia

In the Armenian election, international observers were assigned to polling stations on election day using a method that I did not supervise but that approximates random assignment. If election day fraud occurs in any election, it should have the observable implication of increasing the vote share of the fraud-sponsoring candidate. In the case of Armenia, the incumbent sponsored the majority of election day fraud. Therefore, if international observers have no effect on election day fraud, then the incumbent should perform equally well in both groups of polling stations: those that were monitored and those that were not. If international observers reduce election fraud, the incumbent's average vote share should be lower in monitored polling stations than in unmonitored polling stations.

There are three unique features of the 2003 Armenian elections that allow a test of whether the presence of international observers reduced election day fraud. First, widespread and centrally orchestrated fraud occurred on election day. As the *Economist* described it, the 2003 election was "one of the dirtiest even Armenians can remember."[21] Fraud (and therefore fraud deterrence) can occur at many points in the electoral process.

---

21. *Economist*, "Democracy, It's Wonderful," February 22, 2003.

However, it would be difficult to test for election day costs to a pseudo-democratic government if no fraud occurred.

Eyewitness reports from international observers, domestic observers, and journalists documented many varieties of fraud. The OSCE/ODIHR observed "significant irregularities" in more than 10% of the polling stations they visited, the most blatant of which were ballot box stuffing, "carousel" voting, direct vote buying, individuals voting more than once, the intimidation of witnesses for political parties, the presence inside polling stations of government officials who attempted to intimidate officials and voters, and one isolated incident of the removal of more than fifty passports from a polling station by a policeman.[22] During the counting process, there were numerous attempts to change the vote totals by the polling-station officials, and observers recorded additional evidence of blatant ballot box stuffing. In some cases the international observers were prevented from observing the counting process, which was interpreted as an attempt to conceal illicit behavior.

The second characteristic of the 2003 presidential elections is that the Armenian Central Election Commission made disaggregated election results available. The process of recording and making public polling station-level election results requires a certain level of administrative competence and transparency that is not always present, even in developed democracies. In countries that experience significant amounts of electoral fraud, these data are often "lost" or kept private. The Armenian election data, disaggregated to the level of the polling station, were made public by the election commission on their website.[23]

The third and most important favorable feature of the 2003 Armenian elections for analysis is that the international observers were assigned in a way that approximates random assignment. Although the OSCE/ODIHR mission did not assign observers using a random numbers table or its equivalent, their method would have been highly unlikely to produce a list of assigned polling stations that were systematically different from the polling stations not visited. Each team's assigned list was selected arbitrarily from a complete list of polling stations. Those making the lists did not possess information about polling-station attributes that would have allowed prediction of voting patterns and the choice of polling stations based on those predictions.

In this particular election, the delegation leaders gave each team of the short-term observers a preassigned list of polling stations to visit on

22. OSCE/ODIHR, *Republic of Armenia Presidential Election 19 February and 5 March 2003*, 19.

23. Government-reported election results were made available online at http://www.elections.am by the Central Election Commission of Armenia.

election day. These lists were made with two objectives in mind: (1) to distribute the observers throughout the whole country (including rural and urban areas) and (2) to give each observer team a list of polling stations that did not overlap with that of other teams. Observers were encouraged to go only to those polling stations on their lists and to travel between polling stations in a way that minimized travel time and still ensured coverage of their assigned polling stations. It is important for the validity of the natural experiment that the travel routes not be predictable by external observers, including government officials.

The individuals who made these lists had little knowledge of polling-station characteristics other than their general geographic location. This is critical for the validity of the natural experiment. If the assignment of observers had considered other variables that might be correlated with the performance of the incumbent candidate, then the assignment could not be considered "as-if" random. In addition, the discussion of Armenian politics indicated few observable characteristics of the population (such as socioeconomic status or ethnicity) that might be correlated with the incumbent's popularity. In this case, the staff did not have access to disaggregated data on the demographic characteristics of the Armenian voting population. OSCE/ODIHR staff has assured me that they had no desire to (and did not) choose polling stations on any basis other than the two criteria cited above. In addition, even if this were not true, it is highly unlikely that the mission's office had the capability to choose polling stations that were more or less likely to favor the incumbent or the opposition candidates or that were more likely to experience election day fraud.[24] The fact that Armenian politics are not predictable along partisan or demographic lines underscores that this type of bias in the assignment of international observers would have required enormous effort, access to data that do not exist, and foresight about the trajectory of Armenian politics that would be unusual for foreigners to possess.

Additionally, assigning specific polling stations to each team eliminated much of the agency's influence on the individual observer teams, which, in the absence of a directive, could choose to visit polling sites based on their own selection criteria within their assigned geographic area. When observers are given leeway in choosing polling stations, the two most common alternative selection criteria (based on observation missions outside of the two discussed in this chapter) are to choose polling stations that are considered to be either convenient or interesting. Each of these decision

---

24. Even if this information were inaccurately communicated to me, if observers were more likely to visit stations they believe to be problematic, then this would dampen an observed effect observers have on fraud. For the reasons cited, however, this is an unlikely scenario.

criteria may create significant bias in the types of polling stations that are observed. This has been pointed out as a problem by several critics of election observation.[25] Observer teams that select "interesting" polling stations typically go to areas in which problems are expected; teams using this criteria may disproportionately observe and report irregularities. This is a common strategy among the more ambitious and enthusiastic international observers but was discouraged in this particular mission.

Observer teams that go to convenient areas are criticized for being electoral tourists. Other convenient selection methods may be observing near the observers' hotel in the most comfortable urban areas or going to polling stations that are near tourist destinations. Clearly, these selection criteria are nonrandom and could lead to bias in both the observers' reported observations and in the natural experiment proposed here, particularly because a clever politician could recognize the tendency of observers to travel in certain areas and therefore concentrate any electoral manipulation in places where observers would be unlikely to go. For these reasons it was particularly important for this natural experiment that this type of observer agency was explicitly discouraged.

In sum, the assignment of international observers to polling stations for both rounds of the 2003 presidential elections in Armenia can be characterized as approximating randomization. The selection was made arbitrarily from a list of all polling stations with only geographic logistics in mind, and the assignment was completed with no knowledge of variables that might be correlated with the incumbent's likely vote share. Teams were instructed to visit only the polling stations assigned to them, and because of the relatively small geographic area and limited number of polling stations assigned to each team, they had a high probability of reaching their assigned polling stations on election day.

Checking "As If" Randomization

Ideally, in any experimental research design the assignment of the treatment could be examined in relation to a background covariate in order to test for balance between the treatment and control groups. In this case, the ideal covariate would be an independent measure of the candidates' likely vote share, such as public opinion polling or past election results. These data were not available for Armenia at the polling-station level for the first round, but as table 4.1 shows, observer distribution does not appear to follow a clear pattern that would predict Kocharian vote share. Coverage

---

25. Carothers, "The Observers Observed"; Geisler, "Fair?"

varies by region from a low of 28% of polling stations monitored in Aragatsotn to 70% of polling stations monitored in the capital city of Yerevan. The last column of table 4.1 suggests that much of this difference is due to voter density, because there is relative balance in voters per monitored polling station within each region. Additionally, the OSCE mission observed extensively outside of urban areas where there are fewer voters and travel is more time consuming. To illustrate, an urban polling station is defined as one that is in the region of Yerevan, is a regional capital, or is one of the seven biggest cities (population >40,000). All other polling stations are nonurban, which includes rural and periurban polling stations. Using these criteria, 45% of all polling stations are nonurban. In the first round of the election, international observers visited 38% nonurban polling stations, and 35% nonurban in the second round. Given that there are more voters in each urban polling station, observers covered nonurban areas extensively.

Because the same method of assigning observers was used in both rounds of the election, it is possible to check the second round's randomization against covariates from the first round of the election (table 4.2). Second-round observation, because it occurred three months later and was random, should not be systematically related to any first-round election outcomes. The round two presence of observers is compared with vote share and turnout in round one. These round-one outcomes should be equal between polling stations that were monitored in the second round and those that were not. As expected with near-random assignment, the presence of observers in the second round of the election is unrelated to voter turnout or to vote share for either of the leading candidates.

Table 4.1. Armenia round one observer coverage by region

Region	Total polling stations	Percentage monitored (%)	Average voters per polling station	Voters/total monitored polling stations
Aragatsotn	133	27.82	701	2,520
Ararat	137	53.28	1,355	2,543
Armavir	153	38.56	1,219	3,161
Gegharkunik	148	32.43	1,140	3,515
Kotayk	132	43.18	1,429	3,309
Lori	226	33.63	1,059	3,148
Shirak	273	25.64	907	3,537
Syunik	54	37.04	859	2,319
Tavush	80	28.75	1,152	4,007
Vayots Dzor	40	37.50	1,017	2,712
Yerevan	388	69.59	1,751	2,516

Table 4.2. Logistic regression of round two monitoring on background covariates

Variable	(1)	(2)	(3)
Round 1 Turnout	0.425		
	(0.608)		
Round 1 Kocharian Vote Share		−0.751	
		(0.832)	
Round 1 Demirchian Vote Share			0.114
			(1.083)
Constant	−0.878	−0.220	−0.636
	(0.690)	(0.653)	(0.418)
Observations	1,763	1,763	1,763

Notes: Robust standard errors in parenthesis, clustered by region. *Significant at 5%;
**Significant at 1%

Data and Results

The central measurable effect of observers on election day fraud is to decrease the vote share for the incumbent. With all else constant, if international observers did in fact reduce fraud at the polling stations they visited, then the incumbent should perform worse in observed polling stations. Random assignment (or "as if" random assignment) of the treatment of international observers is equivalent to all else being constant.

Because international observers can be considered randomly assigned to polling stations and because there were two rounds of the presidential election, the natural experimental design involves two rounds of "treatment" and a separate observation of vote share for each round. There was some between-round overlap in the polling stations visited by international observers. This divides the sample of polling station-level election results into four experimental groups based on the treatment of international observation during the course of election day: one group of polling stations was never monitored ($N = 755$), one group was monitored only in the first round ($N = 385$), one was monitored only in the second round ($N = 260$), and one group was monitored in both rounds ($N = 363$).

Groups of polling stations received all possible combinations of the international observer treatment, including no treatment in either round of the election. Therefore, the natural experiment also allows a test of whether first-round observation had any lasting effect in the second round. Approximately 43% of polling stations were not observed in either round of the election, and about 21% were observed in both rounds.[26]

26. Outside of the Yerevan region (where polling stations were equally likely to be visited in both rounds) polling stations that were visited in round one were twice as likely to be visited again in round two.

The Effect of Monitors on Vote Share

The dependent variable is the vote share for the incumbent presidential candidate, Robert Kocharian, in the first and second rounds.[27] The results presented in table 4.3 show clear evidence that during the 2003 presidential elections in Armenia, the presence of international observers reduced the vote share for the incumbent politician by about 6% in the first round (Model 1) and by about 2% in the second round (Model 2). Both results are statistically significant. This allows a rejection of the null hypothesis that there is no difference between observed and unobserved polling stations.

Figure 4.1 illustrates this difference with a kernel density plot of Kocharian's round-one vote share in monitored and unmonitored polling stations. Note the unusual distribution of vote share in unmonitored polling stations.

The results also suggest that the effect of monitoring in the first round of the election carried over into the second round. This type of effect could occur if those committing fraud anticipated that polling stations visited in the first round were more likely to be visited again. If the effect of international observers had lasting effects on fraudulent behavior, the polling stations that were monitored in the first round should also experience less fraud in the second round. If first-round observation had no effect on second-round

Table 4.3. Effects of observations on vote share for President Robert Kocharian

Variables	(1)	(2)	(3)	(4)	(5)
	Round 1 Vote share for Kocharian			Round 2 Vote share for Kocharian	
Observed R1	−0.059**	−0.059**	−0.055**		−0.040**
	(0.010)	(0.010)	(0.009)		(0.008)
Observed R2				−0.020*	
				(0.008)	
Urban			−0.012		
			(0.010)		
Near Nagorno-Karabakh			0.213**		
			(0.019)		
Constant	0.542**	0.542**	0.536**	0.693**	0.702**
	(0.007)	(0.007)	(0.009)	(0.005)	(0.005)
Observations	1,764	1,764	1,764	1,763	1,763
R^2	0.02	0.02	0.07	0.00	0.01

Notes: Robust standard errors in parentheses, clustered by region. *Significant at 5%; **Significant at 1%

27. The same tests for the other candidates are consistent with the conclusions drawn from these results.

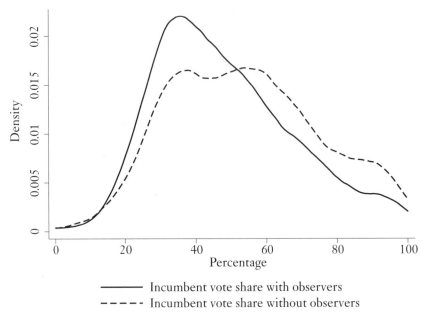

Figure 4.1. Round one vote share for incumbent in monitored vs. unmonitored polling stations

fraud, then the difference in the second-round incumbent vote share be-tween the groups in the first round should be close to zero. Model 5 in table 4.3 illustrates that a first-round visit by observers continued to have a clear effect in the second round. A first-round visit caused the incumbent to perform about 4% worse in the second round among polling stations that were not visited again in the second round. This implies that polling-station officials who were visited by international observers in the first round were less likely to commit fraud in the second round. Overall, the Armenia election shows that under conditions of widespread election day fraud, observers reduced the vote share for the incumbent, therefore making it more difficult or more costly for his government to steal votes. The magnitude of the effect of observers in the first round may have caused the second round runoff, because the national average deterrent effect was greater than the margin by which the incumbent failed to win the first round outright.

The 2004 Presidential Elections in Indonesia

Armenia and Indonesia differ in many ways, most obviously in size. Indonesia is one of the largest and most geographically diverse election-holding countries in the world. There were fewer than 1,800 polling stations for the 2003 Armenian elections. In contrast, elections in Indonesia took place across more than 17,000 islands, approximately 155 million eligible voters, and more than 500,000 polling stations.

The 2004 presidential elections in Indonesia were the first direct presidential elections in the country's history. Legislative elections held in 1999 and in April of 2004 were widely considered successful given the size of the country and the country's newly democratizing status. Prior to these elections, the president was selected indirectly. The incumbent in the 2004 elections, Megawati Sukarnoputri, had been in office since her 2001 appointment by the People's Consultative Assembly. There were two rounds of the 2004 presidential election; due to the fact that first-round election results are unavailable, I focus here on only the second-round runoff between the incumbent candidate Megawati Sukarnoputri (commonly referred to as Megawati or Mega) and the leading challenger, Susilo Bambang Yudhoyono (commonly referred to as SBY). Expectations were high leading up to the 2004 elections, which were viewed as a crucial step in Indonesia's democratization. Many believed that the elections were likely to go well, and the most common concerns in advance of election day pertained to logistical factors and the administration of an election in such a large and diverse country. However, because of the scope of the election reforms leading to the 2004 elections and the recent transition to democratic institutions, some observers worried that the election could deteriorate into violence or fraud.[28]

For the 2004 presidential elections in Indonesia, I had the opportunity to attempt random assignment of international observers for the Carter Center's election day deployment rather than rely on "as if" random assignment as in the Armenian election. To my knowledge, this was the first attempt to randomly assign observers within the field of international election observation.[29] The case of Indonesia was selected because the opportunity to attempt random assignment of international observers was made available by the Carter Center. The introduction of randomly assigned international observers had been met with some skepticism by other practitioners. Although international election observation missions regularly

---

28. European Union, *European Union Election Observation Mission to Indonesia*; Carter Center, *The Carter Center 2004 Indonesia Election Report*.

29. Since that time, randomized assignment of international observers has been conducted by the Carter Center in Nicaragua (2006), by a Yale University student delegation participating in a U.S. Embassy mission in Mauritania (2007), and by the National Democratic Institute (NDI) in the 2006 Palestinian elections.

use randomization to assign international observers to vote-counting centers at the end of election day as part of a parallel vote tabulation,[30] random assignment of international observers during polling was thought unnecessary, logistically too difficult, or contrary to some of the other goals of election observation.[31]

Prior to the election, there were reports of "money politics" and other forms of intimidation, complaints related to restrictions placed on domestic election observers, as well as violations of laws restricting campaign activity. However, overall, the environment leading up to the presidential elections was guardedly optimistic, and observers hoped that the election would be carried out peacefully. Thus, the anticipated effect that international observers could have on election day behavior was moderated by the expectation that the election would be relatively clean. Clear-cut cases of blatant election day fraud would have made this a more straightforward baseline study of whether election observers change election quality, as in the Armenian case. Theoretically speaking, Indonesia was more complicated. Although many experts in Indonesia politics had concerns in advance of the election, blatant election day fraud—such as ballot box stuffing—was not expected. In designing this study, it was not clear in advance of the election which candidate would be more likely to benefit from the presence of observers. In countries that experience widespread election day manipulation, the incumbent party is frequently the primary sponsor, and as shown in the Armenia case, evidence suggests that observers can deter blatant election day manipulation. However, in Indonesia's 2004 election, the incumbent president had never stood for direct election to the presidency and did not have a reputation for carrying out widespread election day

30. The parallel vote tabulation, or quick count, provides an independent measure of the election results, within a margin of error, and is traditionally more reliable than exit polling. Observers (domestic or international) are assigned to a random sample of polling stations to directly observe the counting process, and they report the tallies from the vote count. Because the sample is random, quick counts typically provide very accurate estimations of the election results and thus guard against manipulation during the counting process; Estok, Nevitte, and Cowan, *The Quick Count and Election Observation.*

31. For example, one strategy for election monitoring is to send observers to the areas that are expected to have problems or to send observers to areas that would "benefit from seeing an international presence." These strategies create clear bias in the content of election day observations, but are perceived as politically important. (Personal conversations between the author and international election observation professionals from NDI, the EU, the OSCE/ODIHR, and The Carter Center.) Of course, it would be possible to randomize within regions that are expected to have problems in order to alleviate this concern.

manipulation. Additionally, ahead of the second-round runoff, Megawati had already lost the first round of the election to SBY and was not expected to win. In hindsight, the fact that the incumbent ran, allowed democratic elections, lost, and peacefully transferred power makes clear that she met my definition of a true democrat. Observers should not, therefore, have been costly to Megawati in terms of her election day performance.

Field Experimental Design in Indonesia

The Carter Center's mission for the second round of the election consisted of fifty-seven observers and twenty-eight observer teams, twenty-three of which participated in the randomization. The long-term election observers and the Jakarta-based staff of the Carter Center selected areas of Indonesia (primarily *kabupaten* and *kota*, or districts and cities) to which the Carter Center would send election observers. The selection of districts to be visited by the Carter Center was not random. In order for an area to be selected, it had to be accessible by car or aircraft within one day's travel time and had to have basic accommodations for the observer team that were judged as sufficiently safe.[32] There was also some effort made to avoid extensive overlap with the European Union election observation mission, as well as consideration for whether access was granted to areas in which foreigners are frequently prohibited from traveling, such as Banda Aceh, Ambon, and parts of Papua. For the participating teams, random assignment was applied within each district or pair of districts where Carter Center observers were sent.

The lists of villages and neighborhoods assigned to each participating Carter Center team were generated within each preselected geographic area using systematic random sampling (also called patterned sampling).[33]

---

32. Security concerns are relatively standard on election observation missions but were heightened in Indonesia because of recent Western-targeted bombings of hotels and the Australian embassy.

33. For a given block (city or district) to which a Carter Center team was assigned, a complete list of villages and neighborhoods was compiled. The total number of units within each block, or N_i, was sorted by an identification number that roughly identified the units geographically but was not otherwise organized in any systematic pattern. For each block, a target number of randomly selected units, n_i, was produced in negotiation with regional experts and the Carter Center staff, and for logistical reasons a greater proportion of selected units were allowed within some blocks. Given n_i, every kth unit was selected, with $k = N_i/n_i$ for all i blocks. Randomization requires that every unit within a given block has an equal probability of being selected. The first village chosen in the skipping pattern was selected arbitrarily from all villages within the block.

These lists were not released to anyone other than the Carter Center staff and the observer teams assigned to each area.

The unit of analysis in this study is the village/neighborhood. However, each village or neighborhood contained one or more polling stations, which observers were instructed to select using a method that approximates randomization.

To check the randomization of villages within each experimental block, I used logistic regression with assignment to the treatment group as the dependent variable. Because this was the first direct presidential election in Indonesian history, little historical precedent existed on which to base predictions of vote patterns for the 2004 elections. Only one background covariate is available at the village level: the total number of registered voters. Table 4.4 presents the results of the randomization check. Across all blocks, the null hypothesis—that assignment to the treatment group is not related to the number of registered voters—cannot be rejected. Also in table 4.4, when all blocks are pooled, assignment to the treatment group is unrelated to the number of registered voters, similarly indicating that there is no significant

Table 4.4. Logistic regression of assigned-to-treatment group on registered voters

Variables	(1)	(2)	(3)	(4)	(5)	(6)	(7)
Registered Voters	−0.103	0.028	−0.001	−0.030	0.104	0.124	−0.078
(1,000s)	(0.215)	(0.019)	(0.110)	(0.102)	(0.136)	(0.074)	(0.144)
Constant	−1.125*	−1.704**	−0.072	−1.173**	−1.500**	−1.645**	0.345
	(0.471)	(0.333)	(1.231)	(0.355)	(0.451)	(0.353)	(1.086)
Observations	90	163	23	186	117	136	45

Block	(8)	(9)	(10)	(11)	(13)	(14)	(15)
Registered Voters	0.175	0.006	−0.004	−0.021	−0.029	−0.058	0.160*
(1,000s)	(0.128)	(0.032)	(0.043)	(0.054)	(0.075)	(0.048)	(0.078)
Constant	−1.515*	−1.495**	−1.265**	−1.231	−1.326**	0.339	−2.304**
	(0.674)	(0.379)	(0.202)	(0.674)	(0.513)	(0.801)	(0.524)
Observations	46	156	243	42	31	24	103

Block	(16)	(17)	(18)	(19)	(20)	Pooled estimate	
Registered Voters	−0.007	−0.097	0.170	−0.230	0.016	0.011	
(1,000s)	(0.060)	(0.223)	(0.235)	(0.136)	(0.048)	(0.112)	
Constant	−1.363*	−1.197*	−1.645**	−0.015	−1.527**	−1.34**	
	(0.576)	(0.530)	(0.586)	(0.496)	(0.346)	0.259	
Observations	103	60	52	56	146	1822	

Notes: The "pooled estimate" includes dummy variables for each block (not reported). Standard errors in parentheses. *Significant at 5%; **Significant at 1%

difference in the number of registered voters between treatment and control groups.[34]

Table 4.5 summarizes the areas observed by Carter Center observers at the village level. Out of all villages in the visited regions, Carter Center observers were assigned to visit 482 villages, 95 of which were actually visited. Within these 95 assigned and visited villages, 147 individual polling stations were visited. Note that a small proportion of villages in the control group were visited.[35]

Data and Results for 2004 Indonesian Election

In the second round of the 2004 presidential elections, Susilo Bambang Yudhoyono and his running mate Jusuf Kalla were the leading candidates, having won 34% of the votes cast in the first round in a five-candidate field. The incumbent president, Megawati Sukarnoputri, won 27% in the first round. The runoff was held on September 20, 2004. SBY won the presidency with 61% of the vote. Due to the size of the country, Carter Center observers could not spread out across the entire country, as was attempted by the OSCE/ODIHR mission in Armenia. The randomization within blocks prevents generalization across the country, but within-block comparisons remain valid. Estimating the average effect across included blocks is also possible, although it is more complicated and should not be confused with randomization across the whole country.

Government-reported unofficial election results for the total number of votes cast for each candidate and the number registered voters for all villages were recorded in the second round of the 2004 presidential election. Polling station-level data for the same regions were also collected but are not analyzed here.[36] The unofficial results were made public by the Indonesian *KPU* (the general elections commission) for most of the country. These aggregate results were uploaded by regional election officials to a central government-run website and are subject to the usual disclaimers about unofficial election results. Unfortunately, data were incomplete for three of the districts where teams from the Carter Center were deployed

---

34. Pooling all blocks is more complicated because of variation in the size of the blocks.

35. For some teams, visiting control group villages or neighborhoods was accidental and resulted from visiting polling stations near the border between urban neighborhoods. Other teams encountered logistical (usually transportation related) problems that caused them to choose to visit villages outside of their assigned list. This information is only available anecdotally and was not coded in the dataset.

36. Data were downloaded from the KPU website, http://tnp.kpu.go.id/ (accessed March 2007).

Table 4.5. Carter Center observation coverage of villages in Indonesia

Study or Region	Province	District or city	Assigned treatment group	Assigned control group	Treated	Treated in control group	Total voters
1	Nanggroe Aceh Darussalam	Kota Banda Aceh	19	71	3	1	173,265
2	East Java	Kota Surabaya	34	129	3	0	2,078,486
3	Nusa Tenggara Barat	Kota Mataram	11	12	4	0	241,483
4	East Java	Sampang	41	145	5	0	569,216
5	Bali	Tabanan	27	90	6	0	325,701
6	East Java	Situbondo	32	104	10	0	488,633
7	DI Yogyakarta	Kota Yogyakarta	20	25	4	0	327,873
8	East Java	Kota Kediri	15	31	11	0	200,137
9	North Sumatera	Kota Medan	30	126	5	2	1,525,526
10	Riau	Kampar, Kota Pekan Baru	53	190	5	0	740,924
11	East Kalimantan	Kota Samarinda	8	34	4	2	453,693
13	Central Kalimantan	Kota Palangka Raya	6	25	1	4	123,596
14	West Kalimantan	Kota Pontianak	9	15	4	3	371,780
15	West Sumatra	Kota Padang	20	83	4	1	525,422
16	South Sumatra	Palembang	20	83	11	1	906,169
17	North Sulawesi	Kota Bitung	12	48	3	4	120,637
18	North Maluku	Kota Ternate	11	41	5	1	95,771
19	Maluku	Kota Ambon	18	38	4	1	192,097
20	South Sulawesi	Kota Makassar	28	118	2	2	812,977
	Total		414	1408	94	22	10,273,386

in the second round: Mimika, Kupang, and Manokwari. These regions (and the three corresponding Carter Center teams) were dropped from the analysis, leaving twenty experimental blocks.

Another important issue in analyzing the results pertains to treatment rates. Table 4.5 shows that the treatment rates, or the percentage of villages randomly assigned to be monitored that were, in fact, monitored, vary considerably across blocks. Several issues must therefore be considered in the analysis of the experiment. There is one block in particular (block 12, in Cianjur) in which there was no experiment to speak of, with monitors going only to less than 2% of both the treatment and control groups. It is also a block with an unusually large number of villages, representing a significant portion of all villages in the "failure to treat" category. The reason for the implementation failure in this block was that the team of monitors assigned there did not attempt to comply with the assigned list of villages, a decision that was not influenced by the characteristics of the block. Although I present the summary data for this block in table 4.5, I exclude it from the remainder of the analysis.

Table 4.6 presents aggregate summary statistics for the 1,822 remaining village-level observations. I downloaded, compiled, and merged the international observer data with the unofficial election results. All comparisons include only districts in which Carter Center observers were deployed, where they participated in the randomization, and where village-level elections results were reported for the entire district.

Another issue stems from treatment rates. Given some failure to treat, it is tempting to move the untreated villages into the "control" group and

Table 4.6. Summary statistics for all available village-level variables

Variables	Observations	Mean	Standard deviation	Minimum	Maximum
Observed	1,822	0.064	0.224	0	1
Sample	1,822	0.227	0.419	0	1
Megawati (total votes)	1,822	1,394	1,662	1	22,494
SBY (total votes)	1,822	2,486	2,538	5	19,618
Overall Turnout	1,822	0.715	0.117	0.1	1
Ballots Received	1,822	5,645	5,826	35	59,567
Valid Ballots	1,822	3,880	3,848	6	42,112
Invalid Ballots	1,822	83	131	0	1,582
Extra Ballots	1,822	6	26	0	345
Damaged Ballots	1,822	43	276	0	5,923
Ballots Not Used	1,822	1,645	2,071	0	16,612
Total Registered Voters	1,822	5,639	5,821	35	59,567

simply compare the subset of villages visited by international observers with those that were not. This comparison yields biased estimates when nontreatment is correlated with the dependent variable and does not take advantage of the randomization. To illustrate with this experiment, because it is plausible that some villages were more difficult for observers to locate than others and that this "findability" could be related to voting behavior, it cannot be assumed that the factors determining which villages were actually monitored were completely random. All comparisons must therefore exploit the randomization by using assignment to the treatment group rather than actual treatment. As the central dependent variable of interest, I use the total number of votes cast for Megawati (logged).

The most straightforward method requiring the fewest assumptions is to estimate the intent-to-treat (ITT) effect within each block for one of the candidates. Here, the estimated ITT effect within each block i is the average difference between treatment and control groups in incumbent performance in villages. It would be possible to estimate the ITT effect without accounting for any other observed differences between villages, but regression analysis allows the inclusion of covariates that reduce the unexplained variance in vote share between villages.

I calculate the ITT effect using ordinary-least squares (OLS) regression. The central dependent variable is the performance of the incumbent candidate, measured as the total number of votes cast for Megawati in each village (logged). To account for varying village sizes, an additional independent variable measuring the total number of registered voters in the village (logged) is included in the regression. This basic model can therefore be expressed as:

$$\log (Y_j) = \beta_0 + \beta_1 T_j + \beta_2 \log (X_j) + \mu_j,$$

where Y is the total votes vast for Megawati in village j, $T_j = 1$ if the village was assigned to the treatment group, X is a variable representing the total number of registered voters in the village, and μ represents unobserved causes of votes for Megawati.

Table 4.7 presents estimates of the effect of being assigned to the treatment group within each regional block. Even given the relatively low rate of assigned villages that were actually visited (as shown in table 4.5), assignment to the treatment group is associated with *improved* performance for Megawati in 15 out of the 20 blocks, a result that is unlikely to be due to chance. I also provide a pooled estimate with fixed effects for each experimental block. Note that in these models, *Treatment Group* is a measure of the intent to treat the village, not the actual presence of observers

Table 4.7. Estimated effects of intent to treat on total votes for Megawati (ordinary least squares, ln)

Block	(1)	(2)	(3)	(4)	(5)	(6)	(7)
Treatment Group	0.14	0.02	0.07	0.24*	0.02	0.15*	0.11
	(0.11)	(0.05)	(0.15)	(0.10)	(0.06)	(0.07)	(0.06)
Registered Voters	0.97**	1.04**	0.88**	1.36**	0.85**	0.94**	0.90**
	(0.06)	(0.03)	(0.19)	(0.08)	(0.05)	(0.05)	(0.10)
Constant	−2.16**	−1.65**	−0.69	−4.34**	0.68	−0.81*	−0.50
	(0.42)	(0.26)	(1.78)	(0.60)	(0.40)	(0.41)	(0.89)
Observers	90	163	23	186	117	136	45
R^2	0.77	0.90	0.51	0.64	0.71	0.74	0.66

Block	(8)	(9)	(10)	(11)	(13)	(14)	(15)
Treatment Group	0.11	−0.07	0.03	0.06	0.19	−0.11	0.03
	(0.06)	(0.09)	(0.09)	(0.10)	(0.21)	(0.15)	(0.10)
Registered Voters	0.91**	1.04**	0.86**	0.87**	0.87**	1.14**	0.80**
	(0.05)	(0.03)	(0.04)	(0.05)	(0.05)	(0.10)	(0.06)
Constant	−0.29	−2.00**	−0.88**	−0.52	−0.42	−2.98**	−0.86
	(0.39)	(0.29)	(0.28)	(0.45)	(0.36)	(0.94)	(0.52)
Observers	46	156	243	42	31	24	103
R^2	0.90	0.87	0.70	0.89	0.91	0.88	0.63

Block	(16)	(17)	(18)	(19)	(20)	Pooled estimate	
Treatment Group	−0.04	−0.14	0.19	0.04	0.16	0.065*	
	(0.04)	(0.07)	(0.17)	(0.18)	(0.15)	(0.026)	
Registered Voters	0.89**	0.83**	0.51**	0.99**	0.92**	0.94**	
	(0.03)	(0.03)	(0.09)	(0.08)	(0.07)	(0.014)	
Constant	−0.08	0.28	1.69*	−0.95	−1.80**	−1.95**	
	(0.25)	(0.25)	(0.64)	(0.67)	(0.55)	(0.11)	
Observers	103	60	52	56	146	1822	
R^2	0.91	0.92	0.42	0.73	0.58	0.87	

Notes: Pooled estimate includes block fixed effects. Standard errors in parentheses.
*Significant at 5%; **Significant at 1%

on election day. Because *Treatment Group* is dichotomous, the coefficients represent the percentage of change in total votes cast for Megawati given that *Treatment Group* changes from zero to one and all else is constant. In the pooled estimate in table 4.7, assignment to the treatment group causes a 6.5% positive change in the number of votes cast for Megawati. To put this number in context, the average number of votes cast per village for Megawati is 1,394, and assignment to the treatment group is associated with an average increase of about 91 votes.

This estimation of the intent-to-treat effect is the least biased estimate, but it does not count for actual treatment rates. Because relatively few assigned villages were visited by observers, the estimated effect of observers on villages that were visited is much larger. The average treatment rate across all blocks in the experiment was about 23%: a little more than one out of every five villages assigned to observers was actually visited on election day. Given low treatment rates, as in this case, the figures in table 4.7 likely underestimate the magnitude of the observers' effect.

Following previous applications in field experiments, I use instrumental variable techniques to estimate the magnitude of the treatment effect.[37] Very generally, this estimate can be understood as the ITT effect divided by the actual treatment rates.[38] Table 4.8 presents estimates from two-stage least-squares regression (2SLS). Using 2SLS, for an instrument to be valid it must be correlated with the actual treatment but not correlated with the error term in the model. Assignment to the treatment group of villages within a region is random, and there is therefore no reason that it should be correlated with the error term. Actual treatment, or being visited by international observers, is a function of a village being assigned to the treatment group. When the actual visit by observers to a given village is used as an explanatory variable, assignment to the treatment group satisfies the conditions for a valid instrument.

Like the ITT estimates presented in table 4.7, total registered voters (logged) are included as an independent variable. The difference between the results presented in tables 4.7 and 4.8 is that the table 4.8 results account for the fact that observers did not visit all assigned villages. Consistent with expectations, the estimate of the effect of observers on treated villages in the treatment group (also called the treatment-on-treated effect) is substantively larger and is associated with a +32% change in votes cast for Megawati, an average increase of 446 votes per treated village.[39] Note that this is an estimate of the size of the effect if observers had visited all villages in the assigned-to-treatment group.

The same estimates using vote share rather than votes cast were also conducted, but results are not presented here because the varying size of

37. Angrist, Imbens, and Rubin, "Identification of Causal Effects Using Instrumental Variables"; Gerber and Green, "The Effects of Canvassing, Telephone Calls, and Direct Mail on Voter Turnout: A Field Experiment."

38. This use of experimental treatments as instrumental variables is described in greater detail by Gerber and Green 2000, "The Effects of Canvassing, Telephone Calls, and Direct Mail on Voter Turnout: A Field Experiment," 657–658.

39. Note that both tables 4.7 and 4.8 present pooled estimates in which all blocks are combined.

Table 4.8. Estimated effect of observers on total votes for Megawati in observed villages (two-stage least-squares regression)

Block	(1)	(2)	(3)	(4)	(5)	(6)	(7)
Treated (Observed)	1.04	0.22	0.18	1.96*	0.09	0.50*	0.57
	(0.79)	(0.59)	(0.42)	(0.98)	(0.25)	(0.22)	(0.38)
Registered Voters (ln)	1.00**	1.04**	0.80**	1.37**	0.85**	0.93**	0.90**
	(0.06)	(0.03)	(0.27)	(0.09)	(0.05)	(0.05)	(0.12)
Constant	−2.39**	−1.66**	0.03	−4.40**	0.69	−0.69	−0.48
	(0.49)	(0.26)	(2.40)	(0.69)	(0.40)	(0.42)	(1.07)
Observers	90	163	23	186	117	136	45
R²	0.76	0.90	0.50	0.53	0.71	0.73	0.52

Block	(8)	(9)	(10)	(11)	(13)	(14)	(15)
Treated (Observed)	0.16	−0.49	0.32	0.13	2.41	−0.32	0.17
	(0.09)	(0.61)	(0.93)	(0.23)	(4.08)	(0.43)	(0.55)
Registered Voters (ln)	0.88**	1.05**	0.86**	0.86**	0.45	1.21**	0.80**
	(0.05)	(0.04)	(0.04)	(0.05)	(0.71)	(0.12)	(0.07)
Constant	−0.06	−2.08**	−0.86**	−0.47	2.16	−3.63**	−0.84
	(0.43)	(0.32)	(0.28)	(0.47)	(4.27)	(1.04)	(0.54)
Observers	46	156	243	42	31	24	103
R²	0.89	0.86	0.69	0.88	0.80	0.88	0.62

Block	(16)	(17)	(18)	(19)	(20)	Pooled estimate	
Treated (Observed)	−0.08	−0.72	0.46	0.19	2.89	0.32*	
	(0.08)	(0.46)	(0.43)	(0.89)	(3.24)	(0.13)	
Registered Voters (ln)	0.89**	0.94**	0.48**	0.98**	0.91**	0.93**	
	(0.03)	(0.08)	(0.10)	(0.09)	(0.08)	(0.015)	
Constant	−0.04	−0.46	1.91**	−0.88	−1.76**	−1.87**	
	(0.25)	(0.52)	(0.71)	(0.69)	(0.67)	(0.12)	
Observers	103	60	52	56	146	1822	
R²	0.91	0.87	0.37	0.71	0.40	0.87	

Notes: Instrumented variable: Village visited by international observers. Exogenous variable: Village in treatment group. Pooled estimate includes block fixed effects. Standard errors in parentheses. *Significant at 5%; **Significant at 1%

villages and blocks complicate the analysis. These estimates using alternative specifications of the dependent variable are similar.[40] As an additional check, the estimates presented in Tables 4.7 and 4.8 were also conducted

40. Additionally, I estimated all models with a variable indicating the presence of EU observers. EU observers were not randomly assigned. Out of the 1,822 villages included in this study, EU observers visited 61. Of these 61 villages, 4 were in the treatment group and also visited by Carter Center observers, and 6 of which were in the assigned treatment group but not visited by Carter Center observers. The inclusion of this variable has minimal influence on the sign and significance of the (randomized) Carter Center observation variable.

on total votes cast for SBY and are available on request. There is no significant relationship between observer presence and the performance of the winning candidate, SBY.

Overall, the results of the Indonesia field experiment show that the incumbent candidate performed better and the challenger performed about the same in villages and neighborhoods assigned to be monitored by Carter Center observers. This result was not anticipated and highlights a central advantage of using field experimental methods: the possibility that they can reveal effects that are not anticipated by scholars or practitioners.[41] Such a surprising result nevertheless requires some speculative explanation and analysis of the unique circumstances surrounding this election. Why might the presence of observers increase votes cast for Megawati but not decrease votes cast for SBY? Why did observers influence what was widely viewed as a democratic election?

The reports of international observers, journalists, and analysts suggest several possible explanations. Although all major international observer organizations judged the observed problems with the election to be insignificant, a number of irregularities were documented and described in the postelection reports of international observers. The most plausible explanation for this finding stems from the early closing of polling stations. The official election day was from 7:00 a.m. to 1:00 p.m., but after the first round of the presidential election, the *KPU* ruled that polling stations could close after 11:30 a.m., provided that all eligible voters had voted. If this rule was followed correctly, it should not have produced significant problems, and only those polling stations that reached 100% turnout should have closed early. Reports suggest, however, that a number of polling stations closed before all eligible voters had cast a ballot and well before the earliest legal closing time of 11:30.[42]

During the course of their observation, many Carter Center observers announced or implied that they could return later in the day to observe the closing. The presence of observers could have influenced the decision by election officials to close early by making it more likely that polling stations in visited areas would stay open until the mandated time. If Megawati supporters were less likely to turn out to vote without being mobilized to do so by party representatives or election officials, correctly following the regulations surrounding the length of election day would have disproportionately benefited Megawati voters. Local party officials

41. Banerjee and Duflo, "The Experimental Approach to Development Economics."

42. European Union, *European Union Election Observation Mission to Indonesia*, 58; Carter Center, *The Carter Center 2004 Indonesia Election Report*, 63.

would have more time to mobilize voters, and poll workers would have had greater incentive to prove that all voters had cast a ballot so that they could close early without violating electoral regulations. One potential explanation is therefore that nonobserved villages were more likely to close before less-motivated or reluctant voters had shown up and were less likely to follow the electoral regulations about staying open until 1:00 p.m. or until all registered voters had cast a ballot.

Several additional pieces of evidence support the possibility that Megawati supporters were more reluctant to turn out and also suggest that she was not in control of the party or state machinery that would have been required to engage in widespread election day fraud. First, her party performed poorly in the April legislative elections and in the first-round presidential elections. Second, in the weeks leading up to the runoff election, it was widely speculated in the media that she would lose, with public opinion polls from several organizations predicting support for SBY at about 60% and support for Megawati at around 29%.[43] Third, although Megawati had some incumbency advantages, including the ability to make public appearances throughout the country outside of the legal three-day campaign period, her support from several prominent parties was unstable. For example, Megawati was endorsed by the powerful Golkar party, which won the April 5 legislative elections and which possessed well-developed local party machinery that could have been used to mobilize the vote for Megawati. But several weeks before the election, national and local party leaders split publicly over the decision to endorse Megawati, and before the election, analysts predicted that "Golkar will not be able to fully bring its formidable party machinery behind Megawati."[44] Postelection polling revealed that the vast majority of Golkar voters who cast a ballot voted against their party's endorsement and for SBY.[45] Relative to incumbent presidential candidates in other countries, Megawati's election day advantage was minimal.

If Megawati supporters were reluctant to turn out, she should have performed better in those areas in which turnout was higher. Although it is not conclusive evidence, scatter plots of votes cast for Megawati versus turnout across all 1,822 villages included in the experiment illustrate

---

43. "Indonesia's Megawati Heading for Defeat, Two Polls Show," Associated Press Worldstream, September 15, 2004.

44. "Golkar Party Leaders Split as Internal Rift Deepens," *The Jakarta Post*, September 1, 2004; "What Lies Ahead After Indonesia's Election," United Press International, September 14, 2004.

45. Liddle and Mujani, "Indonesia in 2004."

that Megawati does somewhat better in villages with higher turnout and SBY does worse, on average, in villages with higher turnout. These comparisons do not prove that increasing turnout would have necessarily increased votes for Megawati, but they are consistent with the idea that Megawati's supporters were more reluctant to turn out and that her performance increased when voter mobilization increased.

The results presented here show a clear difference between observed and unobserved villages, but they are subject to interpretation. The most likely explanation for this finding, in my view, is that observers made polling station officials more likely to follow electoral regulations and therefore caused visited polling stations to stay open later than they would have if observers had not visited. Given that the election was expected to be relatively free of election day irregularities, the fact that any significant effect of observers was found is noteworthy. This result does not imply election fraud. If widespread election fraud by one candidate had taken place, and this fraud was deterred by observers, the cheating candidate should have performed worse in areas that were observed. Even though Megawati benefited from observers, the results do not show that SBY performed significantly worse when observers were present, as would be expected if observers reduced ballot box stuffing or other forms of direct election fraud. Rather, I argue that election officials were more likely to follow the letter of the election law pertaining to closing time after having been visited by international observers.

The Carter Center mission concluded that "voters were able to exercise their democratic rights in a peaceful atmosphere and without significant hindrance."[46] The results presented here do not contradict this conclusion.

Inviting Observers Changes Behavior

Taken together, the micro-level results from elections in Armenia and Indonesia show that observers can be more costly to pseudo-democrats than to true-democrats, at least in terms of their election day performance. Particularly for pseudo-democrats who commit election day fraud, this chapter demonstrates that observers can make stealing elections more expensive or more difficult by directly reducing fraud through their presence

---

46. Carter Center, *The Carter Center 2004 Indonesia Election Report*, 13. See also the EU final report *"European Union Election Observation Mission to Indonesia."*

in polling stations. Even in the case of Indonesia, in which the election was viewed as a successful exercise in democracy, the presence of observers had a direct and measurable effect on election day behavior, perhaps inducing increased compliance with government regulations and having an unanticipated effect on turnout among the more reluctant supporters of the incumbent. The Indonesia study demonstrates that the incumbent government was not significantly harmed by the presence of observers, and even benefited from their presence for idiosyncratic reasons.

More generally, these findings indicate that inviting observers can be consequential for leaders who invite monitors and attempt to steal the election and that these costs do not necessarily exist for incumbent true democrats. I also showed that competitive elections outcomes are positively correlated with the presence of observers. In chapter 3, I showed that pseudo-democrats face consequences if they refuse to invite observers or if they are caught cheating by international observers. As I will show in the next chapter, in addition to potentially reducing blatant election day fraud, many leaders now invite observers and work to avoid international criticism, making the changing forms of election manipulation another consequence of internationally monitored elections.

5

THE QUALITY OF MONITORING AND STRATEGIC MANIPULATION

The norm of election monitoring is that governments committed to democratic elections invite international monitors. The corresponding belief is that noninviting states must be electoral autocracies, unless the country has otherwise established a reputation as a consolidated democracy. Because of the belief that all true democrats invite observers, and because there are consequences to being caught manipulating the election by international observers, my theory implies that pseudo-democrats should devote effort to concealing election manipulation such that they are less likely to be caught. In addition, pro-democracy actors should push for increases in the quality of election observation, and international observers should attempt to detect and criticize an expanding range of tactics used to manipulate elections. This chapter continues evaluating the empirical implications of my argument and provides support for the final implication outlined in chapter 1: that the normalization of election monitoring, including improvement in the quality of monitoring and the growing number of pseudo-democrats who invite observers, should increase the use of strategic election manipulation. Chapters 3 and 4 provided evidence of two ways in which election monitoring can be costly to pseudo-democrats: negative reports from observers can lead to reduced international benefits and international observers can reduce election day fraud directly. These findings underscore my argument that inviting international observers is more costly for pseudo-democrats than for true democrats.

Adding to these findings, by documenting strategic action by incumbents in the face of election observers, this chapter illustrates that even well-entrenched autocratic leaders such as Vladimir Putin of Russia and Robert Mugabe of Zimbabwe are willing to devote significant effort to manipulating public perceptions of election-monitors' judgments. This is further evidence that the norm exists and reflects the pseudo-democratic response to the norm. I also document how some incumbent leaders engage in strategic manipulation of elections and observers.

Generally, I document three methods used by incumbents to maintain their hold on power while complying with the norm. First, pseudo-democrats can attempt to use different forms of election manipulation that are less likely to be caught by observers. Second, they can invite low-quality or "friendly" observers in order to ensure that at least one observer group endorses the elections as democratic. Third, if they are caught manipulating the election (or if they choose to cheat blatantly), they can work to discredit the reports of observers after the election.

For example, Russia's efforts to both invite and manipulate observers are perhaps the most baffling, with their efforts extending throughout the post-Soviet sphere. By 2004, Russian elections had been observed on five occasions by the Organization for Security and Cooperation in Europe's Office for Democratic Institutions and Human Rights (OSCE/ODIHR). Since the mid-1990s, the OSCE/ODIHR has developed a reputation as a critical and professionalized observer group that applies relatively consistent standards to the elections it observes within its member states.[1]

In the late 1990s, the Russian government began a campaign arguing that observers from the OSCE/ODIHR are biased and apply inconsistent criteria to countries that are not Western allies. Russia took a position against so-called double standards in international election monitoring and began exerting significant effort to ensure that OSCE/ODIHR observers are shadowed by international observers who are loyal to the Kremlin and whose not-so-secret objective is to contradict the conclusions of OSCE/ODIHR reports.[2]

In response to OSCE/ODIHR monitoring, the Commonwealth of Independent States (CIS), began to monitor elections within its member countries, which are also OSCE members. The CIS is an intergovernmental organization composed of former Soviet states and is headquartered in Belarus. It has earned a reputation for praising blatantly fraudulent elections in former Soviet states and issuing reports that are in direct opposition to the conclusions of the OSCE/ODIHR missions. In what appears to be deliberate effort to create confusion, in 2003 a Russian-based nongovernmental organization (NGO) was founded with the same name as the intergovernmental organization's election-monitoring arm (CIS-EMO), but claimed no connection. The CIS-Elections Monitoring Organization,

---

1. OSCE, *Document of the Copenhagen Meeting of the Conference on the Human Dimension of the CSCE.*
2. Kupchinsky, "CIS: Monitoring The Election Monitors."

registered as an NGO in Nizhny Novgorod, Russia, deploys international observer delegations alongside CIS (the IO) and OSCE/ODIHR delegations. The NGO issues virtually identical election observation reports as the Minsk-based CIS reports, conceivably so that they can claim intergovernmental organization and NGO certification of elections criticized by the OSCE.[3]

Additionally, at meetings of the OSCE, Russia has advocated reduced funding for OSCE/ODIHR missions and otherwise attempted to undermine the organization's work as an independent but pro-democracy judge of election quality. Some pro-Western CIS member states have pushed back against Russian efforts to generate controversy about the quality of their elections. For example, the Moldovan government blocked a train carrying CIS observers at the border prior to their 2004 elections, and Georgia withdrew its membership in the CIS, in part to protest the organization's involvement in elections.

Attempts by incumbents to evade observer criticism have been well documented by other scholars. As Daniel Calingaert argues, "authoritarian regimes have become increasingly adept at keeping up the appearance of meeting democratic norms while subverting the integrity of the electoral process."[4] Similarly, in his widely cited 1997 article critiquing election observation, Thomas Carothers notes that, in part due to an "overemphasis on election day" by observers, "efforts by entrenched leaders to manipulate electoral processes to their advantage have become more subtle as such leaders have been socialized into the new world of global democracy and internationally observed elections."[5]

Building on this work, this chapter provides additional evidence that efforts by pseudo-democrats to conceal election manipulation triggered an evolving game of strategy between international observers, pseudo-democrats, and pro-democracy actors. Pseudo-democrats attempt to invite observers and guarantee their own victory without getting caught, and observers and democracy promoters attempt to catch them, prompting improvements in observation technology, stronger and more overt links between the reports of observers and international benefits, and continuing innovation in the forms of electoral manipulation used by rulers to stay in power. Strategic manipulation includes efforts by leaders to change their methods of manipulation, including the use of new methods,

3. Ibid.
4. Calingaert, "Election Rigging and How to Fight It," 138.
5. Carothers, "The Observers Observed," 22.

recycling of old methods on which observers may no longer be focused, and borrowing techniques from other countries.

Over time, this "arms race" of election monitoring should jointly increase the ability of observers to detect various forms of election fraud as well as the effort required for pseudo-democrats to evade international criticism, introducing further costs to pseudo-democrats. Leaders who do not devote sufficient resources to manipulating the election increase their risk of a negative report from observers, the consequences of which were explored in chapter 3. As in chapter 3, although anticipated costs of negative reports and strategic manipulation by pseudo-democrats are important elements of my theory, they do not lend themselves easily to quantitative hypothesis testing. Instead, I rely on a series of examples drawn from reading of hundreds of election observation reports and case studies of elections, detailed information about the tactics used by pseudo-democrats and observers, and descriptive statistics of election-monitoring missions.

Manipulators versus Monitors

In the remainder of the chapter, I outline over-time interactions between international observers and leaders working to manipulate them, including observer response to strategic manipulation and improvements in the methods and quality of election observation. I then discuss in greater detail strategies used by leaders to invite observers and successfully manipulate elections in front of them, illustrating forms of strategic election manipulation, and then briefly discuss opposition party reactions to international observers.

I have already presented some indirect evidence that both pseudo-democrats and international observers are innovating in the game of strategic manipulation. If it were the case that international observers did not react to more strategic forms of manipulation among pseudo-democrats, the rate of negative reports should have gone to zero as election observation spread, a prediction that is contradicted by the empirical evidence (see introduction, figure I.1). An important effect of the normalization of election observation is that it increased the pressure for leaders to invite observers even as the stakes increased: election monitors improved their methods, negative reports became more likely, and pseudo-democrats became more constrained or more skilled at concealing election manipulation.

Counterintuitively, the fact that observers sometimes legitimate fraudulent elections played a large role in motivating pseudo-democrats to invite international observers, but in the long run it caused the same types of leaders to face a difficult choice between consequences for refusing observers and the risk of a negative report from them. Neither of these options is desirable for pseudo-democrats, who can no longer simply refuse international observers without facing other, more certain, consequences.

Professionalized international monitors are well aware of pseudo-democrats' efforts to evade criticism. By the end of the 1990s, many organizations were actively cautioning their missions to be on alert for leaders attempting to gain international approval for rigged elections. As a European Commission document warned:

> Sometimes politicians in power may be tempted to organise manipulated elections in order to obtain international legitimacy (Togo 1998, Kazakhstan 1999). Care should be taken if…an EU observation mission could contribute to legitimising an illegitimate process.[6]

Despite observers' awareness and the improvements in election-monitoring techniques, it remains difficult to detect all forms of manipulation, weigh their impact on the election quality, and judge the quality of all elections accurately. Most elections fall within the gray area between flawless democratic elections and outright election theft, such as in the Philippines in 1986, Panama in 1989, Georgia in 2003, or Zimbabwe in 2008. Even elections in consolidated democracies are imperfect by a number of objective standards, making the evaluation of elections in countries with new or fluctuating political institutions subjective and challenging.

Transitional elections are particularly difficult to judge. For postconflict countries, some newly independent states, and countries holding their first multiparty elections in decades, any sort of election is viewed as a major accomplishment, even if it is far from democratic. The necessary conditions for democratic elections were arguably not present for the 2006 elections in the Democratic Republic of Congo, yet because they were the first multiparty elections in more than forty years, observers gave the government and the election commission considerable leeway. Despite a number of reported problems, the missions organizing the roughly two thousand international observers issued generally positive evaluations. Even for the best-intentioned observers, evaluating election quality remains a serious challenge, particularly when pseudo-democrats work to manipulate elections subtly, without attracting observer criticism.

---

6. European Commission, "Communication from the Commission on EU Election Assistance," 5.

Despite frequent reference to universal standards for democratic elections, no such black-and-white standards exist.[7] Irregularities in elections can stem from low levels of economic and political development, poor infrastructure, little experience with democracy, or challenges typical in postconflict environments rather than government-sponsored election fraud. Nevertheless, observers have developed a variety of techniques that, although they do not generate automatic and objective judgments of whether elections are free and fair, allow them to document many forms of manipulation and to issue credible and sometimes forceful condemnations of elections. Democracy promoters continue to push for enforcement of existing commitments to democratic elections, as well as more systematic techniques of election observation.[8]

Criticizing and Improving Election Evaluation

Observers' willingness to invest in improved election-monitoring techniques and their willingness to criticize elections increased as election monitoring became a widely shared international norm. Among benefit-seeking states, as election monitoring spread and it became clear that inviting observers was "the only way towards loosening the purse-strings of donors and creditors," criticism of observers increased, including from within election-monitoring organizations.[9] This criticism was followed by changes within many international monitoring groups, including increased professionalization, experience, and improved methodology. Increasingly sophisticated election fraud "has been matched by improvements in the skills and methods of election observers."[10]

Since international election observation was initiated in the 1960s, many observers have recognized their own limitations, and organizations have sought methods to improve their ability to evaluate election quality. Concerns about how accurately observers can judge election quality surfaced in some of the very first election observation missions and those concerns have continued to drive innovations in election observation. Common criticisms of observers include that they legitimize fraudulent elections, engage in electoral tourism, ignore fraud in the pre-election period, issue statements prematurely, distract from more qualified domestic observers,

7. For a recent effort to connect international law to minimal standards for democratic elections, see Davis-Roberts and Carroll, "Using International Law to Assess Elections."

8. Davis-Roberts and Carroll, "Using International Law to Assess Elections"; Donno, "Defending Democratic Norms"; Donno, "Who Is Punished?"

9. Geisler, "Fair?," 614.

10. Calingaert, "Election Rigging and How to Fight It," 138.

and practice "electoral fetishism" by overemphasizing election day with respect to the broader democratization process.[11]

In many cases in the early 1990s, particularly in Africa, reputable observer groups seemed unsure of how to evaluate elections that were clearly flawed.[12] Observers appeared to be aware that some elections were riddled with problems but were unable to determine if the problems affected the outcome of the election or if criticizing the election would generate more problems in the country than would giving the election qualified endorsement. Many reports from this time period in Africa evaluated faulty elections as "a step in the right direction." Jon Abbink and Gerti Hessling refer to this as "one of the most worn-out metaphors in [election observation]."[13] Observers were widely criticized for their failure to highlight accurately the widespread problems in the 1992 elections in Kenya, Ghana, and Angola, among others, and complaints were made that "the presence of observers and their often hesitant reports can be easily misappropriated by African governments and bent in their favour."[14] Although the possibility that observers will endorse flawed elections is a common criticism of observers, according to my theory this possibility is an important reason why election monitoring spread to pseudo-democratic countries in the late 1980s and early 1990s.

In response to criticism of election observation, many organizations began to undertake more systematic and comprehensive election-monitoring missions. For example, the Commonwealth, which once issued statements on the quality of elections before election day was over, significantly revised its election observation methodology and became more likely to criticize problematic elections.[15] The more professionalized observer groups continue to respond to criticism and work to improve election observation methods, but debates over the mandate of international observers, their appropriate role, and criteria for democratic elections are unlikely to disappear. In table 5.1, I summarize common tactics used to bias elections and the corresponding methods used by observers to mitigate them. In general, improvements in election monitoring should lead to less direct forms of election manipulation. Generally speaking, election fraud that takes place on election day is easiest for observers to

11. Abbink and Hesseling, *Election Observation and Democratization in Africa*; Geisler, "Fair?"; Carothers, "The Observers Observed."

12. Geisler, "Fair?"

13. Abbink and Hesseling, *Election Observation and Democratization in Africa*, 12.

14. Ibid., 8.

15. Sives, "A Review of Commonwealth Election Observation."

detect and condemn. As manipulation moves away from the casting and counting of votes, it becomes more difficult for observers to detect, more difficult for them to demonstrate that significant election fraud took place, and less likely (although not impossible) that election manipulation will be condemned. Thus, the diffusion of the norm of election observation should be associated with a parallel change in the most likely types of election fraud used by political actors seeking to manipulate the election in their favor.

To illustrate, when the count and tabulation process is not observed, one of the easiest ways to steal elections in front of foreign observers is to hold entirely democratic elections and then falsify vote totals at the end of election day. This concern was recognized by international observers as early as 1966:

> Our concern...is that the process of the final tally of votes is beyond the possibility of verification by foreign observers. If fraud took place, it would seem to be more likely at the point of reporting from the province and/or reporting from the [Central Election Commission].[16]

Election monitors have since developed methods of reliably detecting—and therefore deterring—this tactic. The expectation that Ferdinand Marcos would steal the 1985 elections by falsifying the vote totals led a domestic election-monitoring group, NAMFREL, to attempt a comprehensive independent tally of votes from all polling stations. They planned to station nonpartisan observers from their organization at all polling stations in the country for the counting of votes and produce their own tally. It quickly became clear that the large number of polling stations would make aggregation unwieldy and time consuming. Recognizing this challenge, National Democratic Institute (NDI) staff recommended that observers be stationed in a random sample of polling stations for the count, allowing observers to produce an independent estimate of the election results, within a specified margin of error, well before official results were released.[17] In the Philippines, this method was instrumental in demonstrating that Marcos lost the 1986 elections. In part because of advocacy of the method by international and domestic observers, these "quick counts" or parallel vote tabulations spread rapidly with election monitoring in the late 1980s and early 1990s and represent one of the first and most

---

16. Roe, "The Committee on Free Elections," 63.

17. Bjornlund, *Beyond Free and Fair*; Estok, Nevitte, and Cowan, *The Quick Count and Election Observation*; Garber and Cowan, "The Virtues of Parallel Vote Tabulations."

important innovations in election-monitoring technology. When quick counts are correctly administered, fraud in the vote tabulation process is very difficult to get away with.

Another concern is that observers were focusing their attention on capital cities and other urban areas, clearing the way for widespread fraud in rural areas. Although international observer coverage is not comprehensive in most cases, the average number of short-term observers has increased dramatically, as illustrated in figure 5.1, at the same time that election-monitoring technology has improved, and since the early 1990s, long- and short-term observers spend significant time in rural and urban areas.

Responding to concerns about pre-election manipulation, international observers introduced a variety of improvements, including long-term observers, or LTOs. Beginning in the early 1990s and becoming widespread by 1995, LTOs are deployed throughout the country months in advance of an election and report on all aspects of the electoral process, including the registration of candidates and voters, campaigning, and the state of administrative preparations for elections countrywide. The qualitative evaluations provided by LTOs make the reports of international observers more credible.

Some organizations also conduct media monitoring. Media monitoring can be used to evaluate whether all candidates have sufficient access to media time, to judge imbalance in coverage, and to evaluate the veracity of content in campaign-related advertising. In each election observation mission, other tactics may be employed if they are deemed useful.

In part because of the example set by NAMFREL in the Philippines, nonpartisan domestic election monitoring has also spread rapidly since the mid-1980s, and many critics of international observation believed domestic election monitoring to be a superior alternative.[18] In the mid-1990s, many democracy promoters viewed international observers as temporary substitutes until domestic observers could become better established. It soon became clear, however, that in many countries domestic election-monitoring organizations are relatively easy for pseudo-democrats to discredit as biased, refuse to credential, or falsify by allowing only loyal government supporters to be credentialed as domestic observers. International monitors, because their reputations are established outside the monitored country, are harder to discredit. By the late 1990s it was widely recognized by election-monitoring experts that domestic and international

18. Bjornlund, *Beyond Free and Fair;* Carothers, "The Observers Observed"; Nevitte and Canton, "The Role of Domestic Observers."

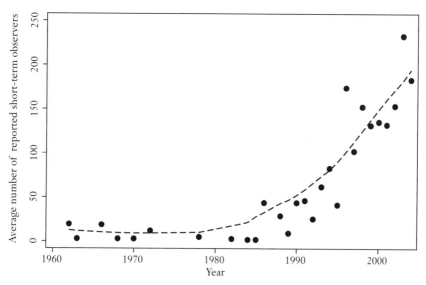

Figure 5.1. Average number of reported short-term observers per observed election, 1960–2004

Note: The dashed line represents a locally weighted regression curve, known as a lowess smoother.

monitors were complementary, and coordination between reputable domestic and international observers became increasingly common.[19] For pseudo-democrats, coordination between international and domestic observers makes manipulating either group more difficult, and the complementary advantages of both types of observers further increase the forms of manipulation that are likely to be criticized.

The expanding mandate of election observation missions also increased attention to postelection dispute resolution and acceptance of the results. Whereas election monitors in the early 1990s were more likely to issue a postelection statement immediately after the election and close their in-country offices, international observer organizations in the late 1990s were more likely to stay in the country for weeks or months after an election, continuing to evaluate the government's conduct in handling election-related disputes. Countries with relatively frequent elections may invite constant observer presence, with monitoring of the upcoming election beginning while monitoring of the previous election is completed.

19. Bjornlund, *Beyond Free and Fair.*

Table 5.1. Election manipulation and observer response

Proximity to election day	Form of election manipulation	Response by international observers
Vote count, tabulation, and acceptance of results	Changing vote totals and manipulating the count Refusal to accept the election results or adjudicate postelection disputes	Parallel vote tabulation or quick count Postelection monitoring until results are accepted by all parties and winner assumes office
Election day	Ballot box stuffing, vote buying, and election day intimidation Election day fraud in rural areas or in areas difficult to reach, clean elections in capital city Subtle forms of manipulation difficult for foreigners to pick up on, limitation on the number of international observers, and intimidation of or refusal to credential nonpartisan domestic observers	Increased numbers of short-term observers trained to look for such election day manipulation Increased numbers of short-term observers deployed throughout the country in rural and urban areas Coordination with nonpartisan domestic election observers
Election day and pre-election period	Government efforts to dictate observer access to aspects of the electoral process, numbers of international observers, composition of delegation, or ability to release their findings Pre-election fraud or manipulation, failure to distribute balloting materials to all parts of the country, pre-election violence Monopolization and inappropriate use of media Misuse of state resources to campaign or bias the election	Well-publicized and coordinated observer statements refusing to deploy a mission if restrictions were placed on international monitors Long-term observers stationed throughout the country months in advance of the election Media monitoring Long-term observation and willingness to criticize an election for misuse of state resources
Pre-election period	Manipulation of the voter register Manipulation of the electoral system or election rules Efforts to weaken or divide opposition political parties Accusations of inconsistent standards, inviting low-quality observers	Voter registration audits Evaluation of the electoral system, including recommended changes given existing problems Meetings with representatives from all parties before elections, criticism of government efforts to weaken them Linking election monitoring to enforcement of international agreements already signed by individual countries, advocacy of consistent practices in election monitoring

Observer organizations also sought to coordinate across organizations and countries. A common charged leveled against international observers, frequently by incumbent governments, is that they apply inconsistent criteria across elections, a problem Thomas Carothers highlights as the "elusive standards" of democratic elections.[20] In response to this criticism, individual observer organizations published their own criteria and methodology for election monitoring, and academics contributed recommendations for how elections could be more uniformly judged.[21]

International Human Rights Law Group's 1984 publication of *Guidelines for International Election Observing* was perhaps the first effort to standardize election-monitoring practices across organizations, and it set out some very basic guidelines for election observation.[22] The Inter-Parliamentary Union published *Free and Fair Elections: International Law and Practice* in 1994, written by a prominent international human rights lawyer Guy Goodwin-Gill and updated in 2006.[23] The OSCE/ODIHR's *Election Observation Handbook*, now in its fifth edition, was first published in 1996.[24] NDI contributed a number of guides and handbooks on election-monitoring techniques (also aimed at domestic observers), including the quick count, monitoring of voter registration, and media monitoring. The *Handbook for European Union Election Observation* was first published in 2002 and is now in its second edition.[25] Initiated by the Carter Center, NDI, and the UN, and commemorated in 2005 at the UN headquarters in New York, twenty-three organizations signed on to the *Declaration of Principles and Code of Conduct for International Election Observation*, a document that individual election observers are now expected to sign and to which they must adhere.[26]

However, despite the improvements in election-monitoring technology and the increased investment by international actors in improving election monitoring, observers remain far from perfect judges of election quality. For leaders engaging in blatant and premeditated forms of election manipulation, inviting low-quality election observers represented a reliable strategy. By 2000, the reputations of most observer organizations had become clear, and leaders planning blatant election fraud could either

20. Carothers, "The Observers Observed," 23.

21. Elklit and Reynolds, "A Framework for the Systematic Study of Election Quality"; Elklit and Svensson, "What Makes Elections Free and Fair."

22. Garber, *Guidelines for International Election Observing.*

23. Goodwin-Gill, *Free and Fair Elections.*

24. OSCE/ODIHR, *Election Observation Handbook.*

25. European Commission, *Handbook for European Union Election Observation.*

26. Carter Center, *Building Consensus on Principles for International Election Observation.*

invite observers that were not reputed to be critical or invite organizations of varying quality so that conflicting reports between observers were more likely. Even following widespread improvement in election-monitoring techniques, low-quality observers remained and, in some regions, proliferated. For a number of African states, such as Zimbabwe, the Organization for African Unity (now the African Union) represented a friendly organization that was highly unlikely to criticize, although their reputation has improved in recent years. The Arab League has sent delegations to elections in Northern Africa and is also unlikely to criticize election fraud. Although La Francophonie has issued several critical reports, their observers can more often be relied upon to validate questionable elections. The Russian controlled Commonwealth of Independent States is one of the most blatantly artificial observer groups. The Shanghai Cooperation Organization, which is composed of China, Kazakhstan, Kyrgyzstan, Russia, Tajikistan, and Uzbekistan, has also deployed election-monitoring delegations in recent years, but the organization has no stated objective of promoting democracy.

In figure 5.2, I show the trends in multiple monitors and in the use of "friendly" organizations.[27] I use a conservative definition of critical observers, including only those groups that have reputations for regularly criticizing election manipulation: the OSCE/ODIHR (including observers representing the Parliamentary Assembly Council of Europe), the Organization of American States (OAS), the EU, the Carter Center, the Commonwealth, and the NDI or International Republican Institute (IRI). Each of these groups has also been criticized for failing to condemn elections that others believed were fraudulent.[28] However, relative to other organizations, their reputations are much more professional, and they condemn elections more frequently than do any other organizations. If I instead code each organization as "critical" after it has condemned at least one election, more organizations qualify as critical after 1995 and substantially fewer elections are observed by only uncritical observers.

As in the Russian case described in the introduction to this chapter, governments frequently accuse observers of bias, applying double standards, or of not understanding elections or democracy in the region. Although these criticisms are sometimes well deserved, such government-sponsored criticism is more likely to be leveled by leaders seeking to distract media attention from their own behavior. Some leaders actively

---

27. See also Kelley, "The More the Merrier?"

28. Kelley, "D-Minus Elections: The Politics and Norms of International Election Observation."

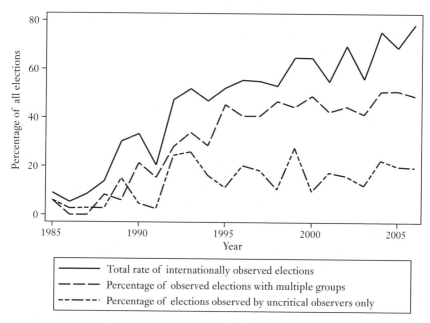

Figure 5.2. Trends in international observation missions

court professionalized observer organizations, convince them to monitor the election, and then try to discredit them after they arrive in the country. For example, the Zambian government sought European Union observers for the 2001 presidential elections, welcomed them into the country, and then almost immediately accused them of favoring the opposition candidate before they had made any statements.[29]

The reputed master manipulator of elections and international observers is Robert Mugabe of Zimbabwe.[30] Over the course of elections in 2000, 2002, 2005, and 2008 the Mugabe government attempted to control, manipulate, and discredit international observers using a variety of tactics. Despite his efforts, Mugabe did not succeed at eliminating criticism of the elections, but on several occasions these efforts appear to have muddied the waters sufficiently to lessen the effects of international condemnation.

Mugabe's tactics against observers vary. By the late 1990s, some observer groups were in the habit of deploying pre-election missions to

29. "Zambia: EU Denies Supporting Opposition Candidate," *Africa News*, January 7, 2002.

30. This section relies heavily on information from Bjornlund, *Beyond Free and Fair*, chapter 9.

evaluate whether they should send an observer mission should they receive an invitation from the host government. This practice of sending pre-election missions before government invitations were issued was in many cases welcome and noncontroversial, yet it was not strictly compliant with the norm that observers should be invited by the host government. U.S.-based NGOs NDI and IRI deployed a pre-election mission for the planned 2000 Zimbabwean elections, but they chose to announce that the conditions for credible democratic elections did not exist, provoking a forceful reaction from the Zimbabwe government. The government revoked NDI and IRI staff visas before the election and launched a comprehensive campaign to manipulate foreign observers. It is noteworthy that Zimbabwe did not simply ban all foreign observers from the country, which would have been a violation of the norm. By 2000, refusing observers would have been an unambiguous sign that the election would not be democratic and likely would have led to immediate sanctions.

Instead of banning observers outright, Mugabe issued a blanket invitation to observers and then changed the requirements continuously until election day, attempting to dictate their nationality and their numbers and decreasing the likelihood they would criticize the election. Ultimately, the government banned all NGOs from monitoring the election, refused to credential any observer from the United Kingdom, and mandated that the EU delegation contain members from EU member countries only, effectively banning observers from Kenya and Nigeria who had planned to serve on the EU delegation.[31] The election was eventually observed by the EU, the Commonwealth, the Organization of African Unity (OAU), and the Southern African Development Community (SADC).

After giving up their pursuit of credentials, IRI condemned the election based on their pre-election observation: "The process is so flawed that it cannot adequately reflect the will of the people. Those responsible for elections in Zimbabwe have failed their country."[32] In contrast, the OAU and SADC missions praised the elections as free and fair, and the Commonwealth mission issued what the EU later called a "wishy-washy" report.[33] Citing pre-election violence, the Commonwealth report said that there were "impediments placed in the way of enabling the electorate to freely choose their representatives,"[34] but did not argue the election was

---

31. Bjornlund, *Beyond Free and Fair.*
32. Ibid., 199.
33. Bjornlund, *Beyond Free and Fair,* 201.
34. Commonwealth Observer Group, *Parliamentary Elections in Zimbabwe: 24–25 June 2000,* 34.

fundamentally flawed. Of the groups permitted in the country, the EU issued the most critical report, citing "serious flaws and irregularities in the electoral process,"[35] but they were subsequently criticized on all sides: by African observer groups for "not allowing Africans to express themselves," from Mugabe himself for applying biased standards, and by the banned observer groups for implicitly condoning the manipulation of observers by failing to withdraw their mission.[36]

For the 2002 presidential elections, tensions increased, as did the Mugabe government's sometimes impressive and confusing tactics. Mugabe reportedly met with the EU team about potential deployment of an EU mission but stormed out of the meeting, telling them to "keep out," that "Zimbabwe would not allow other countries to run our elections," and protesting after the meeting that "some of them were our former colonizers."[37] The government later backpedaled on Mugabe's statements and the EU observer ban, announcing they were only opposed to "monitors" but would accept "observers."[38] Zimbabwe later prohibited observers from Denmark, Finland, Germany, the Netherlands, Sweden, and the United Kingdom, causing the EU to withdraw its efforts to deploy a mission, instead imposing economic sanctions.

The quality of the 2002 elections was again quite poor, with widespread government-sponsored violence and election fraud. Unsurprisingly, the Organization for African Unity found it to be "transparent, credible, free and fair." In contrast to the 2000 elections, however, the Commonwealth and SADC Parliamentary Forum condemned the elections, along with the EU and other groups that had refused to deploy observers. The Commonwealth suspended Zimbabwe from the organization for twelve months. Within a month of the elections, economic sanctions or aid suspensions were instituted by Germany, Norway, Japan, Canada, Switzerland, the United States, and Denmark, and it was estimated that Zimbabwe lost $4 billion in development aid in the year after the 2002 elections.

Mugabe's efforts to manipulate observers succeeded on some fronts, because he was able to gain a positive report from international observers

35. European Union, "Elections in Zimbabwe on 24–25 June 2000."

36. Bjornlund, *Beyond Free and Fair,* 201.

37. "Zimbabwe; Foreigners 'Welcome' to Observe Poll," *Africa News,* November 26, 2001.

38. This is a common rhetorical distinction in diplomatic circles and is sometimes emphasized by governments attempting to avoid high-quality election observation. Some organizations use monitoring and observing interchangeably. Other organizations use only the word *observation,* which is meant to imply a less interventionist method of poll watching. However, because no international observer groups adopt an interventionist approach to international election monitoring, the rhetorical distinction loses practical value for researchers.

from the OAU and generated voluminous media attention to the question of whether Westerners could fairly judge African elections. It is impossible to know for certain whether Mugabe would have faced the same forms of international condemnation if international observation had not become an international norm, yet it is clear that international condemnation of the elections from foreign observers caused the government to forgo a variety of international benefits, including severe reductions in foreign aid, suspension from international organizations, travel bans on Mugabe and other prominent government officials, freezing of their assets, and the labeling of Zimbabwe as a pariah state. Zimbabwe presents a clear example of government efforts to manipulate observers as well as the international response when leaders fail to evade international criticism.

Strategies of Election Manipulation

Willful manipulation of elections and electoral processes is widespread, diverse, sometimes obvious, and frequently innovative. As Andreas Schedler emphasizes, "rulers may choose any number of tactics to help them carve the heart out of electoral contests."[39] Within electoral authoritarian regimes, case-based research and recent theoretical work documents the use of a variety of tactics used by governments to maintain their hold on power.[40] Observers do not cause election manipulation to exist. Rather, observers influence the form of manipulation employed by governments and parties to bias elections in their favor. In my theory, pseudo-democratic governments that invite observers should attempt to manipulate elections without getting caught or criticized, an effort I refer to as "strategic manipulation."[41]

As American politics literature has documented, strategic manipulation is not confined to the developing world.[42] For example, in urban political

---

39. Schedler, "The Menu of Manipulation," 41.

40. Schedler, "The Menu of Manipulation"; Magaloni, *Voting for Autocracy*; Brownlee, *Authoritarianism in an Age of Democratization*; Schedler, "The Nested Game of Democratization by Elections"; Schedler, *Electoral Authoritarianism*; Simpser, "Making Votes Not Count"; Schaffer, *Elections for Sale*; Taylor, "Patterns of Electoral Corruption in Peru"; Alvarez, Hall, and Hyde, *Election Fraud: Detecting and Deterring Electoral Manipulation*; Calingaert, "Election Rigging and How to Fight It."

41. Schedler, *Electoral Authoritarianism*; Beaulieu and Hyde, "In the Shadow of Democracy Promotion."

42. Alvarez, Hall, and Hyde, *Election Fraud; Detecting and Deterring Electoral Manipulation*; Campbell, *Deliver the Vote*; Cox and Kousser, "Turnout and Rural Corruption."

machines, Jessica Trounstine cites various biasing strategies in voter access to information, voting, and the ways in which votes are translated into seats, many of which are difficult to prove or are not perceived as illegal. Trounstine lists media control, suppression of civic groups, vote bribery, obscure polling sites, misuse of government resources, violence aimed at voter suppression, ghost voting and the discarding of ballots, candidate disqualification, gerrymandering, and malapportionment.[43] Similarly, but illustrated in the comparative politics literature on electoral authoritarianism, Schedler describes the "menu of manipulation" used by leaders, which includes overt election fraud, political repression, manipulating the ability of politicians to participate, manipulating the forum for debating policies or access to the relevant means of communicating with voters, manipulating the rules of competition, and making competition unfair.

As Michael Bratton points out with respect to elections in Africa, incumbents use executive power not simply to break electoral rules, but to bend the rules in their favor, including, for example "the disqualification of leading candidates, the spotty coverage of voter registration, the lack of internal democracy in ruling parties, [and] the abuse of government resources during the campaign."[44] Leaders possess an array of tactics and rely on diverse strategies in order to maintain a "semblance of democratic legitimacy" in the presence of international observers.[45]

As election monitoring has evolved, so have the strategies used by pseudo-democrats to evade international condemnation of their elections. For example, as election monitoring began to spread rapidly throughout Africa in the early 1990s, Gisela Geisler criticized the disproportionate focus by observers on election day and the fact that elections in Kenya and Ghana were "already 'rigged' before the votes were cast and counted."[46] This and related criticism lead observers to increase emphasis on observation of the pre-election period.[47]

It would be impossible to define and measure all strategies of manipulation, because strategic manipulation should, by definition, include unobservable forms. Strategic manipulation may also be obvious and observable, but it is distinguishable from outright election theft because it is intended

43. Trounstine, "Challenging the Machine-Dichotomy"; Cox and Kousser, "Turnout and Rural Corruption"; Campbell, *Deliver the Vote*; Alvarez, Hall, and Hyde, *Election Fraud; Detecting and Deterring Electoral Manipulation.*

44. Bratton, "Second Elections in Africa," 60–65.

45. Schedler, "The Menu of Manipulation," 36.

46. Geisler, "Fair?," 615.

47. Bjornlund, *Beyond Free and Fair.*

to evade detection and criticism. Strategic election manipulation may include tactics that are legal, such as electorally targeted manipulation of fiscal policy, changing the electoral system, or gerrymandering. For example, following three previously unsuccessful attempts at running for president, Daniel Ortega was elected as president of Nicaragua only after he spearheaded a change in the electoral rules so that a president could be elected with 35% rather than the previously necessary 45% of votes cast. In 2006 he won with 38% of the vote in an election that was endorsed by reputable international monitoring missions despite the blatant manipulation of the electoral rules to engineer his own victory.[48]

Cleverly, some governments change election-related laws in order to make their intended manipulation strategies legal, such as passing obscure candidate citizenship requirements, modifying voter registration laws, or requiring opposition candidates to pay enormous registration fees. Of course, some leaders manipulate elections blatantly in order to demonstrate their strength or dominance or for other domestic reasons.[49] President Alexander Lukashenko of Belarus has boasted that he is so popular that he had to commit election fraud by artificially lowering his own vote share so as to be credible to international observers.[50] Lukashenko has also engaged in more traditional forms of election fraud, banned any criticism of his regime in public discourse, employed a widespread campaign of violence and intimidation against suspected regime opponents, branded opposition party members as traitors, and kept tight control of state-run media.[51] Lukashenko, and leaders like him, make little effort to conceal such manipulation. They employ a different form of strategic manipulation by instead waging a war of public opinion and arguing, for example, that their popularity makes political repression irrelevant because they would win even in free and fair elections, or by attempting to discredit international observers.

In order to bias elections in their favor while avoiding the most extreme and obvious forms of election theft, governments have intimidated journalists and shut down independent media outlets; monopolized or misused state-run television; falsely accused their opponents of crimes; threatened and intimidated opposition candidates, their families, and their

48. Birch, "Electoral Systems and Electoral Misconduct."

49. Lust-Okar, *Structuring Conflict in the Arab World*; Magaloni, *Voting for Autocracy*; Simpser, "Making Votes Not Count."

50. Jan Maksymiuk, "Belarus: Lukashenka—Father of the Nation, Or Loudmouthed Autocrat?," *Radio Free Europe*, Prague, November 24, 2006.

51. OSCE/ODIHR, *Republic of Belarus Presidential Election 19 March 2006, OSCE/ODIHR Election Observation Mission Report*.

supporters; and taken other actions aimed at increasing their own chances at winning the election without being condemned for election fraud. I discuss how these tools are used strategically below.

Candidate exclusion and dividing the opposition represent very effective forms of biasing election outcomes because they are not on their own likely to provoke severe international criticism, as their use is often hard to prove. At its most extreme, candidate exclusion includes indefinite disappearance of candidates, jailing, actual or attempted murder, intimidation, or "voluntary" exile. These extreme forms of candidate exclusion provoke international condemnation if the government is clearly responsible, but perpetrators frequently remain unknown. The suicide bombing and assassination of leading Pakistani opposition candidate Benazir Bhutto at a campaign rally led international observers to condemn violence leading up to the 2008 elections, but the overall evaluation of the election was ultimately positive, in part because the ruling party was defeated.

If leading opposition candidates do not "choose" to compete, it is much easier for the incumbent party to win without using other forms of manipulation. Screening candidates through intimidation, political imprisonment, or even murder is a highly effective tactic. In countries with extreme levels of political violence, such as Afghanistan, prospective politicians face an increased risk of assassination. Less violently but just as effectively, candidates in the 1995 Haitian elections could be barred from competing if they were members of the ruling party during the Duvalier dictatorship; however, the determination about which candidates fit this description was subjective, and some argue that the criterion was applied unfairly. In Côte d'Ivoire, the leading opposition candidate and former prime minister (1990–1993), Alassane Dramane Ouattara, was disqualified as a candidate from the 1995 and 2000 presidential elections because of a newly introduced nationality clause in the electoral law that required candidates to prove that they and their parents were Ivorian. Eligible opposition parties boycotted the Indonesian election of 1997 because, they claimed, one popular opposition candidate had been barred from competing in the election, ostensibly due to his health, even though the government argued these exclusions were within the scope of the law.

Underscoring the success of these strategies, recent research on electoral authoritarian regimes has shown that unless opposition parties are able to form a coalition to challenge the incumbent regime with a united front, "liberalizing electoral outcomes" are unlikely.[52] Although the methods vary,

---

52. Howard and Roessler, "Liberalizing Electoral Outcomes."

it is frequently the case that "incumbents find ways to engineer the failure of opposition parties."[53] Because electoral autocrats are rarely beaten by divided or weak opposition parties, engineering a weak or divided opposition remains one of the most powerful strategies for incumbent governments to stay in power.

Another form of indirect manipulation of elections reflects the importance of information in campaigns and elections. Governments can monopolize state-run media to campaign for government candidates, and they are frequently criticized for such actions by international observers. Drawing less attention is the more subtle, but potentially just as effective, method of exploiting state-run media in a manner that harms the opposition but is not technically campaign related. For example, in Cambodia in 1993, the government played the movie *The Killing Fields* on state television just days before the election, which was arguably intended to discredit Communist Party candidates.[54] Playing a movie on state-run television sounds relatively innocuous, but this type of strategy can bias the election using resources available only to the state, while avoiding overt or illegal forms of election manipulation. Alberto Simpser and Daniela Donno argue that international election observation can actually harm governance by leading incumbents to resort to the rigging of courts, media repression, and control of other administrative bodies.[55]

Violence and political repression can be used to display dominance of the regime, but it can also be employed in manner intended to avoid international condemnation. As Schedler writes, "irregular episodes of harassment and intimidation make fewer international headlines than systematic human rights violations, and they may be equally effective in dissuading dissidence and imposing self-censorship."[56] This method of manipulation is clearly not part of a democratic political process and is likely to be condemned by observers if it is blatantly or systematically undertaken by the government. Prior to the 2006 election in Belarus, President Lukashenko preemptively threatened any supporters of a postelection attempt to overthrow the government, saying that "we will break the neck [of protesters] immediately—like a duckling's."[57] Although the statement

---

53. Schedler, "The Menu of Manipulation," 41.
54. Roberts, "The Cambodian Elections of 1993."
55. Simpser, "Unintended Consequences of Election Monitoring"; Simpser and Donno, "Can International Election Monitoring Harm Governance?"
56. Schedler, "The Nested Game of Democratization by Elections," 106.
57. "Belarus Leader to 'Break Neck' of Election Demonstrators," Agence Free Press, March 17, 2006.

obviously threatened protestors, its actual effect on the behavior of voters, journalists, and opposition political parties is hard to gauge, and observers have difficulty distinguishing between opposition supporters who are intimidated and those who are simply indifferent. Threats of violence have a chilling effect on competition that may be impossible to prove because successful intimidation leaves little observable evidence.[58] Similarly, in an effort to justify the use of violence toward opposition party supporters, governments have been discovered planting armed agitators at otherwise peaceful rallies, a charge levied at the Ethiopian government following the 2005 elections. Subsequent government crackdowns on "violent protestors" are then less likely to be criticized by international observers.

State bureaucracies sometimes enact discriminatory policies aimed at biasing the election without giving the appearance of impropriety. Because many bureaucracies in developing countries already have existing reputations as being incompetent (or they can quickly earn them), claims that opposition candidates did not properly file candidate registration papers, cumbersome voter registration processes, lost election materials, supposedly broken computers (famously following the 1988 Mexican elections), duplicate voter registrations for government supporters, and similarly ambiguous election irregularities are potential forms of intended election fraud that are difficult to prove as such. If an outdated voter register favors the incumbent, it can be an effective form of strategic manipulation simply to underemphasize the importance of voter registration or divert bureaucratic energies elsewhere and blame the out-of-date rolls on a lack of time and money. Politically captured election administration bodies can falsify vote counts or adjudicate electoral disputes in favor of the incumbent. Intent matters, particularly in countries with little electoral experience. When intentional manipulation and administrative incompetence are observationally equivalent, it becomes difficult for observers to condemn an election without additional evidence that administrative problems were in fact intentional manipulation of the electoral process.

Similarly, partisan control of the election administration body may be gained through legal measures, although it can be used to confer an unfair advantage and manipulate electoral outcomes. For example, in Azerbaijan in 1998, President Aliev's control of the central election commission was cited as the central opposition party complaint. Although OSCE/ODIHR observers criticized the administration of the election, Aliev retained control of the election commission, which disqualified several

58. Kuran, *Private Truths, Public Lies.*

opposition parties from participating in the 2000 election, including the most popular party.

Vote or abstention buying are also relatively common strategies used both by government and opposition parties, some of which can be well concealed from international observers.[59] Although these techniques are not new, when campaigns pay voters to stay home in an effort to suppress turnout for supporters of their opponent, international observers may note that turnout is unexpectedly low; however, a well-orchestrated effort could realistically be concealed from international observers. For example, a widespread vote-buying strategy with a diverse pedigree goes by many locally known names, including the "Tasmanian dodge," the "caterpillar" in Russia, the "shuttle" in the Philippines, and chain voting or carousel voting in other countries.[60] The goal of this vote-buying scheme is to allow vote buyers to evade the secret ballot and decrease uncertainty that vote sellers followed through on their side of the transaction. The scheme begins with a ballot that has been stolen or smuggled out of a polling station. The vote buyer marks the ballot and gives it to a vote seller, who then smuggles the premarked ballot into the polling station, casts it as his or her own, and then must smuggle out the voter's own ballot, still unmarked, in order to be paid by the vote buyer. The newly obtained blank ballot is then marked and cast by the next vote seller. Although this tactic has been documented and criticized by international observers on a number of occasions, it is possible to conceal it from international monitors. It serves as an example of election manipulation that can evade the protections of the secret ballot, take place in otherwise functioning polling stations, and not be observable by anyone but the participants in the vote-buying scheme.

Efforts to engage in strategic manipulation are not foolproof, and sometimes they fail spectacularly. In the 2000 elections in Côte d'Ivoire, coup leader and presidential candidate General Robert Guei attempted to win his election through fraud and gain international certification, but he managed to fail at both. To limit competition without eliminating it entirely, the Guei regime ensured that fourteen of the nineteen prospective presidential candidates, including those from the two largest political parties, were barred from running by the Supreme Court. These actions led the UN-coordinated observer mission to withdraw from the country

59. Schaffer, *Elections for Sale.*
60. Schedler and Schaffer, "What Is Vote Buying?," 23.

and issue a strong condemnation. However, Guei apparently did not cheat enough to win the election, and in a surprise outcome, one of the four remaining opposition candidates won the elections with 59% of the vote.

Although some forms of election manipulation are uniquely available to the incumbent because they require government complicity or the exploitation of state resources, opposition political parties or other civic groups are capable of election fraud, and some governments diffuse criticism of their own fraud by accusing the opposition of cheating as well. International observers at the 1999 Nigerian elections witnessed widespread election fraud, including ballot box stuffing, voter intimidation, and inflation of the voter register. In part because both sides were cheating, however, they had difficulty determining whether the observed irregularities influenced the winner of the election. Despite the poor quality of the elections, the Carter Center's postelection statement reflected their uncertainty about the overall effect of widespread election fraud committed by multiple parties and did not condemn the election as strongly as it might have had only the government had been caught cheating:

> While we witnessed a number of abuses, the delegation has no systematic evidence indicating that these abuses would have affected the overall outcome of the election. Nevertheless these abuses may have substantially compromised the integrity of the process in the areas where they occurred.[61]

Incumbents who are caught and criticized by international observers frequently attempt to diffuse criticism. Incumbent governments may argue that observers are biased and imperialist, that they are too few in number to accurately judge elections, and that they act only for their host country's interests.

In addition to these examples, many forms of strategic manipulation may be unobservable. Like a perfect crime, perfectly orchestrated strategic manipulation leaves no evidence but guarantees victory for the government and defeat for the opposition. Because of the potential for this dynamic to exist, and because of the possibility that opposition parties are better equipped to document such covert manipulation, I briefly explore the reaction of opposition parties to international observers and strategic manipulation.

---

61. Carter Center and National Democratic Institute, *Observing the 1998-99 Nigeria Elections, Final Report,* 59.

Opposition Parties, Observers, and Election Fraud

Across all observed elections, the reaction of opposition parties to international observers is diverse. Opposition parties may actively pressure their government to invite international election monitors, as in Jamaica in 1997. If they think that observers will legitimize what they anticipate will be a seriously flawed process, they lobby against them. Writing on opposition parties in Africa, Oda van Cranenburgh notes that initially "opposition parties were the primary actors urging for international observation to ensure a free and fair process..." but that "many opposition groups have become disenchanted with election observation."[62]

Opposition parties also engage in election fraud, although the dynamics between observers and opposition parties are distinct from those between pseudo-democratic leaders and the observers they invite. When the government holds democratic elections, it is rare for opposition parties to engage in nationally orchestrated election fraud and even less likely that an election will be internationally condemned for opposition-only election fraud. Nevertheless, documented forms of opposition party manipulation include local schemes in areas of opposition party control, clientelism and vote buying, or intimidation and violence perpetuated by nonstate groups.

The strategy of opposition parties hinges on whether they anticipate that observers will judge election fraud accurately. For opposition political parties, the worst possible outcome is that the government rigs the election and international observers nevertheless praise it. Observer praise of an election makes postelection complaints by opposition parties less credible, and successful strategic manipulation by the government reduces their ability to win political representation. Indeed, this is precisely the outcome that pseudo-democrats are trying to achieve.

Thus when governments are engaging in strategic manipulation, the opposition has an increased incentive to signal their complaints to observers and to demonstrate that their complaints are valid. This dynamic, as recent research shows, led to increases in opposition party election boycotts during the 1990s when observers were present and their ability to judge election fraud was still in question.[63] More so than postelection protest, successful pre-election boycotts are costly for opposition parties. Not only do successful boycotts involve significant organization, they require that the parties forgo any possibility of representation. Threatening or

---

62. Abbink and Hesseling, *Election Observation and Democratization in Africa*, 31.
63. Beaulieu and Hyde, "In the Shadow of Democracy Promotion."

carrying out an election boycott has been used in many countries to draw attention to unfairness in the electoral process, to pressure governments to rectify problems in the administration of elections, and to draw international and domestic attention to election manipulation.[64]

False accusations of government-sponsored election fraud may also be triggered by the presence of international observers because the possibility of causing negative international media attention increases the incentive for opposition groups to invent claims of election fraud, particularly if their chances of winning are otherwise low. Pre-election complaints of fraud inoculate the opposition against the possibility that they will perform poorly in the election. If the opposition party wins, the complaints become irrelevant, and if they lose, their performance can be blamed on unfair competition. This strategy is not foolproof, and it backfires if opposition complaints of fraud are believed to be exaggerated. Opposition parties suspected of such falsified complaints themselves become targets of observer criticism.

Nevertheless, some complaints made by opposition parties cannot be proven or disproven. Some involve complicated conspiracies or point to types of manipulation that are legal, such as targeted increases in government spending. Other opposition complaints are hard to believe. In the Dominican Republic in 1966, one observer faithfully reported opposition party claims that "they had been warned to expect white phosphorous to be placed in the ballot envelopes causing them to burst into flames when opened."[65] No burning ballots were documented in the Dominican election, but similarly creative accusations have continued along with government innovation in the use of strategic manipulation.

In short, opposition response to observers is not uniform, but rather it reveals that opposition parties have an interest in exposing government-sponsored manipulation when it exists, sometimes accuse the government of fraud that it did not commit, and are generally wary of participating in a process that could be manipulated but not criticized by the international community. If they believe that foreign observers will improve the quality of the process in either the short or the long term, and thereby improve their chances of winning, opposition parties are also likely to pressure governments to invite high-quality election observers.

---

64. Lindberg, "Tragic Protest"; Beaulieu, "Protesting the Contest: Election Boycotts Around the World, 1990–2002."

65. Keys, "Observing the Elections," 77.

Strategic Interaction under the Norm of International Observation

Many forms of strategic manipulation follow the letter of the law, but they bend the laws governing democracy such that the playing field is steeply tilted. Other forms of strategic manipulation that may be encouraged by election monitoring are clearly illegal and violate the letter and the spirit of rules governing democratic elections, such as bringing about the mysterious disappearance of opposition candidates, engaging in well-concealed vote buying, and manipulating the voter registration lists in opposition strongholds. As I have shown in this chapter, observers have responded to this diversity in tactics and have become more likely to criticize many forms of election manipulation that take place before and after election day.

The evolving game of strategy between international observers and pseudo-democrats suggests continuing innovation on the part of leaders, observers, and democracy-promoting international actors. As election monitoring became more widespread, international actors invested in improving election observation, thus increasing the scope and quality of election monitoring and giving leaders the incentive to modify their methods of strategic manipulation. After the norm became established, few leaders chose not to invite observers, and many leaders who were not otherwise inclined to signal their democratizing intentions invited reputable international observers. The fact that monitoring is costly to pseudo-democrats makes it an effective signal, and it is a central reason that international actors accepted the practice. Overall, for pseudo-democrats, the norm of election monitoring—and the widespread international support for democratic regimes—increases pressure on all governments to hold elections and increases the uncertainty over the outcome of those elections. To comply with international expectations, leaders must now hold elections, invite observers, and receive a positive report. For leaders who do not wish to give up power but who cannot afford to shun pro-democracy international actors or become a pariah state, the norm of election monitoring means they must devote increased effort to conceal election manipulation, risk the consequences of a negative report, overcome any direct deterrent effect that observers have on election fraud, and still guarantee their hold on power. This calculation is increasingly complicated as observers and pseudo-democrats interact under the norm of election monitoring.

CONCLUSION

Constrained Leaders and Changing International Expectations

Prior to the 2006 Belarusian election, President Aleksander Lukashenko invited observers from the Organization for Security and Cooperation in Europe (OSCE), the National Democratic Institute, and the Commonwealth of Independent States. Reportedly a popular incumbent, Lukashenko nevertheless engaged in many forms of electoral manipulation, including vote buying, intimidation, mass arrests, and monopolization of the media. The OSCE criticized the electoral process, saying that that it was "severely flawed due to arbitrary use of state power and restrictions on basic rights."[1] The United States responded to the fraudulent elections by declaring the results invalid, refusing to accept Lukashenko as the winner, and calling for a new election.[2] The European Union barred President Lukashenko and thirty of the country's officials from entering EU member states, and vowed to support Belarus's opposition movement and the development of an independent press.[3]

This international involvement in the Belarusian election is not unique. In fact, the elections are typical in that an incumbent who planned on manipulating the election willingly invited high-quality international observers. Predictably, the fraudulent elections were denounced by international observers, the international community responded by attempting to delegitimize the elections, and pro-democracy actors used the reports

---

1. OSCE/ODIHR, "Belarusian Election Severely Flawed Due to Arbitrary Use of State Power and Restrictions on Basic Rights," news release, Minsk, March 20, 2006.

2. C. J. Chivers and Steven Lee Myers, "U.S. Calls Belarus Vote for Leader Invalid," *New York Times*, March 20, 2006.

3. "Europe Bars Its Doors to Belarus President and 30 Officials," *New York Times*, April 22, 2006; "Election in Belarus Did Not Meet Standards, Observers Say," *New York Times*, March 20, 2006.

of observers to justify the imposition of costs on the government. In some cases, similar scenarios following fraudulent elections have resulted in massive domestic uprisings and the eventual removal of the incumbent government. In other cases, the parallel vote tabulations organized by domestic and international observers have prevented the incumbent government from falsifying the results during the tabulation process, also resulting in the ouster of the incumbent government.

Over the past fifty years, the trajectory of election observation reflects a widespread increase in global support for democracy. Democracy has become the world's most popular form of government. Long-standing democracies devote significant resources toward encouraging the development of democratic political institutions in other countries, and regimes not already perceived as consolidated democracies face direct and indirect pressure to liberalize their political institutions. How do leaders react to this pressure? More generally, when the preferences of powerful states change, how do other governments respond and what are the lasting consequences? Motivated by these questions, this book examines how the movement toward democracy and international pressure on states causes behavioral changes among governments seeking foreign support. I argue that an important outcome of this pressure is that efforts by regimes to increase their share of international benefits can generate lasting changes in global governance through the creation of new and self-enforcing international norms.

This book opened with an empirical puzzle. Leaders throughout the developing world are now expected to invite international observers and receive their endorsement, and those few leaders who refuse now send an unambiguous signal to international and domestic audiences that they are holding undemocratic elections and they reject international engagement. Strikingly, even the majority of leaders planning to commit widespread election fraud comply with the norm, risking international condemnation of their elections. Many leaders now face "the pseudo-democrat's dilemma," in which they must choose between two undesirable outcomes: inviting observers and risking the consequences of a negative report or refusing to invite observers and sending an unambiguous signal that their country's elections will not be democratic.

Now tied to broader international support for democracy, good governance, and political stability, inviting foreign observers has become linked to a variety of internationally allocated benefits, including membership in international organizations, foreign aid, international investment, increased trade, tourism, normal diplomatic relations, and international legitimacy. Similarly, refusing foreign observers or earning their criticism now leads to reduced or eliminated international support.

The case of international election monitoring illustrates why states invite potentially costly foreign intrusions into their domestic affairs and how actions intended to signal a government's type become international norms. Increasing global integration and the widely held view that states can and should influence the domestic politics and policies of other states make this argument particularly relevant to modern international relations theory. Norms help govern international interactions in the absence of global government. The international relations literature to date has focused almost exclusively on two types of international norms: those that facilitate cooperation within international institutions or that are imposed by powerful states and those that result from the work of norm entrepreneurs, motivated by principled ideas, whose efforts bring about desired change in the state behavior.

At least one other class of norms is important in global governance, and it does not fit neatly into either of the previous categories. Signaling norms are distinct both because of the mechanism that creates them and because of their consequences, as I have argued throughout this book and as I summarize below. Signaling norms are diffusely motivated behaviors that are initiated as a strategic response to changes in the international environment but that become widely shared—and enforced—"standards of appropriate behavior for actors with a given identity."[4] In explaining the norm of international election monitoring, I have argued that the global movement toward democracy triggered a game between leaders seeking international benefits and democracy-promoting actors, ultimately resulting in the widely held expectation that leaders holding credible elections should invite international election monitors to judge them. In the remainder of this chapter, I summarize my theory and the findings presented in the book and evaluate the implications of my argument, including the implications for theories of international norm formation, the quality of elections, the behavior of pseudo-democrats, and the policies related to election observation and democracy promotion.

Theory in Brief

My central argument is that that states seeking international benefits can generate unintended yet consequential international norms. In my model of norm development, states are divided into two groups: those

---

4. Finnemore and Sikkink, "International Norm Dynamics and Political Change," 891.

seeking foreign support and those allocating international benefits. Actors within each group behave independently, without explicit coordination with other actors in their group. Benefit-seeking states are further divided into "good" types of regimes, which are preferred by benefit-giving states, and "bad" types of regimes, which international actors would prefer not to support. In explaining the norm of election monitoring, good types of leaders or regimes are committed to democratization and bad leaders are pseudo-democrats, or leaders who hold elections but who are willing to violate the rules of democracy.

Leaders of many states in the international system work to maximize their share of international benefits. These international benefits are targeted toward states possessing desirable characteristics and withdrawn from states that are revealed not to possess them. Information between states is asymmetric: governments possess accurate information about their own type, but other international actors can have difficulty judging whether another state is a desirable type. Thus, even when international actors prefer to interact with specified types of states, they cannot always distinguish good from bad regime types and, all else equal, prefer to avoid states of uncertain value that might possess undesirable characteristics. Benefit-seeking states with desirable characteristics are thus motivated to find credible signals of their type to other international actors.

If an attempted signal is successful in communicating a state's valued characteristic to international audiences, it is rewarded. Mimicry of successful signals causes the new behavior to spread. The behavior becomes an international norm when benefit-giving actors believe that all good governments send the signal. More states are motivated to adopt the signal, even those that must fake it, and the behavior becomes widespread and expected, even in the absence of explicit advocacy or pressure on states to adopt the new behavior. Acceptance of the signal as an internationally held norm reinforces the incentives for states to continue the signaling behavior.

The normalization of a signal also ties the behavior more closely to a characteristic that is valued by powerful international actors. Initially, these benefit-giving international actors may be indifferent to the signal, but once it is accepted as a means by which they can more efficiently target their support to states possessing desirable characteristics, they are motivated to invest in the quality of the signal, making it more difficult for undesirable types to fake it. Therefore, when a signal becomes a norm, it increases the costs for leaders who refuse to signal and simultaneously makes it riskier for undesirable types to attempt to signal.

Although this theory can be applied to other signaling-based norms, I have developed and evaluated it using international election observation.

Reacting to increases in international benefits tied to democracy, governments seeking increased Western support were motivated to find a signal that demonstrated their commitment to democracy. Although other signals were attempted, government invitations to nonpartisan foreign election monitors became a successful—and therefore widely imitated—signal of a government's commitment to democratic elections. Foreign observers are not perfect judges of election quality, but because they are frequently willing to condemn elections that are stolen, their reports are a valuable source of information to democracy-promoting actors, and inviting observers and receiving their endorsement became recognized as a credible signal that a government was committed to democratization. Because election observation was initiated by state leaders and observers continue to be invited by host governments, the practice evaded concern among democracy promoters regarding the issue of international intervention in the domestic affairs of sovereign states.

My theory also provides a direct theoretical link between the causes and consequences of signaling norms. More than arguing that norms matter, I show that the fact that election monitoring is risky for electoral autocrats is not only an interesting feature of international election monitoring, but it is also a central reason why inviting observers became a widely accepted international norm. This feature of signaling norms is counterintuitive because it implies that the bad types who would least prefer a signal to become a widely held norm—in this case the pseudo-democrats—are the driving force in spreading the behavior and in demonstrating to international actors that the signal is informative. To illustrate, if inviting monitors was costless for pseudo-democrats, it would be cheap talk and easier for them to mimic, but the potential rewards of signaling would be diminished. If election observation were not riskier for pseudo-democrats, the practice would not have become an informative signal of a government's commitment to democracy, inviting observers would not have been rewarded by pro-democracy actors, and pseudo-democrats would not have had the incentive to mimic the signal. Thus, the fact that election monitoring is a useful but imperfect tool to separate true democrats and pseudo-democrats is both a consequence of the norm and a central reason why it became an international norm at all.

By initiating a new and potentially costly signal of an internationally valued characteristic, states seeking democracy-related international benefits generated the norm of election observation. Norm generation was not the explicit goal of democratizing leaders or democracy-promoting actors; yet over time, the response by individual states to changes in the international environment led to an important change in internationally held expectations about the behavior of governments throughout the developing world.

Findings

I presented a variety of evidence in support of my argument, including cross-national data on the spread of election observation; detailed descriptions of the characteristics of inviting and noninviting countries; evidence of three ways that election monitoring is costly to pseudo-democrats, including several detailed cases demonstrating the existence of democracy-contingent international benefits; micro-level experimental tests showing that observers can deter fraud and otherwise improve the quality of elections (an effect that is more costly to pseudo-democrats than true democrats); and qualitative evidence illustrating the escalating game of strategic manipulation between pseudo-democrats, international monitors, and pro-democracy international actors. Additionally, I rely on diverse sources of documentation, including the rhetoric from leaders who discuss their decision to invite observers, archives of international organizations and nongovernmental organizations (NGOs), reports from individual observers, and a variety of election-based cases, to show that election monitoring was initiated as a signal to international audiences by governments that were committed to holding democratic elections but whose reputations were not well established. As international benefits tied to democracy increased, and as the number of governments inviting observers and receiving international endorsements increased, more governments began to invite international election monitors.

During the Cold War, Western reticence to support governments that were not overtly anti-communist outweighed their relatively weak preference for supporting democratic governments. Consistent with my theory, nearly all early inviters were governments that were already recognized as anti-communist Western allies and who could therefore marginally increase their value by signaling their commitment to democratization. Countries that were not already anti-communist were unable to improve their share of international benefits by signaling their commitment to democracy because of the disproportionate weight given to a country's opposition to communism.

As Cold War politics waned, the relative weight of a country's commitment to democracy increased, as did the overall amount of international benefits devoted to promoting democracy. Governments throughout the world felt international pressure to democratize, and invitations to international election observers spread rapidly, becoming a widely recognized signal of a country's commitment to democratize. In the 1990s most newly independent states and countries holding their first multiparty elections invited international observers. By the late 1990s, more than 80% of elections in the developing world were internationally monitored. Without pressure from powerful states or morally motivated activism, and at the invitation of leaders seeking international endorsement of their elections, inviting international observers became an international norm.

Using cross-national data on election observation, I explore several observable implications of my theory pertaining to the causes of internationally observed elections. I show that leaders were more likely to invite observers as international pressure for democracy increased, particularly if their regime type was highly uncertain (previous elections were suspended, country was run by transitional leadership, the elections were the country's first for which multiparty competition was allowed); if they were not already recognized as a democratizing country; and if they had invited observers previously. The central alternative explanations for the norm of election observation, including other theories of norm development, the regional and international diffusion of policies, and existing work on election monitoring, are undermined by a lack of evidence. Although norm entrepreneurs were active in promoting democracy and human rights, there is little evidence that activists helped initiate and spread the practice of election observation. Most organizations sending international observers were at first reluctant participants in election observation and declined invitations from leaders of sovereign states to send election monitors. Election monitors sent by human rights NGOs, rather than advocating election monitoring for its own sake, appeared to be exploiting leaders' enthusiasm for election observers in order to gain access to otherwise restricted information on human rights abuses. Evidence of overt pressure on states to invite observers (rather than pressure to democratize), exerted by either international or domestic actors, did not appear until the later stages of norm development, as election monitoring became a widely expected practice. In contrast to the literature on diffusion, I also find that the regional rate of election monitoring does not predict observed elections.[5]

The final alternative explanation that I consider in the book is that it is costless for leaders to invite international election observers, and the norm of election monitoring is therefore entirely inconsequential. I evaluated this alternative explanation by examining the domestic political

---

5. Simmons, Dobbin, and Garrett, *The Global Diffusion of Markets and Democracy.*

implications of my theory. Evidence of significant domestic consequences of election monitoring refutes the alternative explanation that it is costless for pseudo-democrats, and tests several key empirical implications of my theory. For election monitoring to be an effective signal of a government's type, it must be costly for undesirable types to imitate. Although election monitoring does not separate types perfectly, I exploit subnational experimental evidence in order to demonstrate that observers can deter fraud directly and therefore cost cheating parties a significant number of votes that they would have received in the absence of election observers. This is just one of many ways that election monitors can be costly to pseudo-democrats, but it presents clear causal evidence that inviting observers is not cheap talk and that it is more costly for pseudo-democrats to invite observers than it is for true democrats.

Not only do observers criticize elections, but consistent with my theory, a variety of international actors began reacting to negative reports from observers by withdrawing international benefits or by refusing to reopen channels of foreign support following elections that did not meet international standards. The norm of election monitoring means that pseudo-democrats must choose between inviting observers and risking a negative report and refusing observers and facing a virtually nonexistent chance that their elections will be recognized as democratic. I further explore the types of leaders who do not invite observers and show that, after the norm developed, the countries most likely to refuse observers were holding elections in which competition is banned or severely restricted, such as Cuba, Laos, North Korea, Singapore, Turkmenistan, and Vietnam. Other governments, such as Iran and Malaysia, hold somewhat competitive elections but represent rare cases in which the parties in power receive domestic support for refusing international engagement. I also show that this second strategy is less likely than one might expect. Even countries such as Belarus, Russia, and Zimbabwe devote significant effort to inviting observers and manipulating their reports, rather than simply refusing to invite them.

In addition to generating observable implications about the spread of election monitoring, my theory also predicts an evolving game of strategy between pseudo-democrats, who try to mimic the signal of inviting observers without being criticized, and international observers, who improve their ability to catch election manipulation over time by expanding their mandate and improving election-monitoring techniques. I demonstrate that pseudo-democrats engage in strategic manipulation by providing numerous examples of government attempts to manipulate elections without being caught and illustrate the changing practices of international election observers by focusing on how they respond to innovations in strategic manipulation. If pseudo-democrats had successfully fooled international election observers, the over-time trends should show negative reports becoming increasingly rare. In contrast, if my predictions of an evolving game of strategy in which innovations in cheating are met with improvements in election monitoring are correct, the rate of negative reports should remain relatively constant after the norm is created. The pattern of internationally criticized elections is relatively stable after about 1995, implying that pseudo-democrats are not entirely successful in evading observer criticism.

The types of evidence presented in this book are diverse and range from micro-level tests of whether observers reduce rates of blatant election fraud to cross-national examinations of whether international pressure for democracy coincided with governments choosing to invite observers. By evaluating the evidence at several levels of analysis and by employing multiple methods, I demonstrate significant support for my argument: leaders initiated election monitoring as a signal to international audiences of their commitment to democratization. Other leaders, including pseudo-democrats, mimicked the signal in order try to gain the endorsement of observers and increase their access to international benefits. Because election monitoring was risky for pseudo-democrats and provided valuable information about leaders' types to pro-democracy actors, it was rewarded by pro-democracy audiences. The fact that observers were invited by host governments rather than forced upon them by democracy promoters sidestepped early concerns that election monitoring violated sovereignty, and eventually this fact was used by democracy promoters to make internationally certified elections a necessary condition for an even greater range of international benefits, further raising the stakes and expanding the dilemma faced by pseudo-democrats.

The Norm of Election Observation

The consequences of the norm of international election monitoring continue to evolve. Two trends in particular underscore the acceptance of election observation as an international norm, highlight its near-global acceptance by even the most powerful states in the world, and reflect how democracy promoters respond to efforts by pseudo-democrats to manipulate the institution of election observation.

The first trend resulting from the norm is that international observers are now invited to monitor elections in many long-standing democracies.

The empirical analysis provided in this book covers 1960–2006. From 2002 to 2010, election observation spread most rapidly among the developed democracies such as Belgium, France, Italy, Norway, the United Kingdom, and the United States. The diffusion of election observation to long-standing democracies has not yet been fully explained, in part because it can only recently be described as a trend and because observation in recognized democratic states is by one account "still largely unnoticed by the general public."[6] *OSCE Magazine* published a 2010 article intended to highlight and explain the practice to the OSCE community.[7] Among democracy promoters, election observation in developed democracies remains controversial. On one hand, supporters of election observation are reluctant to devote scarce resources to observing elections that they know they will judge to be democratic. On the other hand, countries such as Cuba, Iran, Malaysia, and perhaps most vocally, Russia, supported a narrative that accused the developed democracies of hypocrisy for supporting observation in other states but not welcoming observation of their own elections. As election observation became more widely accepted as an international norm, pseudo-democratic governments increasingly complained about double standards in election observation. Although it is possible that the Russian government was genuinely concerned with promoting democracy and improving the quality of elections when they proposed a number of changes to OSCE Office for Democratic Institutions and Human Rights (ODIHR) observation practices, a more likely interpretation is that the Russians were attempting to undermine criticism of their own elections, as well as diffuse international support for pro-democracy movements in former Soviet states.

Thus, in part to guard against charges of hypocrisy and double standards, many democracy-promoting states with well-established reputations as democracies now invite observers. This trend is consistent with widespread acceptance of the international norm of election observation, decreasing domestic sovereignty costs associated with inviting observers, and a desire on the part of democracy-promoting OSCE member states to demonstrate that they are not exempt from the rules. As the director of the ODIHR, Ambassador Janez Lenarčič, explained, "all OSCE participating states are under the same obligation to implement election-related commitments and to invite international observers to verify this..." and that "established democracies are not immune from election-related

---

6. Eschenbächer, "Assessing Elections in Established Democracies," 30.
7. Ibid.

problems."[8] He went on to state that OSCE member states that have long democratic transitions can, "as mature and self-confident democracies…serve as positive examples for countries which still meet election observation with suspicion and fear of international interference."[9]

The OSCE missions to the U.S. elections, for example, have been formally documented since 2002, with the first national deployment of an OSCE mission taking place in 2004. Prior to 2002, some OSCE states viewed the invitation to observers to be implicit in their 1990 commitment to the Copenhagen Document. An official report pertaining to the 2004 U.S. elections states that the United States has invited observers from the OSCE to "every presidential and midterm election in the U.S. since 1996."[10] Although there remain questions about the equality of missions deployed across countries, with leaders of countries such as Armenia, Belarus, Russia, and Uzbekistan within the OSCE, as well as the governments of Algeria, Malaysia, and Zimbabwe attempting to challenge the legitimacy of election observation by arguing that observers employ inconsistent standards, observation in even the developed democracies undercuts their argument.

The second trend relates to the supply of observer missions. Even China has become involved in sending international observers through the Shanghai Cooperation Organization (SCO), an international organization composed of China, Kazakhstan, Kyrgyzstan, Russia, Tajikistan, and Uzbekistan.[11] The Chinese government's apparent interest in supporting international election observation missions is noteworthy primarily because China is the world's largest and best-known autocracy, as well as one of the few remaining countries in the world that does not itself hold direct national elections.[12] Election observation by the SCO, along with the observation missions sponsored by the Commonwealth of Independent States, make clear that one consequence of the norm is the adoption of international election observation by international actors who have no interest in promoting democracy. Although some practitioners worry that this trend undermines the practice of election observation, I would argue that the deployment of election observers by autocratic governments is an indication of the strength of the norm of international election

8. Ibid., 30.
9. Ibid., 31.
10. Jones, *Observation of U.S. Elections*, as delivered by Chargé d'Affaires Paul W. Jones to the *Permanent Council, Vienna*.
11. Cooley, "Cooperation Gets Shanghaied: China, Russia, and the SCO."
12. See appendix B.

observation. Since the late 1990s, rather than reject the norm, even auto-cratic governments have attempted to influence the content of election observer reports, going so far as to sponsor election observation missions through clearly anti-democratic international organizations.

Extending the Theory to Other International Norms

Although I have focused on international election observation as a sub-stantively important topic and an informative case of norm creation, the theory outlined in this book can be applied to other issue areas. In democracy promotion alone, government efforts to signal their type and increase internationally allocated benefits have led to the normalization of a variety of behaviors, including the spread of national elections to nearly all countries in the world, the adoption of independent election commissions, the widespread use of transparent ballot boxes and indelible ink, the public release of precinct-level election results, and even reserved parliamentary seats for women and minorities.[13] Like election monitoring, some of these practices are adopted by governments because they want to be perceived as democratizing countries, not necessarily because they are committed to democratization.

There are other characteristics that are valued by international actors, such as transparency, stability, rule of law, good governance, and business-friendly investment climates. The theory offered in this book suggests that benefit-seeking states should respond to changes in the relative value of such characteristics, and my theory can help explain the widespread adoption of independent central banks, bilateral investment treaties, liberalization of the media, the use of credit-rating agencies, and even perceptions about countries that refuse to allow international weapons inspectors. Similarly, governments and transnational actors such as corporations invite international monitoring in areas as diverse as child-labor practices, pollution, the production of coffee, and compliance with inter-national trade agreements.[14] The theoretical issues surrounding signaling and monitoring within other issue areas are similar in many ways to those surrounding international election monitoring, including questions of why states give access to international actors so that they can judge their internal processes, and even more interestingly, why states often seek

---

13. S. Bush, "International Politics and the Spread of Quotas for Women in Legislatures."
14. Auld, "Assessing Certification as Governance"; Cashore, Auld, and Newsom, *Governing Through Markets: Forest Certification and the Emergence of Non-State Authority.*

various forms of international monitoring even when negative judgments can be very costly. Although it is outside the scope of this book to provide complete documentation of these extensions, I briefly discuss the application of my theory to several other issue areas.

Attracting Foreign Direct Investment and Bilateral Investment Treaties

Like election monitoring, bilateral investment treaties (BITS) have grown from a nonexistent phenomenon in the late 1950s to being widely practiced throughout the world. Bilateral investment treaties are "agreements establishing the terms and conditions for private investment by nationals and companies of one country in the jurisdiction of another."[15] For governments that do not already possess well-established property rights protections for foreign investors, BITs are now expected by multinational corporations to signal that foreign investments in the country will be protected. As Zachary Elkins, Andrew Guzman, and Beth Simmons write, before BITs existed, for governments seeking foreign investment the existing system of customary international law "did not allow potential hosts voluntarily to signal their intent to contract in good faith."[16] Similarly, as Tim Büthe and Helen Milner argue with respect to preferential trade agreements and BITs,

> A government can make a more credible commitment regarding present and future economic policies by entering into international agreements that commit its country to the liberal economic policies that are seen as desirable by foreign investors.[17]

Because BITs possess an international enforcement mechanism, the treaties are arguably less costly for states whose commitment to property rights protections is genuine and therefore represent a credible signal of a government's commitment to the property rights of investors. Also like election monitoring, a number of powerful states, including the United States, initially opposed BITs. Yet despite their opposition, many host governments embraced BITs as a method to attract foreign direct investment. Although scholars do not typically refer to BITs as an international norm, I would argue that this is a result of insufficient interaction between

---

15. Elkins, Guzman, and Simmons, "Competing for Capital: The Diffusion of Bilateral Investment Treaties, 1960–2000," 220.

16. Ibid., 221.

17. Büthe and Milner, "The Politics of Foreign Direct Investment," 742.

scholars working on quantitative international political economy and those working on international norms. BITs represent a neglected international norm in the international relations literature and provide an example of a signaling-based norm. The definition of international norms can easily be applied: under the norm of BITs, foreign investors now share the expectation that governments that desire foreign direct investment and intend to respect property rights will sign BITs. Additionally, foreign investors expect that only those countries that do not intend to respect the rights of foreign investors refuse BITs, thus generating pressure on less-desirable types of investment-seeking countries to sign BITs in order to lure investors. Elkins, Guzman, and Simmons explain the diffusion of BITs through a competitive process that is similar to my argument, although they do not use the term "international norm" or try to explain the diffusion of BITs. According to their argument, BITs were initiated and spread precisely because they represented a credible signal of a government's commitment to enforce property rights protections for foreign investors. Those countries most in need of Foreign Direct Investment (FDI), most likely to lose investment to competitors, and without an excellent reputation in the eyes of foreign investors (what they refer to as "inherent credibility") were the most likely to sign on to such treaties. Additionally, like the increase in democracy-contingent benefits that triggers my theory, they predict that BITs should spread rapidly when there is an increase in the global amount of capital seeking foreign investment opportunities.

Although rationalist and institutionalist scholars of international political economy have been somewhat reluctant to discuss international norms, this is not because international norms do not exist or because these scholars necessarily think that norms are inconsequential. The added value of applying my theory to other substantive areas such as BITs is that it provides a more complete understanding of international norm formation and provides a more thorough casual explanation of the diffusion and persistence of new behaviors within the international system.

Applying my theory of norm formation also tentatively reconciles two divergent findings in the political economy literature that explain the diffusion of BITs and their effects on levels of FDI. Several scholars argue that BITs diffused because they are more costly for governments that will not respect property rights and that signing a BIT represents a credible signal of a government's commitment to respect property rights.[18] Yet

---

18. Elkins, Guzman, and Simmons, "Competing for Capital"; Büthe and Milner, "The Politics of Foreign Direct Investment."

other scholars, such as Susan Rose-Ackerman and Jennifer Tobin, have found that BITs increase FDI only for countries that already have a stable business environment and have little effect on low- and middle-income countries.[19] If BITs in fact signal a credible commitment of respect for property rights, why are they not associated with increased FDI for all governments?

One answer to this puzzle is suggested by the dynamics of the argument in this book. Foreign direct investors have difficulty judging whether a given government will respect property rights. All else equal, investors prefer countries in which the risk of property rights violations are low. However, once BITs were identified by investors as a signal that the government was committing itself to respect investors' property rights, refusing to sign a BIT became a signal that a government would not respect property rights. BITs diffused widely, even to countries in which the business environment was less than desirable. The signaling dynamics between investors and investment-seeking governments created pressure toward an equilibrium in which all governments that might respect property rights offered BITs to investors. In the competitive market for FDI, investors developed the belief that governments that did not offer BITs were undesirable places to invest (and that many less-desirable countries also offered BITs). This over-time dynamic should ultimately generate pressure on governments to find additional signals of the quality of their investment climates. The signaling theory of norm formation also offers a possible explanation for Rose-Ackerman and Tobin's paradoxical finding that BITs do not increase FDI to low- and middle-income countries (which I assume are also less likely to be able to send other costly signals of the quality of their investment climate).[20]

Independent Central Banks

Independent central banks combined with transparent political institutions have spread relatively widely throughout the world and are generally interpreted as a method by which governments can commit to a low-inflationary monetary policy.[21] Kathleen McNamara has argued that

19. Rose-Ackerman and Tobin, "Foreign Direct Investment and the Business Environment."

20. Ibid.

21. Bernhard, Broz, and Clark, "The Political Economy of Monetary Institutions"; Franzese, "Partially Independent Central Banks"; Keefer and Stasavage, "Checks and Balances"; Broz, "Political System Transparency and Monetary Commitment Regimes"; Bernhard and Leblang, "Political Parties and Monetary Commitments."

adopting "central bank independence is one way of signalling to investors a government is truly 'modern', ready to carry out extensive reforms to provide a setting conducive to business."[22] Sylvia Maxfield has made a similar argument.[23] McNamara criticizes literature that explains the diffusion of independent central banks as a credible commitment device by highlighting that governments sometimes adopt central banks when they do not necessarily need the policy credibility. She also demonstrates that central banks have not necessarily been successful—as the most extreme functionalist argument of central bank independence (CBI) would predict—at ameliorating inflation or improving economic conditions in countries that adopt them. Alternatively, McNamara argues that central banks and other organizational structures "diffused across borders through the perceptions and actions of people seeking to replicate others' success and legitimise their own efforts at reform by borrowing rules from other settings, even if these rules are materially inappropriate to their local needs."[24] Her argument implies that the adoption of central banks could have diffused for reasons similar to my explanation for the diffusion of election monitoring. Like the spread of election monitoring to pseudo-democratic regimes, and like the diffusion of BITs, central bank independence is associated with lower inflation in only a subset of cases.[25]

Applying my theory of norm development to the diffusion of CBI would suggest that one potential reason why CBI does not always have its intended effect of reducing inflation is in part because some governments adopted the policy of independent central banks in order to appear like other states that adopted business-friendly neoliberal economic reforms. These governments may try to influence the decisions of the central bank for political gain or appoint central bankers who will not necessarily maintain a low-inflation policy.

Other state behaviors have become signals of neoliberal economic policies, and my argument would suggest that if an important audience (in this case, either domestic constituents or international investors) develops the belief that all good types of neoliberal democratic states adopt independent central banks, fixed exchange rates, capital account liberalization or other such policies, and these policies are rewarded by international actors, failing to adopt these policies begins to signal that a given government is

---

22. McNamara, "Rational Fictions," 60.
23. Maxfield, *Gatekeepers of Growth.*
24. McNamara, "Rational Fictions," 48.
25. Jácome and Vázquez, "Is There Any Link Between Legal Central Bank Independence and Inflation?"; McNamara, "Rational Fictions."

not committed to neoliberal or proinvestment policies. If international actors believe that all states that have good investment climates send such signals, the behaviors can be understood as international norms.

International Weapons Inspectors

Former Iraqi President Saddam Hussein's interactions with international weapons inspectors illustrate the strength of connections between signals, norms, and internationally held beliefs about whether a state possesses desirable or undesirable characteristics. In this case, an international norm surrounding the possession of biological and nuclear weapons is that states that are not carrying out covert weapons programs will allow the International Atomic Energy Agency (IAEA) free access to inspect their country, a norm that could also be explained by the signaling theory outlined in this book.

Like the norm of election monitoring, the corollary to the norm of weapons inspection is that any government that refuses or resists IAEA inspectors must possess weapons of mass destruction (WMDs), as was famously illustrated by the U.S. government's belief under the Clinton and Bush administrations that Iraq possessed them. As George W. Bush argued to Congress in the 2002 State of the Union Address, "The Iraqi regime has plotted to develop anthrax and nerve gas and nuclear weapons for over a decade.... This is a regime that agreed to international inspections then kicked out the inspectors. This is a regime that has something to hide from the civilized world."[26] As has now been documented, although Hussein refused IAEA inspectors, it was not because he actually possessed WMDs. Rather, he wanted to maintain the illusion that he did in order to appear more threatening and powerful to domestic audiences and regional rivals.[27]

As recent scholarship recognizes, a number of political, economic, and military behaviors have diffused throughout the international system. I have briefly outlined how my argument can be applied to weapons inspection, the diffusion of bilateral investment treaties, the spread of neoliberal economic institutions, and how it can explain some paradoxical findings in these literatures. This argument could also help explain the widespread reliance on sovereign credit-rating agencies; the spread of mechanized armies to nearly all countries in the world, despite their

---

26. George W. Bush, "State of the Union Address," January 29, 2002.

27. Glenn Kessler, "Hussein Pointed to Iranian Threat: Specter of Arms Allowed Him to Appear Strong, He Told U.S.," *Washington Post*, July 2, 2009.

disadvantages in fighting insurgents; and the signing of various international treaties and agreements, even by states that continue to violate the provisions of the treaties.[28] Understanding and explaining these phenomena as global signaling-based norms illustrates why states adopt new behaviors when they are costly, even when there is not coercive or moral pressure to do so. My theory also explains how such international actors can simultaneously serve as effective and credible signals for a subset of governments *and* be associated with empirical findings that are puzzling to scholars looking at only whether costly signals have their intended effects. My theory generates dynamic over-time predictions across issue areas: Signaling norms should be initiated by desirable types. If benefit-giving actors believe that all good types send the signal, marginal types will also have the incentive to send the signal, and over time, nonsignaling types will be perceived as nonvaluable types. When less desirable types mimic the signal, benefit-giving actors and valued regime types should work to increase the cost of the signal by making the required signal more costly for them to imitate. Although the signal may have initially allowed audiences to separate good regimes from bad, the norm—or the belief that all good regime types send the signal—should lead to diffusion of the signal among both types of governments, diluting the information provided by the original signal and generating demand for more costly (more informative) signals.

Implications and Future Research

I now turn to a discussion of the implications of this book for future research on international norm development, democratization, international diffusion of costly behaviors, democracy promotion policy, election monitoring, and other international efforts to motivate change in state behavior.

Pathways to International Norms

The central contribution of this book to the international relations literature is an alternative theory of norm development. My theory does

---

28. For descriptions of the empirical puzzles in these issue areas, see Hathaway, "Do Human Rights Treaties Make a Difference?"; Lyall and Wilson, "Rage Against the Machines"; Tomz, *Reputation and International Cooperation;* Vreeland, "Political Institutions and Human Rights."

not subsume or contradict existing theories of norm formation. Rather, I have argued that some types of norms, specifically those that grow out of signaling dynamics, are relatively neglected in the international relations literature. This focus on the existing theories raises questions about when the alternative logics of international norm formation are most likely to operate. In addition to the theory presented in this book, there are at least two other paths to the creation of new international norms now identified in the existing literature. In the first theory, norms are generated because they encourage or reinforce mutually beneficial international cooperation. Individual states serve both as norm compliers and norm enforcers, and these cooperative norms tend to exist within broader sets of international institutions.

The second existing theory centers on norms initiated and spread by the work of norm entrepreneurs. These activist-centered norms are often intended to modify or prevent existing behaviors, such as the use of land mines, torture, child slavery, or nuclear weapons. How are these theories related to my argument? If they do not directly contradict each other, and instead explain norm formation under varying conditions, when is each theory most likely to apply? I offer a preliminary answer to these questions in part by making the simplifying assumption that states or governments are motivated to comply with new behaviors (potential norms) because they think it is in their interest to do so. This is a conservative rationalist assumption, indicating only that governments do not knowingly adopt a new behavior if they believe that doing so will make them worse off. The assumption says nothing about the composition of potential benefits, which may include material gains, such as foreign aid and international investment, or nonmaterial gains, such as legitimacy or prestige.

The interesting question, in my view, is not whether adopting a new behavior is in a state's interest but rather which factors within the environment changed such that modifying existing behavior is perceived to be a better option than the status quo. The three (simplified) theories of norm formation differ most clearly on why states are motivated to change their behavior. For cooperative norms, opportunities to institutionalize mutually beneficial cooperation are in a state's best interest because they directly benefit the norm-complying government through gains from cooperation or they help institutionalize such gains from cooperation. For advocacy-based norms, the desired change in behavior is typically not in the state's interest without pressure from norm entrepreneurs. Norm entrepreneurs work to make compliance with the new behavior more beneficial to target states or to increase the costs for noncompliers. Thus, activists cause changes in the international environment and pressure states to adopt the new norm, changing their decision calculus in a manner that is distinct from the reason why states begin complying with cooperative norms.[29]

For signaling-based norms, as I argue in this book, changes in preferences among benefit-giving actors provide diffuse incentives for individual states to signal their type in order to increase their share of international benefits, triggering a dynamic process that ultimately leads to international norm formation. In comparing the reasons that states begin to change their behavior and comply with a potential norm, I find that singling norms fall between cooperative and advocacy norms. For signaling norms, the driving force for states to change their behavior is a change in the preferences of benefit-giving actors, although the change is not imposed or coerced. The broader changes in preferences among international actors can be caused by norm advocacy, although my theory is noncommittal on this point. Changes in preferences among international actors occur for a number of reasons and are treated in my argument as exogenous. In contrast to advocacy norms in which the behavioral change is caused by pressure from activists or cooperative norms in which the behavioral change is caused by the belief that there are mutually beneficial gains from such a change, my argument is defined by states changing their behavior because it signals something to international actors about their own characteristics. The signal itself does not necessarily have advocates (although this is a point at which the two theories can converge) nor does it necessarily cause or enforce mutually beneficial cooperation. Complying states perceive the behavior to be in their interest because it is informative to international or domestic audiences or because international actors have developed the belief that all good regime types send the signal.

This distinction suggests a possible pattern in the conditions under which each theory is most likely to apply. When the formation of a new norm would facilitate or enforce mutually beneficial cooperation, international benefits are reciprocal and cooperative norms are most likely. In contrast, if complying with a new standard of behavior is not perceived to be in a state's interest, but other actors wish to bring about a specific change in the behavior of states, new international norms are most likely the work of norm entrepreneurs. Situated between these two causal paths to international norms are signaling norms, which are likely when there are (new) potential gains for actors possessing certain characteristics but when it is difficult to judge which actors possess those characteristics.

---

29. Note that norm entrepreneurs can also motivate change in behavior by reframing an issue rather than by changing preferences over strategies, as argued in Payne, "Persuasion, Frames and Norm Construction."

Note that the suggested relationship between existing theories does not imply that norm formation is automatic under any conditions. In the best of circumstances, the formation of new international norms remains unlikely. However, defining the varying logics by which new and consequential international norms are generated is a valuable theoretical contribution.

Constraining Election Manipulation and Pseudo-Democrats

International election monitoring attracts a variety of criticism, much of it warranted. This book has presented evidence suggesting that despite its faults—and in some cases because of them—international election monitoring can improve the quality of elections and constrain the behavior of pseudo-democrats by decreasing their scope for manipulation.

Criticisms of election monitoring are widespread. Some scholars argue that international election monitors fail in their objectives when they observe election fraud because they have not eliminated it entirely,[30] have been critical of election monitoring because observer organizations have not condemned clearly problematic elections,[31] and criticize the lack of consistent and universal standards for democratic elections.[32] The findings in this book suggest a more nuanced view of election monitoring in which both its strengths and its shortcomings are reasons why it has become a widespread practice and an internationally held and enforced norm.

Manipulating elections and receiving a positive report remain the central aims of pseudo-democrats. In the early stages of election monitoring, perfect detection of election manipulation by observers would have eliminated this strategy, and according to my theory, election monitors never would have been invited to low-quality elections. Thus, one of the central criticisms of observers—that they sometimes legitimize fraudulent elections—is also a reason why election monitoring spread to countries for which their reports now matter and in which they can deter fraud and improve the quality of elections.

I also explored why leaders invite observers, cheat in front of them, and get caught. This is not a preferred strategy for any type of leader. However, the fact that leaders are now regularly caught and criticized

---

30. Pastor, "Mediating Elections."

31. Abbink and Hesseling, *Election Observation and Democratization in Africa*; Geisler, "Fair?"

32. Elklit and Reynolds, "A Framework for the Systematic Study of Election Quality"; Elklit and Svensson, "What Makes Elections Free and Fair"; Davis-Roberts and Carroll, "Using International Law to Assess Elections"; Goodwin-Gill, *Free and Fair Elections*.

by international observers—and face a loss of international benefits as a result—is a direct consequence of the fact that election monitoring has become an international norm. The most direct and obvious forms of stealing elections are less likely because of the spread of election monitoring. Although it is possible that some forms of strategic manipulation may be even more pernicious, some forms of strategic manipulation can exist in stable and functioning democracies, such as gerrymandering or less-than factual campaign advertisements.[33] The fact that pseudo-democrats work to conceal election manipulation and international observers work to detect and criticize it means that observers have expanded the scope of their observation over time, have improved their methods, and have become somewhat more willing to criticize elections even when the election manipulation is not blatant. Thus, the methods available to pseudo-democrats to invite observers, steal the election, and not get caught are constrained by improvements in election monitoring.

Taken together, international pressure for democracy and the norm of international election monitoring make it substantially more difficult for leaders to steal elections. Election monitoring constrains pseudo-democrats by limiting the tools that they can use to bias elections in their favor without getting caught. The types of election manipulation that are less likely to be caught and criticized tend to be less direct and less certain forms of election manipulation. Direct election fraud, as shown in chapter 4, is reduced by the presence of international observers. International pressure for democracy raises the stakes for election-holding leaders by making it more difficult for pseudo-democrats to avoid criticism by international observers and simultaneously more costly for them to receive a negative report.

Implications for Election Observation

For reputable organizations engaging in election monitoring, this book presents some good news. Even short-term international monitors can have a direct deterrent effect on election day fraud simply by visiting polling stations on that day. This finding suggests that when blatant election day fraud is suspected, maximizing the number of short-term election observers could be a wise investment. It also implies the possibility that those engaging in election manipulation are sensitive to being watched, and targeted observation—potentially including long-term observation and

---

33. For the argument that election observation has pernicious effects, see Simpser and Donno, "Can International Election Monitoring Harm Governance?"; Simpser, "Unintended Consequences of Election Monitoring."

media monitoring—could successfully reduce manipulation in other elements of the electoral process, including voter registration, campaigning, or preparation of electoral materials. These untested propositions could be evaluated using similar field-experimental methods.

Observer organizations, if they are so inclined, could learn a great deal about the conditions under which their work is effective by randomly assigning international observers or other related elements of election monitoring when it is possible. There are still a number of questions about the effectiveness of election observation that could be answered with further use of field experimental methods and the randomization of various components of election observation: Are domestic and international observers substitutes or compliments? Does the length of time observers spend in a polling station matter? What is the most effective combination of long- and short-term observers? Do observers displace election day fraud? Is widespread publicity that observers will be monitoring a region more or less effective than actually deploying high-quality long- and short-term observers?

My argument also suggests that it is important for observers to continue to innovate their technologies and to avoid setting out rigid universal standards for democratic elections. Although some organizations and scholars are working toward universally applied standards, the evidence in this book highlights some challenges inherent in this objective. Because of the extensive menu of manipulation provided to pseudo-democrats and their incentives to engage in strategic manipulation, predictable observer methodology and universal standards for democratic elections would make it easier for pseudo-democrats to comply with the letter of these standards while violating their spirit and continuing to covertly manipulate elections in their favor. By retaining some agency in the application of methods and interpretation of standards, observers are able to tailor their judgments to the context of each country and therefore require pseudo-democrats to continue innovating and to employ an increasingly constrained set of tools to manipulate elections in their favor. This may leave them more exposed to charges of being unfair but may allow them further leeway to criticize pseudo-democrats who engage in more creative but no less effective forms of election manipulation.

Implications for Democracy Promotion and International Pressure

The history of international election monitoring also suggests several implications for democracy promotion and international pressure more generally. First, democracy promotion need not be overt in order to be effective. Much of the literature on democracy promotion focuses on direct democracy assistance within other countries or democracy promotion via military invasion or coercive tactics. This book focuses instead on how changes in the broader international environment can indirectly motivate states to change their behavior. Even in the absence of direct intervention, when powerful states make their preferences on an issue known, other states react, particularly those states working to maximize their share of international benefits. Powerful states may or may not anticipate this reaction, but efforts to gain increased foreign support will continue to provoke behavioral changes and can eventually produce new, international norms regarding the appropriate behavior of governments.

In addition to exploring the consequences of international support for democracy, my theory also supports existing methods of democracy promotion and efforts to change the policies or behaviors of other regimes. Governments and organizations wishing to promote democracy in other states should make their preferences known, support governments that appear to be successfully democratizing, and advertise their support of countries that successfully changed their policies or behavior. In some sense, this has already been demonstrated by studies of EU membership conditionality and programs such as the Millennium Challenge Corporation, which sets explicit requirements with which states must comply in order to receive foreign aid. Similar methods could be used outside of foreign aid and EU membership in order to influence states without intervening directly.

The Pseudo-Democrat's Dilemma Explained

This book was motivated by the empirical puzzle of why incumbent leaders invite international election observers and cheat in front of them. During the period of research for this study, election observation continued to spread to elections in even more countries, including some developed democracies, and the reports of observers garnered increasing international attention. One of the contributions of this book is simply to document the global trend of election observation since its inception in sovereign states. It is perhaps always something of a risk to study a new and rapidly changing phenomenon. International election observation in sovereign states grew from an unheard of activity fifty years ago to a nearly universal practice, and it could just as easily disappear. For the time being, however, international observers continue to play an integral role in many elections throughout the world and will likely to do so as long as democracy-contingent benefits exist and as long as democracy promoters gain valuable information from observer reports.

The reasons why international observers are invited have changed over time, and the decision by an incumbent government to invite observers is closely tied to the availability of international benefits for countries perceived as democracies. Election observation began in countries with relatively clean elections. Today, a positive judgment from reputable international observers confers legitimacy to the elected leaders and to the country. Especially for those countries with previously poor reputations, an internationally endorsed election brings increases in internationally allocated benefits. A negative report can lead to suspension from international organizations, reduction in foreign aid, and in extreme cases, it can be used to legitimize or support postelection electoral revolutions.

I have also shown that international observers can, but do not always, reduce election day fraud and that they have a variety of effects on forms of election manipulation. Taken as a whole, this study has offered a theory of why international observers are invited and, in this context, provided empirical tests of the argument and of the domestic consequences it implies. In conclusion, one might ask whether election observation is good for democracy. In the past twenty years, international observers have been involved in a variety of historically important elections, and by most accounts, they have had both positive and negative effects. This book contributes to the debate by providing a clearer picture of the mechanisms of international involvement in democratization. International observers are consequential players in the field of elections, not only because of their reports on election quality but also because they represent a broader trend among the election-holding states that are attempting to gain international support for their domestic political institutions.

Appendixes

APPENDIX A

Formalization of Signaling Game

The theory presented in chapter 1 is based on a signaling game, which is outlined briefly in this appendix. The game models the decision by incumbent governments to invite international observers. It is a finite game of imperfect information, in which incumbent governments can signal their commitment to democratic elections by inviting observers and receiving their endorsement. Because it is not modeled as a dynamic game, it does not formalize the over-time changes in the norm of election observation. However, equilibria from the game can be used to approximate different periods of the election-monitoring norm development and are helpful in highlighting both the conditions under which leaders should be expected to invite observers and how changing parameters in the model influence the decision calculus of incumbent leaders and democracy promoters.

Actors and Game Sequence

Incumbent regimes are represented by i, and can be one of two types, a true democrat (T) or a pseudo-democrat (P), $i \in \{T, P\}$. Democracy promoters are denoted by D and are the intended recipients of signals sent by the incumbent. The incumbent chooses whether to invite observers and whether to cheat. International observers may be invited by the incumbent and issue reports on the quality of the election, but they are not the sender or the receiver of a signal.

The sequence of moves is as follows. Prior to the start of the game, democracy promoters set the level of the democracy premium, or the contingent benefits, available to a government recognized as democratizing. In the first stage, the type of the incumbent is determined by chance.

The probability that the incumbent is of type T is represented by γ, where $0 \leq \gamma \leq 1$ and the corresponding probability of P is $1-\gamma$.

In order to focus on the decision to invite observers, I limit the model to the simplest case in which true-democrats never cheat ($M = 0$), and the pseudo-democrat always cheats ($M > 0$). Excluding the long-term consolidated democracies, democracy promoters prior beliefs are that $\gamma < 1/2$.

The incumbent chooses whether to invite international observers ($J = 1$) or not ($J = 0$). All governments pay a marginal cost when inviting observers, called a *sovereignty cost*, denoted by Y, with $Y \geq 0$. All cheating is costly, and cost of fraud is a function of whether observers are invited $c(J)$.

After choosing whether to invite observers, the incumbent chooses the level of manipulation, which includes any effort required to conceal election fraud ($M > 0$). Pseudo-democrats cheat at some optimal level, M^*, and the probability of victory increases in M. All cheating is costly, and the level of cheating is assumed to be directly proportional to its cost.

Nature moves, and the incumbent can win or lose the election, or $e \in \{L, W\}$. The base probability that an incumbent wins the election is denoted by p. For simplicity, I assume that the probability of victory is the same for both types, absent fraud. The probability of victory with fraud is denoted as q. Fraud increases the probability of victory, so q is always greater than p. Observers can influence the probability of victory indirectly by deterring fraud or making it more expensive to commit the equivalent level of fraud. If the incumbent loses the election, the payoff is zero, even if observers are invited.[1] I assume that when observers are invited ($J = 1$), the costs of fraud, or $c(1)$ is greater. When observers are present, they are assumed to make election fraud more difficult or more costly, thereby requiring more fraud in order to generate the same probability of victory, as illustrated in figure 1.1 (chapter 1).

Following the election, democracy promoters update their beliefs about the government's type based on whether the incumbent government won or lost, whether observers were invited, and whether observers criticized the election or not. The report of observers is denoted by R. If cheating is detected, observers issue a negative report, $R = -1$, and if cheating is not detected, observers issue a positive report, $R = 1$. If observers are not invited, R is denoted as 0. The probability that observers find evidence of cheating is r. If there is no fraud, no evidence of cheating is produced. The reports issued by observers inform the updated beliefs of democracy-promoters

---

1. Note that the decision to hold elections is not included in the model. This assumption could be relaxed in future iterations.

about a government's commitment to democracy. The international community reverts back to its prior beliefs about the incumbent's type ($\gamma < 1/2$) when beliefs are not pinned down by Bayes' rule off the equilibrium path. Given the observed behavior of the incumbent, the outcome of the election, and the reports of observers, if any, democracy promoters accept the results of the election ($X = 1$), or reject them ($X = 0$). If the incumbent does not win, observers always accept the result of the election as a sign that the country is democratizing, but the incumbent is no longer in office to receive benefits.

Summary of Timeline

Stage 1: The incumbent, i, determines whether to invite J.
Stage 2: The election outcome is realized.
Stage 3: If i wins, observers issue a report on the election, R based on whether fraud was uncovered.
Stage 4: D accepts or rejects the results of the election.
Stage 5: Payoffs are accrued.

Payoffs

International benefits are allocated to the incumbent regime after they have chosen whether to invite observers, they have won or lost, and after democracy promoters have accepted or rejected the results of the election. The size of international benefits tied to democracy are exogenous, set before elections take place, and are denoted by $A \geq 0$. They are based on the relative value of a country's characteristics to international actors and whether democracy promoters' accept or reject the results of the election, which is informed by the observer report R. B denotes the benefits of winning office such as salary and domestic prestige that are not dependent on the government's type. Let B denote the benefits of winning office such as salary and domestic prestige that are not dependent on the government's type. The payoff to an incumbent is:

$$\begin{cases} B + A - Y \text{ if } W = 1, J = 1 \text{ \& } X = 1; \\ B - Y \text{ if } W = 1, J = 1 \text{ \& } X = 0; \\ B \text{ if } W = 1 \text{ and } J = 0; \\ 0 \text{ if election is lost.} \end{cases}$$

Democracy promoters are better off when they accurately support democratizing states. They gain V when they accurately reward democratic governments and avoid rewarding pseudo-democratic governments. I assume that $V > 0$ when any democracy premium exists. Thus, the payoff to democracy promoters is:

$$\left| \begin{array}{l} V \text{ if } X = 1 \text{ and } i = T; \\ V \text{ if } X = 0 \text{ and } i = P; \\ \quad 0 \text{ otherwise.} \end{array} \right.$$

Proposition 1: There is a unique equilibrium to this game, depending on the value of the democracy premium (A) and the sovereignty costs of inviting observers (Y):

If $A = 0$, then neither T nor P invites. D rejects the results of the election.

If $\dfrac{(Y + c\,(1) - c\,(0))}{q\,(1 - r)} > A > \dfrac{Y}{p}$, then T invites and P does not. D accepts the results of the election if and only if the incumbent invites observers and no fraud is detected.

If $A > \dfrac{(Y + c\,(1) - c\,(0))}{q\,(1 - r)} > \dfrac{Y}{p}$, then T and P invite observers. D accepts the results of the election if and only if the incumbent invites observers and no fraud is detected.

PROOF: The incumbent invites when the expected utility of inviting observers is greater than the utility of not inviting observers, or $EU_i\,(1, R) > EU_i\,(0,0)$.

For T, if no democracy premium exists, or $A = 0$, then $EU_T\,(1,1) = pB - Y$ and $EU_T\,(0,0) = pB$. By assumption, $Y > 0$, so $EU_T\,(1,1) \not> EU_T\,(0,0)$. If the democracy premium is sufficiently greater than the sovereignty cost, T invites. Recall that T never cheats. Thus, T invites when $A > \dfrac{Y}{p}$. In the simplified case in which T is certain of victory, T invites when $A > Y$.

For P, if $A = 0$, $EU_P\,(0,0) = qB - c(0)$, and $EU_P\,(1,R) = qB - c(1) - Y$. By assumption, $c\,(1) > c\,(0)$ and $Y > 0$. Thus, $EU_P\,(1, M_1) \not> EU_P\,(0, M_0)$, because $qB - c\,(M_1) - Y \not> qB - c(M_0)$. Even if T invites, and $A >$

$\frac{Y}{p}$, P does not invite when the additional cost of cheating in front of observers is too high. Even in the most likely case in which P is certain of victory ($q = 1$) and certain that no fraud will be discovered by observers ($r = 0$), P does not invite so long as $c(1) - c(0) + Y > A$. P invites if and only if the democracy premium, A, is sufficiently large to outweigh the sovereignty costs and the additional cost of cheating in front of observers.

D accepts the results of the election if and only if $\mathcal{J} = 1$ and $R = 1$. If $\mathcal{J} = -1$, D rejects the results of the election, as $\mu(T|1,-1) = 0$. If $R = 0$, and the incumbent wins the election, D's post-election belief about the incumbent's type is $\mu(T|0,0) = \gamma$. By assumption, $\gamma < 1/2$. Therefore, D rejects the results of the election when observers are not invited.

APPENDIX B

Codebook

Data used in the cross-national empirical analysis come from both original data collection efforts and pre-existing sources. All sources are cited, summarized, and referenced in relation to individual variable definitions, which are also provided below.

Sources

Elections and Election Observation Data

Original data collection efforts took place in two stages. First, it was necessary to collect data on national level election events from 1960 to 2006. Second, I coded whether an election was internationally observed or not. When possible, data also indicate which organizations observed the election and the content of their summary judgment about the quality of the election process.

In evaluating whether the government of a country invited international observers, it is necessary to distinguish between first and multi-round elections. Because the invitation to observers in the final round of an election is nearly perfectly determined by whether the election was observed in the first round, data were collected on multiple rounds, with emphasis on first-round elections. Data on election events were coded from a variety of sources, beginning with Tatu Vanhannen's Polyarchy manuscript.[2] The Oxford University Press data handbooks on elections, edited by Dieter Nohlen and a series of coauthors, were principal sources

---

2. See http://www.prio.no/sptrans/-929210677/file42502_contents.pdf.

of information on multiple rounds and precise election dates.[3] The IFES election guide was the primary source for election dates in the post-1998 period.[4] For this book, the original data collection on national election events used in Hyde (2006) was updated based on the NELDA dataset, described below, and fully reconciled. International system membership data are from Gleditsch and Ward (1999).

The original data collection excluded the developed democracies, which have been added based primarily on Matt Golder's dataset on elections and electoral systems.[5] Dates of these elections were then updated, cleaned, and converted into the format used in the NELDA dataset.

Observed elections were coded in the following manner. First, observer organizations' official reports were sought as primary sources. Except in rare cases, if an observer organization reported that they observed an election, it was coded as observed. However, a number of observer organizations have lost records of some observed elections or make only a subset of their reports public. For every election held between 1962 and 2006, newswire reports and other news sources were searched for mention of the election and the words *international, foreign, observer,* and *monitor.* The secondary literature on election observation was searched extensively for comparison,[6] with articles such as Amanda Sives's analysis of election observation by the Commonwealth Secretariat serving as the principle record of early election observation by that organization.[7] For elections in which it was still difficult to determine whether observers were present, academic writing on elections and personal accounts written by individual observers were searched for references to elections.

If it was clear from news reports that international election observers were invited and actually monitored a given election, it was recorded as observed even if it was never made clear which organization monitored the election. Out of the 522 observed first-round national elections

3. Nohlen, *Elections in the Americas;* Nohlen, Krennerich, and Thibaut, *Elections in Africa;* Nohlen, Grotz, and Hartmann, *Elections in Asia and the Pacific.*

4. See http://www.electionguide.org/.

5. Golder, "Democratic Electoral Systems Around the World, 1946–2000."

6. Beigbeder, *International Monitoring of Plebiscites, Referenda and National Elections;* Bjornlund, *Beyond Free and Fair;* Lean, "External Validation and Democratic Accountability"; Legler, Lean, and Boniface, *Promoting Democracy in the Americas;* Pastor, "Mediating Elections"; Carothers, "The Observers Observed"; Abbink and Hesseling, *Election Observation and Democratization in Africa;* McCoy, "Monitoring and Mediating Elections during Latin American Democratization"; Middlebrook, *Electoral Observation and Democratic Transitions in Latin America;* Santa-Cruz, "Monitoring Elections, Redefining Sovereignty"; Santa-Cruz, "Constitutional Structures, Sovereignty, and the Emergence of Norms."

7. Amanda Sives, "A Review of Commonwealth Election Observation."

recorded in the dataset, I was unable to identify the observer organization for 33 elections, or 6.3% of observed elections.

Embassy delegations and delegations sent from individual countries were not considered official observers unless they joined a multinational delegation, a delegation sponsored by an intergovernmental organization, an international nongovernmental organization, or participated in "coordination and support" under the umbrella of the United Nations. Similarly, journalists, individual academics, and nonpartisan domestic observers are not considered international observers.

The National Elections across Democracy and Autocracy (NELDA) Dataset

In cooperation with Nikolay Marinov, data were collected on 58 variables and attributes for each election event occurring in the developing world between 1960 and 2006. The dataset, variables, sources, and intercoder reliability tests are described in detail on the project's website, http://hyde.research.yale.edu/nelda. The NELDA data were used to update and reconcile the list of election dates originally collected for this project. In addition, six of the variables used in chapter 2 originated in the NELDA data, as cited below.

POLITY and Regime Type Data

Data on regime types come from several sources. Data on long-term developed democracies were compiled from Arend Lijphart's book and from OECD membership data.[8] As an alternative measure of regime type and level of democratization, the *POLITY* dataset was used.[9]

The Democracy Assistance Project

Sector-specific data on foreign aid are from the Democracy Assistance Project, a USAID-funded investigation of the effectiveness of democracy assistance. The data and codebook for this project are available on the project's website, http://www.pitt.edu/~politics/democracy/democracy.html.

Data were downloaded from Phase II of the project, and they include two-year averages of the total amount of aid devoted to democracy and governance and nondemocracy and governance for 1990–2005 and for U.S. and non-U.S. bilateral foreign aid donors.[10]

---

8. Lijphart, *Patterns of Democracy*; OECD, "Ratification of the Convention on the OECD."
9. Marshall and Jaggers, "Polity IV Project."
10. Finkel et al., "Effects of US Foreign Assistance on Democracy Building."

The Democracy Assistance Project was also used as the source for data on the U.S. policy priority for each aid-receiving country in terms of military assistance, as described below.

Variables

Observed

Coded by the author, this variable is equal to one if the election was observed by an official delegation of foreigners invited to observe and report on the electoral process.

Pre-election Concerns about Election Fraud

Coded from NELDA11, the variable is equal to one if the answer to the following question was yes, and zero otherwise: "Before elections, are there significant concerns that the election would not be free and fair?" If the variable was coded as "no," "unclear," or "unknown," it was zero.

Opposition Competition

This variable measures whether opposition parties were allowed to compete, and was coded from three variables in the NELDA data, NELDA 3–5. If all three variables were coded as "yes," *Opposition Competition* was equal to one, and zero otherwise. The three variables answer the following questions:

NELDA3: "Was opposition allowed?"
NELDA4: "Was more than one party legal?"
NELDA5: "Was there a choice of candidates on the ballot?"

Previous Elections Suspended

This variable measures whether elections had previously been suspended in the country and was coded from NELDA1: "Were regular elections suspended before this election?" It is equal to one if NELDA1 is yes, and zero otherwise.

First Multiparty

This variable measures whether the elections were the first multiparty elections held in a country and was coded from NELDA2: "Were these the first multiparty elections?" It is equal to one if NELDA2 is yes, and zero otherwise.

Transitional Government

This variable measures whether the elections were organized by transitional leadership and was coded from NELDA10: "Was the country run by 'transitional leadership' tasked with 'holding elections'?" It is equal to one if NELDA10 is yes, and zero otherwise.

Uncertain Type

This variable is a composite of *Previous Elections Suspended, First Multiparty*, and, *Transitional Government*. If any one of these variables is coded as "yes," *Uncertain Type* is coded as one, and is zero otherwise.

Consolidated Democracy

This is a dummy variable that indicates governments widely considered to be long-term consolidated democracies. This group of countries includes the long-term developed democracies, which are defined as countries that have been continuously democratic for forty years or more, as coded by Arend Lijphart,[11] and that were also OECD members before 1975. These 23 countries are Australia, Austria, Belgium, Canada, Denmark, Finland, France, Germany, Greece, Iceland, Ireland, Italy, Japan, Luxembourg, Netherlands, New Zealand, Norway, Portugal, Spain, Sweden, Switzerland, United Kingdom, and United States. *Consolidated Democracy* also includes countries after they have joined the European Union or countries after they were officially informed by a respected international election observer organization that they no longer need to invite international observers because they were widely considered consolidated democracies. I also consider Israel and India to be long-term consolidated democracies.

Democracy and Governance/ODA

This variable was constructed from data provided by the Democracy Assistance Project and collected from USAID. For each aid recipient, it measures the percentage of aid devoted to democracy and governance as a percentage of total development assistance in the previous year. The four variables used from the Democracy Assistance Project dataset are *aid100* (total Democracy & Governance aid from the United States, or D & G aid), *aid000* (total non-D & G aid from the United States), *oda100* (total non-U.S. D & G aid), and *oda000* (total non-U.S. non-D & G aid). All four variables are two-year averages of aid in year t and year $t-1$ and were reported in millions of 2000 U.S. constant dollars.[12] Thus, for each election holding country,

$$\textit{Democracy and Governance/ODA} = (\textit{aid100} + \textit{oda100}) / \\ (\textit{aid100} + \textit{oda100} + \textit{aid000} + \textit{oda000})$$

11. Lijphart, *Patterns of Democracy*.

12. Finkel et al., *Cross-National Research on USAID's Democracy and Governance Programs—Codebook (Phase II)*.

U.S. Military Assistance Priority

This variable was constructed by Finkel et al. and represents the percentage of global U.S. military assistance (including counternarcotics) devoted to a given country in the previous year.[13]

GDP (logged) and GDP per capita (logged)

Both *GDP* variables are from the World Development Indicators, as published by the World Bank.[14]

POLITY and POLITY Squared

The POLITY2 variable from the Polity IV dataset was used as a measure of regime type. Because the *POLITY* variables lag by one year, for newly independent states I assume that that the POLITY2 score for the current year (year of independence) can be substituted for the previous year.

Regional Percentage Observed

This variable was computed from the original data on observed elections and represents the total percentage of elections observed in a country's region in the previous year, excluding the country's own elections, if any.

Table B.1. Descriptive statistics for table 2.3

Variables	Observers	Mean	Standard deviation	Minimum	Maximum
Observed	727	.567	.496	0	1
Previously Observed	727	.495	.500	0	1
Opposition Competition	727	.915	.279	0	1
Consolidated Democracy	727	.184	.388	0	1
Previous Elections Suspended	727	.124	.330	0	1
First Multiparty	727	.0867	.282	0	1
Transitional Government	727	.0825	.275	0	1
Uncertain Type	727	.190	.392	0	1
Democracy and Governance/ ODA$_{t-1}$	727	.0865	.118	0	1
U.S. Military Assistance (Current USD)$_{t-1}$	727	.755	4.55	0	48.67
GDP (logged)	714	23.7	2.17	18.84	30.09
GDP per capita (logged)	710	7.54	1.57	4.62	11.09
Year	727	1998	4.27	1991	2005

13. Ibid.
14. World Bank, *World Development Indicators.*

Table B.2. Countries included in analysis

Afghanistan	Djibouti	Laos	Republic of Vietnam
Albania	Dominican Republic	Latvia	Romania
Algeria	East Timor	Lebanon	Russia
Angola	Ecuador	Lesotho	Rwanda
Argentina	Egypt	Liberia	Senegal
Armenia	El Salvador	Libya	Serbia (Yugoslavia)
Australia	Equatorial Guinea	Lithuania	Sierra Leone
Austria	Estonia	Macedonia (FYROM)	Singapore
Azerbaijan	Ethiopia	Madagascar	Slovakia
Bahrain	Fiji	Malawi	Slovenia
Bangladesh	Finland	Malaysia	Somalia
Belarus	France	Mali	South Africa
Belgium	Gabon	Mauritania	Spain
Benin	Gambia	Mauritius	Sri Lanka
Bolivia	Georgia	Mexico	Sudan
Bosnia-Herzegovina	German Dem. Rep.	Moldova	Swaziland
Botswana	Ghana	Mongolia	Sweden
Brazil	Greece	Morocco	Switzerland
Bulgaria	Guatemala	Mozambique	Syria
Burkina Faso	Guinea	Myanmar (Burma)	Taiwan
Burundi	Guinea-Bissau	Namibia	Tajikistan
Cambodia	Guyana	Nepal	Tanzania
Cameroon	Haiti	Netherlands	Thailand
Canada	Honduras	New Zealand	Togo
Central African Republic	Hungary	Nicaragua	Trinidad and Tobago
Chad	Iceland	Niger	Tunisia
Chile	India	Nigeria	Turkey
Colombia	Indonesia	Norway	Turkmenistan
Comoros	Iran	Oman	Uganda
Congo	Iraq	Pakistan	Ukraine
Costa Rica	Ireland	Panama	United Kingdom
Côte d'Ivoire	Israel	Papua New Guinea	United States
Croatia	Italy	Paraguay	Uruguay
Cuba	Jamaica	People's Republic of Korea	Uzbekistan
Cyprus	Japan	People's Republic of Yemen	Venezuela
Czech Republic	Jordan	Peru	Yemen
Czechoslovakia	Kazakhstan	Philippines	Zambia
Democratic Republic of Congo	Kenya	Poland	Zimbabwe
Democratic Republic of Vietnam	Kuwait	Portugal	
Denmark	Kyrgyz Republic	Republic of Korea	

Table B.3. Excluded countries by reason for exclusion

Micro-states with population < 500,000	Countries holding no national elections between 1960–2006
Antigua and Barbuda	China
Andorra	Eritrea
Barbados	Qatar
Bahamas	Saudi Arabia
Bhutan	
Belize	
Brunei	
Cape Verde	
Dominica	
Federated States of Micronesia	
Grenada	
Kiribati	
Liechtenstein	
Luxembourg	
Maldives	
Malta	
Monaco	
Marshall Islands	
Nauru	
Palau	
Seychelles	
Saint Kitts and Nevis	
Saint Lucia	
San Marino	
São Tomé and Principe	
Saint Vincent and the Grenadines	
Solomon Islands	
Surinam	
Tonga	
Tuvalu	
Vanuatu	
Samoa / Western Samoa	

SELECTED BIBLIOGRAPHY

Note that all newspaper and news wire sources are cited in the relevant footnotes rather than in the bibliography.

Abbink, Jon, and Gerti Hesseling, eds. *Election Observation and Democratization in Africa.* Houndmills, England: Macmillan Press, 2000.

Abbott, Kenneth W., and Duncan Snidal. "Values and Interests: International Legalization in the Fight against Corruption." *Journal of Legal Studies* 31 (2002): 141–178.

Aguila, Juan M. del. *Cuba: Dilemmas of a Revolution*, 3rd edition. Boulder, CO: Westview Press, 1994.

Akerlof, George A. "The Market for 'Lemons': Quality Uncertainty and the Market Mechanism." *Quarterly Journal of Economics* 84, no. 3 (August 1970): 488–500.

Alvarez, R. Michael, Thad E. Hall, and Susan D. Hyde, eds. *Election Fraud: Detecting and Deterring Electoral Manipulation.* Washington DC: Brookings Institution Press, 2008.

Anglin, Douglas G. "International Election Monitoring: The African Experience." *African Affairs* 97, no. 389 (October 1998): 471–495.

Angrist, Joshua D., Guido W. Imbens, and Donald B. Rubin. "Identification of Causal Effects Using Instrumental Variables." *Journal of the American Statistical Association* 91, no. 434 (June 1996): 444–455.

Auld, Graeme. "Assessing Certification as Governance: Effects and Broader Consequences for Coffee." *Journal of Environment Development* 19, no. 2 (June 1, 2010): 215–241.

Axelrod, Robert. "An Evolutionary Approach to Norms." *American Political Science Review* 80, no. 4 (1986): 1095–1111.

Ball, M. Margaret. *The OAS in Transition.* Durham, NC: Duke University Press, 1969.

Banerjee, Abhijit V. and Esther Duflo. "The Experimental Approach to Development Economics." CEPR Discussion Paper No. DP7037 (2008). Washington DC: Center for Economic and Policy Research.

Barnett, Michael N. *Dialogues in Arab Politics: Negotiations in Regional Order.* New York: Columbia University Press, 1998.

Beaulieu, Emily. "Protesting the Contest: Election Boycotts Around the World, 1990–2002." PhD Dissertation, University of California–San Diego, 2006.

Beaulieu, Emily, and Susan D. Hyde. "In the Shadow of Democracy Promotion: Strategic Manipulation, International Observers, and Election Boycotts." *Comparative Political Studies* 42, no. 3 (2009): 392–415.

Beck, Nathaniel, Jonathan N. Katz, and Richard Tucker. "Taking Time Seriously: Time-Series-Cross-Section Analysis with a Binary Dependent Variable." *American Journal of Political Science* 42, no. 4 (October 1998): 1260–1288.

Beigbeder, Yves. *International Monitoring of Plebiscites, Referenda and National Elections: Self-Determination and Transition to Democracy.* The Hague: Martinus Nijhoff Publishers, 1994.

Bernhard, William, J. Lawrence Broz, and William Roberts Clark. "The Political Economy of Monetary Institutions." *International Organization* 56, no. 4 (Autumn 2002): 693–723.

Bernhard, William, and David Leblang. "Political Parties and Monetary Commitments." *International Organization* 56, no. 04 (2002): 803–830.

Birch, Sarah. "Electoral Systems and Electoral Misconduct." *Comparative Political Studies* 40, no. 12 (December 1, 2007): 1533–1556.

Bjornlund, Eric. *Beyond Free and Fair: Monitoring Elections and Building Democracy.* Washington, DC: Woodrow Wilson Center Press, 2004.

Boutros-Ghali, Boutros. *An Agenda for Democratization.* New York: United Nations, 1996.

Braddock, Daniel M. "1958 Elections: Electoral Outlook Six Weeks Prior to Elections, 136." *Dispatch From the Embassy in Cuba to the Department of State* (October 3, 1957).

Bratton, Michael. "Second Elections in Africa." *Journal of Democracy* 9, no. 3 (1998): 51–66.

Brownlee, Jason. *Authoritarianism in an Age of Democratization.* Cambridge: Cambridge University Press, 2007.

Broz, J. Lawrence. "Political System Transparency and Monetary Commitment Regimes." *International Organization* 56, no. 04 (2002): 861–887.

Burnell, Peter J. "From Evaluating Democracy Assistance to Appraising Democracy Promotion." *Political Studies* 56, no. 2 (2008): 414–434.

———. *Democracy Assistance: International Co-Operation for Democratization.* Democratization studies. London: F. Cass, 2000.

Bush, George W. "State of the Union Address," January 29, 2002.

———. "Remarks on the 100th Anniversary of Cuban Independence in Miami, Florida," May 20, 2002.

Bush, Sarah. "International Politics and the Spread of Quotas for Women in Legislatures." *International Organization* 65, no. 1 (2011).

Büthe, Tim, and Helen V. Milner. "The Politics of Foreign Direct Investment into Developing Countries: Increasing FDI through International Trade Agreements." *American Journal of Political Science* 52 (October 2008): 741–762.

Calingaert, Daniel. "Election Rigging and How to Fight It." *Journal of Democracy* 17, no. 3 (2006): 138–151.

Campbell, Tracy. *Deliver the Vote: A History of Election Fraud, an American Political Tradition—1742–2004.* New York: Basic Books, 2005.

Carothers, Thomas. *Critical Mission: Essays on Democracy Promotion.* Washington DC: Carnegie Endowment for International Peace, 2004.

———. "The Observers Observed." *Journal of Democracy* 8, no. 3 (1997): 17–31.

Carter Center. *Building Consensus on Principles for International Election Observation.* Atlanta: The Carter Center, 2006. http://www.cartercenter.org/.

———. *The Carter Center 2004 Indonesia Election Report.* Atlanta: The Carter Center, 2005. http://www.cartercenter.org/documents/2161.pdf.

Carter Center and National Democratic Institute for International Affairs. *Observing the 1998–99 Nigeria Elections, Final Report.* Atlanta: The Carter Center, 1999.

Cashore, Benjamin, Graeme Auld, and Deanna Newsom. *Governing Through Markets: Forest Certification and the Emergence of Non-State Authority.* New Haven, CT: Yale University Press, 2004.

Checkel, Jeffrey T. "International Norms and Domestic Politics: Bridging the Rationalist—Constructivist Divide." *European Journal of International Relations* 3, no. 4 (1997): 473–495.

Committee on International Relations, and Committee on Foreign Relations. "Legislation on Foreign Relations Through 2002." Washington, DC: U.S. Government Printing Office, July 2003.

Commonwealth Observer Group. *The Parliamentary Elections in Zimbabwe: 24–25 June 2000,* London: Commonwealth Secretariat, 2000.

Cooley, Alexander. "Cooperation Gets Shanghaied: China, Russia, and the SCO." *Foreign Affairs* (December 14, 2009).

Cooper, Andrew F., and Thomas Legler. *Intervention without Intervening? The OAS Defense and Promotion of Democracy in the Americas.* New York: Palgrave Macmillan, 2006.

Cox, Gary W. "Authoritarian Elections and Leadership Succession, 1975–2000." Typescript. University of California, San Diego, 2008.

Cox, Gary W., and J. Morgan Kousser. "Turnout and Rural Corruption: New York as a Test Case." *American Journal of Political Science* 25, no. 4 (November 1981): 646–663.

Cox, Michael, G. John Ikenberry, and Takashi Inoguchi, eds. *American Democracy Promotion: Impulses, Strategies, and Impacts.* Oxford: Oxford University Press, 2000.

Crawford, Gordon. *Foreign Aid and Political Reform: A Comparative Analysis of Democracy Assistance and Political Conditionality.* New York: Palgrave Macmillan, 2001.

CSCE. *Implementation of the Helsinki Accords: Hearing before the Commission on Security and Cooperation in Europe.* Paris Human Dimension Meeting: Commission on Security and Cooperation in Europe, July 18, 1989.

Daguzan, Jean-François. "France, Democratization and North Africa." *Democratization* 9 (Spring 2002): 135–148.

Davis-Roberts, Avery, and David J. Carroll. "Using International Law to Assess Elections." *Democratization* 17, no. 3 (2010): 416–441.

Diamond, Larry J. *Developing Democracy: Toward Consolidation.* Baltimore, MD: The Johns Hopkins University Press, 1999.

Dimitrova, Antoaneta, and Geoffrey Pridham. "International Actors and Democracy Promotion in Central and Eastern Europe: The Integration Model and Its Limits." *Democratization* 11 (December 2004): 91–112.

Donno, Daniela. "Defending Democratic Norms: Regional Intergovernmental Organizations, Domestic Opposition and Democratic Change." PhD Dissertation, Yale University, 2008.

——. "Who Is Punished? Regional Intergovernmental Organizations and the Enforcement of Democratic Norms." *International Organization* 64 (Fall 2010): 593–625.

Drake, Paul W. "The International Causes of Democratization, 1974–1990." In *The Origins of Liberty; Political and Economic Liberalization in the Modern World,* edited by Paul W. Drake and Mathew D. McCubbins, 70–91. Princeton, NJ: Princeton University Press, 1998.

Druckman, James N., Donald P. Green, James H. Kuklinski, and Arthur Lupia. "The Growth and Development of Experimental Research in Political Science." *American Political Science Review* 100, no. 04 (2006): 627–635.

Dunning, Thad. "Improving Causal Inference: Strengths and Limitations of Natural Experiments." *Political Research Quarterly* 61, no. 2 (June 1, 2008): 282–293.

Dunning, Thad, and Susan D. Hyde. "The Analysis of Experimental Data: Comparing Techniques." Manuscript, Yale University, 2008.

Elkins, Zachary, Andrew T. Guzman, and Beth A. Simmons. "Competing for Capital: The Diffusion of Bilateral Investment Treaties, 1960–2000." In *The Global Diffusion of Markets and Democracy*, edited by Beth A. Simmons, Frank Dobbin, and Geoffrey Garrett, 220–260. Cambridge: Cambridge University Press, 2008.

Elklit, Jurgen, and Andrew Reynolds. "A Framework for the Systematic Study of Election Quality." *Democratization* 12 (April 2005): 147–162.

Elklit, Jurgen, and Palle Svensson. "What Makes Elections Free and Fair." *Journal of Democracy* 8, no. 3 (1997): 32–46.

Estok, Melissa, Neil Nevitte, and Glenn Cowan. *The Quick Count and Election Observation: An NDI Handbook for Civic Organizations and Political Parties.* Washington DC: National Democratic Institute for International Affairs, 2002.

European Commission. "Communication from the Commission on EU Election Assistance and Observation." Brussels: European Union, 2000.

——. *Handbook for European Union Election Observation.* 2nd edition. Brussels: European Commission, 2008.

——. "Programming Guide for Strategy Papers: Democracy and Human Rights." Brussels: European Commission, 2008.

European Union. *Compendium of International Standards for Elections.* 2nd edition. London: Electoral Reform International Services, 2007.

——. *European Union Election Observation Mission to Indonesia.* Brussels: European Union, 2004.

European Union Election Observation Mission. *Final Statement on the Zambia Elections 2001.* Lusaka: European Union, May 5, 2002.

——. *Peru Presidential and Congressional Elections—EU Observation.* Brussels: European Union, April 6, 2001.

Fazal, Tanisha M. "State Death in the International System." *International Organization* 58, no. 02 (2004): 311–344.

Fearon, James. "Rationalist Explanations for War." *International Organization* 49 (1995): 379.

Fearon, James, and Alexander Wendt. "Rationalism v. Constructivism: A Skeptical View." In *Handbook of International Relations*, edited by Walter Carlsnaes, Thomas Risse, and Beth A. Simmons, 52–72. London: Sage, 2002.

Finkel, Steven E., Andrew Green, Aníbal Pérez-Liñán, and C. Neal Tate. *Cross-National Research on USAID's Democracy and Governance Programs—Codebook (Phase II)*, 2007, http://www.pitt.edu/~politics/democracy/democracy.html.

Finkel, Steven E., Aníbal Pérez-Liñán, and Mitchell A. Seligson. "Effects of US Foreign Assistance on Democracy Building, 1990–2003." *World Politics* 59, no. 3 (2007): 404–439.

Finnemore, Martha. "International Organizations as Teachers of Norms: The United Nations Educational, Scientific, and Cultural Organization and Science Policy." *International Organization* 47, no. 4 (1993): 565–597.

Finnemore, Martha, and Kathryn Sikkink. "International Norm Dynamics and Political Change." *International Organization* 52, no. 04 (1998): 887–917.

Fox, Gregory H., and Brad R. Roth. "Democracy and International Law." *Review of International Studies* 27, no. 03 (2001): 327–352.

Franck, Thomas M. "The Emerging Right to Democratic Governance." *American Journal of International Law* 86, no. 1 (January 1992): 46–91.

Franzese, Robert J. "Partially Independent Central Banks, Politically Responsive Governments, and Inflation." *American Journal of Political Science* 43, no. 3 (July 1999): 681–706.

Freedom House. "Freedom House: Methodology," 2006. http://www.freedomhouse. org/template.cfm?page=35&year=2006.

Fukuyama, Francis. *The End of History and the Last Man*. New York: Free Press, 1992.

Garber, Larry. *Guidelines for International Election Observing*. Washington, DC: International Human Rights Law Group, 1984.

Garber, Larry, and Glenn Cowan. "The Virtues of Parallel Vote Tabulations." *Journal of Democracy* 4, no. 2 (1993): 95–107.

Geisler, Gisela. "Fair? What Has Fairness Got to Do with It? Vagaries of Election Observations and Democratic Standards." *Journal of Modern African Studies* 31, no. 4 (December 1993): 613–637.

Gerber, Alan S., and Donald P. Green. "The Effects of Canvassing, Telephone Calls, and Direct Mail on Voter Turnout: A Field Experiment." *American Political Science Review* 94, no. 3 (September 2000): 653–663.

Gillespie, Richard, and Richard Youngs. "Themes in European Democracy Promotion." *Democratization* 9, no. 1 (2002): 1–16.

Gleditsch, Kristian Skrede, and Michael D. Ward. "A Revised List of Independent States since the Congress of Vienna. *International Interactions* 25, no. 4 (1999): 393–413.

——. "Diffusion and the International Context of Democratization." *International Organization* 60, no. 04 (2006): 911–933.

——. "Diffusion and the Spread of Democratic Institutions." In *The Global Diffusion of Markets and Democracy*, edited by Beth A. Simmons, Frank Dobbin, and Geoffrey Garrett, 261–302. Cambridge: Cambridge University Press, 2008.

Goemans, Hein E., Kristian Skrede Gleditsch, and Giacomo Chiozza. "Introducing Archigos: A Data Set of Political Leaders." *Journal of Peace Research* 46, no. 2 (2009): 269–283.

Goertz, Gary, and Paul F. Diehl. "Toward a Theory of International Norms: Some Conceptual and Measurement Issues." *Journal of Conflict Resolution* 36, no. 4 (December 1, 1992): 634–664.

Golder, Matt. "Democratic Electoral Systems around the World, 1946–2000." *Electoral Studies* 24, no. 1 (March 2005): 103–121.

Goodwin-Gill, Guy S. *Free and Fair Elections: International Law and Practice*. Geneva: Inter-Parliamentary Union, 2006.

Green, Joseph Coy, Papers. Seeley G. Mudd Manuscript Library, Princeton University, Princeton, NJ. *Report of the Allied Mission to Observe the Greek Elections*. Athens, 1946.

Guan, Mei, and Donald P. Green. "Noncoercive Mobilization in State-Controlled Elections: An Experimental Study in Beijing." *Comparative Political Studies* 39, no. 10 (December 1, 2006): 1175–1193.

Hafner-Burton, Emilie M., and Kiyoteru Tsutsui. "Human Rights in a Globalizing World: The Paradox of Empty Promises." *American Journal of Sociology* 110, no. 5 (2005): 1373–1411.

Hathaway, Oona A. "Do Human Rights Treaties Make a Difference?" *Yale Law Journal* 111, no. 8 (June 2002): 1935–2042.

Howard, Marc M., and Philip G. Roessler. "Liberalizing Electoral Outcomes in Competitive Authoritarian Regimes." *American Journal of Political Science* 50, no. 2 (2006): 365–381.

Humphreys, Macartan, William A. Masters, and Martin E. Sandbu. "The Role of Leaders in Democratic Deliberations: Results from a Field Experiment in São Tomé and Príncipe." *World Politics* 58, no. 4 (2006): 583–622.

Huntington, Samuel P. *The Third Wave: Democratization in the Late Twentieth Century.* Norman: University of Oklahoma Press, 1991.

Hurd, Ian. "Legitimacy and Authority in International Politics." *International Organization* 53, no. 02 (1999): 379–408.

Hyde, Susan D. "Experimenting with Democracy Promotion: International Observers and the 2004 Presidential Elections in Indonesia." *Perspectives on Politics* 8, no. 2 (2010).

——. "The Observer Effect in International Politics: Evidence from a Natural Experiment." *World Politics* 60, no. 1 (2007): 37–63.

——. "Observing Norms: Explaining the Causes and Consequences of Internationally Monitored Elections." PhD Dissertation, University of California–San Diego, 2006.

Hyde, Susan D., and Nikolay Marinov. "National Elections Across Democracy and Autocracy: Which Elections Can be Lost?" *SSRN eLibrary* (2010). http://ssrn.com/paper=1540711.

Ikenberry, G. John. "Why Export Democracy?" *Wilson Quarterly* 23, no. 2 (1999): 56.

Institute for Democracy and Electoral Assistance. "Focus: Democracy Forum 2000, Attacking Poverty by Supporting Democracy." *IDEA Newsletter Archive,* January 2000.

Jácome, Luis I., and Francisco Vázquez. "Is There Any Link Between Legal Central Bank Independence and Inflation? Evidence from Latin America and the Caribbean." *European Journal of Political Economy* 24, no. 4 (December 2008): 788–801.

Jensen, Nathan M. "Political Risk, Democratic Institutions, and Foreign Direct Investment." *Journal of Politics* 70, no. 04 (2008): 1040–1052.

——. "Democratic Governance and Multinational Corporations: Political Regimes and Inflows of Foreign Direct Investment." *International Organization* 57, no. 03 (2003): 587–616.

Jens-Hagen Eschenbächer. "Assessing Elections in Established Democracies: Why ODIHR Sends Observers and Experts to Countries Across the Entire OSCE Region." *OSCE Magazine,* 2010.

Jones, Paul W. *Observation of U.S. Elections, as delivered by Chargé d'Affaires Paul W. Jones to the Permanent Council, Vienna.* Report to the Permanent Council. Vienna, November 4, 2004.

Katzenstein, Peter J., ed. *The Culture of National Security: Norms and Identity in World Politics.* New York: Columbia University Press, 1996.

Katzenstein, Peter J., Robert O. Keohane, and Stephen D. Krasner. "International Organization and the Study of World Politics." *International Organization* 52, no. 4 (1998): 645–685.

Keck, Margaret E., and Kathryn Sikkink. *Activists Beyond Borders: Advocacy Networks in International Politics.* Ithaca, NY: Cornell University Press, 1998.

Keefer, Philip, and David Stasavage. "Checks and Balances, Private Information, and the Credibility of Monetary Commitments." *International Organization* 56, no. 4 (Autumn 2002): 751–774.

Kelley, Judith. "Assessing the Complex Evolution of Norms: The Rise of International Election Monitoring." *International Organization* 62, no. 02 (2008): 221–255.

——. "D-Minus Elections: The Politics and Norms of International Election Observation." *International Organization* 63, no. 4 (2009): 765–787.

——. "The More the Merrier? The Effects of Having Multiple International Election Monitoring Organizations." *Perspectives on Politics* 7, no. 01 (2009): 59–64.

——. "Supply and Demand of Election Monitoring." Manuscript, Duke University, 2008.

Keohane, Robert O. *After Hegemony: Cooperation and Discord in the World Political Economy.* Princeton, NJ: Princeton University Press, 1984.

——. "Reciprocity in International Relations." *International Organization* 40, no. 1 (1986): 1–27.

Keys, Donald. "Observing the Elections." In *The Lingering Crisis: A Case Study of the Dominican Republic,* edited by Eugenio Chang-Rodriguez. New York: Las Americas Publishing Company, 1969.

Klotz, Audie. *Norms in International Relations: The Struggle Against Apartheid.* Ithaca, NY: Cornell University Press, 1995.

Knack, Stephen. "Does Foreign Aid Promote Democracy?" *International Studies Quarterly* 48, no. 1 (March 2004): 251–266.

Koh, Harold Hongju. "Why Do Nations Obey International Law?" *Yale Law Journal* 106, no. 8 (June 1997): 2599–2659.

Krasner, Stephen D., ed. *International Regimes.* Ithaca, NY: Cornell University Press, 1983.

Krasner, Stephen D. "Structural Causes and Regime Consequences: Regimes as Intervening Variables." *International Organization* 36, no. 2 (1982): 185–205.

Kupchinsky, Roman. "CIS: Monitoring The Election Monitors." *Radio Free Europe,* April 2, 2005.

Kuran, Timur. *Private Truths, Public Lies: The Social Consequences of Preference Falsification.* Cambridge, MA: Harvard University Press, 1995.

Lake, David A. *Hierarchy in International Relations.* Ithaca, NY: Cornell University Press, 2009.

Lake, David A., and Angela O'Mahony. "The Incredible Shrinking State: Explaining Change in the Territorial Size of Countries." *Journal of Conflict Resolution* 48, no. 5 (October 1, 2004): 699–722.

Lean, Sharon. "External Validation and Democratic Accountability." In *Promoting Democracy in the Americas,* edited by Thomas Legler, Sharon F. Lean, and Dexter S. Boniface, 152–174. Baltimore, MD: The Johns Hopkins University Press, 2007.

Legler, Thomas, Sharon F. Lean, and Dexter S. Boniface, eds. *Promoting Democracy in the Americas.* Baltimore, MD: The Johns Hopkins University Press, 2007.

Levitsky, Steven, and Lucan Way. "International Linkage and Democratization." *Journal of Democracy* 16, no. 3 (2005): 20–34.

Liddle, R. William, and Saiful Mujani. "Indonesia in 2004: The Rise of Susilo Bambang Yudhoyono." *Asian Survey* 45, no. 1 (February 2005): 119–126.

Lieberman, Joseph. "Iran Presidential Election." Interview by Shepard Smith, Fox News Channel, June 15, 2009.

Lijphart, Arend. *Patterns of Democracy: Government Forms and Performance in Thirty-Six Countries.* New Haven, CT: Yale University Press, 1999.

Lindberg, Staffan I. "Tragic Protest: Why Do Opposition Parties Boycott Elections?" In *Electoral Authoritarianism: The Dynamics of Unfree Competition,* edited by Andreas Schedler, 267. Boulder, CO: Lynne Rienner Publishers, 2006.

Lust-Okar, Ellen. *Structuring Conflict in the Arab World: Incumbents, Opponents, and Institutions.* Cambridge: Cambridge University Press, 2005.

Lyall, Jason, and Isaiah Wilson. "Rage Against the Machines: Explaining Outcomes in Counterinsurgency Wars." *International Organization* 63, no. 01 (2009): 67–106.

Magaloni, Beatriz. *Voting for Autocracy: Hegemonic Party Survival and Its Demise in Mexico.* Cambridge: Cambridge University Press, 2006.

Mansfield, Edward D., Helen V. Milner, and B. Peter Rosendorff. "Free to Trade: Democracies, Autocracies, and International Trade." *American Political Science Review* 94, no. 2 (June 2000): 305–321.

Mansfield, Edward D., and Jon C. Pevehouse. "Democratization and International Organizations." *International Organization* 60, no. 01 (2006): 137–167.

March, James G., and Johan P. Olsen. "The Institutional Dynamics of International Political Orders." *International Organization* 52, no. 4 (Autumn 1998): 943–969.

Marshall, Monty G., and Keith Jaggers. *Polity IV Project: Dataset Users Manual.* College Park, MD: University of Maryland (2002).

Maxfield, Sylvia. *Gatekeepers of Growth.* Princeton, NJ: Princeton University Press, 1998.

McCleary, Rachel M. "Guatemala's Postwar Prospects." *Journal of Democracy* 8, no. 2 (1997): 129–143.

McCoy, Jennifer. "Monitoring and Mediating Elections during Latin American Democratization." In *Electoral Observation and Democratic Transitions in Latin America,* edited by Kevin J. Middlebrook, 53–90. Boulder, CO: Lynne Rienner Publishers, 1998.

McFaul, Michael. "Democracy Promotion as a World Value." *Washington Quarterly* 28, no. 1 (2004): 147–163.

McNamara, Kathleen R. "Rational Fictions: Central Bank Independence and the Social Logic of Delegation." *West European Politics* 25 (January 1, 2002): 47–76.

Middlebrook, Kevin J. *Electoral Observation and Democratic Transitions in Latin America.* Boulder, CO: Lynne Rienner Publishers, 1998.

Miguel, Edward, and Michael Kremer. "Worms: Identifying Impacts on Education and Health in the Presence of Treatment Externalities." *Econometrica* 72, no. 1 (January 1, 2004): 159–217.

Milner, Helen V. *Interests, Institutions, and Information: Domestic Politics and International Relations.* Princeton, NJ: Princeton University Press, 1997.

Milner, Helen V., and Keiko Kubota. "Why the Move to Free Trade? Democracy and Trade Policy in the Developing Countries." *International Organization* 59, no. 01 (2005): 107–143.

Monten, Jonathan. "The Roots of the Bush Doctrine: Power, Nationalism, and Democracy Promotion in U.S. Strategy." *International Security* 29, no. 4 (2005): 112–156.

Montgomery, Tommie Sue. *Revolution in El Salvador.* Boulder, CO: Westview Press, 1995.

Morrow, James D. "The Strategic Setting of Choices: Signaling, Commitment, and Negotiation in International Politics." In *Strategic Choice in International Relations,* edited by David A. Lake and Robert Powell, Princeton, NJ: Princeton University Press, 1999.

——. "When Do States Follow the Laws of War?" *American Political Science Review* 101, no. 03 (2007): 559–572.

Nadelmann, Ethan A. "Global Prohibition Regimes: The Evolution of Norms in International Society." *International Organization* 44, no. 4 (1990): 479–526.

National Democratic Institute. "National Democratic Institute/Carter Center Joint Post-Election Statement on Withdrawal from 1993 Togolese Elections." National Democratic Institute for International Affairs, September 1, 1993.

——. "Statement by the National Democratic Institute on the July 7 and 8 Presidential Election in Niger." Washington, DC: National Democratic Institute, July 19, 1996.

National Democratic Institute and The Carter Center. *Peru Elections 2000: Final Report of the National Democratic Institute/Carter Center Joint Election Monitoring Project.* Atlanta: NDI/Carter Center, 2000.

Nevitte, Neil, and Santiago A. Canton. "The Role of Domestic Observers." *Journal of Democracy* 8, no. 3 (1997): 47–61.

Nohlen, Dieter, ed. *Elections in the Americas: A Data Handbook.* Oxford: Oxford University Press, 2005.

Nohlen, Dieter, Florian Grotz, and Christof Hartmann, eds. *Elections in Asia and the Pacific: A Data Handbook.* Oxford: Oxford University Press, 2001.

Nohlen, Dieter, Michael Krennerich, and Bernhard Thibaut, eds. *Elections in Africa: A Data Handbook.* New York: Oxford University Press, 1999.

OECD. *Ratification of the Convention on the OECD,* Paris: Organization for Economic Cooperation and Development, 1960.

Olken, Benjamin A. "Monitoring Corruption: Evidence from a Field Experiment in Indonesia." *Journal of Political Economy* 115, no. 2 (April 2007): 200–249.

Organization of American States. "Fifth Meeting of Consultation of Ministers of Foreign Affairs, Santiago, Chile, August 12–18, 1959. Final Act." Washington DC: Pan American Union, 1960. Reprinted in *American Journal of International Law* 55, no. 2 (April 1961): 537–539.

——. "Eighth Meeting of Consultation of Ministers of Foreign Affairs, Punta del Este, Uruguay, January 22–31, 1962. Final Act," OEA/Ser.F/II.8 Eng. Washington DC: Pan American Union, 1962. Reprinted in *American Journal of International Law* 56, no. 2 (April 1962): 601–616.

——. "Supporting the Electoral Process," 2006. http://www.oas.org/key_issues/eng/KeyIssue_Detail.asp?kis_sec=6.

OSCE. *A Decade of Monitoring Elections: The People and the Practice.* Warsaw: OSCE Office for Democratic Institutions and Human Rights, 2005.

——. *Document of the Copenhagen Meeting of the Conference on the Human Dimension of the CSCE,* Copenhagen: Organization for Security and Cooperation in Europe, 1990OSCE/ODIHR.

——. *Election Observation Handbook.* 5th edition. Warsaw: OSCE Office for Democratic Institutions and Human Rights, 2005.

——. *Republic of Armenia Presidential Election March 16 and 30, 1998, Final Report.* Warsaw: OSCE Office for Democratic Institutions and Human Rights, April 9, 1998. http://www.osce.org/documents/odihr/1998/04/1215_en.pdf.

——. *Republic of Armenia Presidential Election 19 February and 5 March 2003.* Warsaw: OSCE Office for Democratic Institutions and Human Rights, April 28, 2003. http://www.osce.org/documents/odihr/2003/04/1203_en.pdf.

——. *Republic of Belarus Presidential Election 19 March 2006, OSCE/ODIHR Election Observation Mission Report.* Warsaw: OSCE Office for Democratic Institutions and Human Rights, 2006. http://www.osce.org/documents/odihr/2006/06/19393_en.pdf.

Pan American Union. *Report of the Technical Assistance Mission of the Organization of American States on the Presidential Elections in the Republic of Costa Rica*. Washington, DC: General Secretariat, Organization of American States, 1962.

Pastor, Robert A. "Mediating Elections." *Journal of Democracy* 9, no. 1 (1998): 154–163.

Payne, Rodger A. "Persuasion, Frames and Norm Construction." *European Journal of International Relations* 7, no. 1 (2001): 37–61.

Peceny, Mark. *Democracy at the Point of Bayonets*. University Park, PA: Pennsylvania State University Press, 1999.

Pevehouse, Jon C. *Democracy from Above: Regional Organizations and Democratization*. Cambridge: Cambridge University Press, 2005.

——. "Democracy from the Outside-In? International Organizations and Democratization." *International Organization* 56, no. 03 (2003): 515–549.

Pinto-Duschinsky, Michael. "Foreign Political Aid: The German Political Foundations and Their US Counterparts." *International Affairs (Royal Institute of International Affairs 1944-)* 67, no. 1 (January 1991): 33–63.

Price, Richard. "Reversing the Gun Sights: Transnational Civil Society Targets Land Mines." *International Organization* 52, no. 03 (1998): 613–644.

Program on International Policy Attitudes. "World Publics Strongly Favor International Observers for Elections, Including Their Own." Washington DC: World Public Opinion.org, September 8, 2009.

Przeworski, Adam. *Democracy and the Market: Political and Economic Reforms in Eastern Europe and Latin America*. Cambridge: Cambridge University Press, 1991.

Przeworski, Adam, Michael E. Alvarez, Jose Antonio Cheibub, and Fernando Limongi. *Democracy and Development: Political Institutions and Well-Being in the World, 1950–1990*. Cambridge: Cambridge University Press, 2000.

Rabe, Stephen G. *The Most Dangerous Area in the World: John F. Kennedy Confronts Communist Revolution in Latin America*. Chapel Hill: University of North Carolina Press, 1999.

Rich, Roland. "Bringing Democracy into International Law." *Journal of Democracy* 12, no. 3 (2001): 20–34.

Risse-Kappen, Thomas, Steve C. Ropp, and Kathryn Sikkink, eds. *The Power of Human Rights: International Norms and Domestic Change*. Cambridge: Cambridge University Press, 1999.

Roberts, David. "The Cambodian Elections of 1993." *Electoral Studies* 13, no. 2 (1994): 157–162.

Roe, Charlotte, "The Committee on Free Elections." In *The Lingering Crisis: A Case Study of the Dominican Republic*, edited by Eugenio Change-Rodriguez. New York: Las Americas Publishing Company, 1969.

Rose-Ackerman, Susan, and Jennifer Tobin. "Foreign Direct Investment and the Business Environment in Developing Countries: The Impact of Bilateral Investment Treaties." *SSRN eLibrary* (May 2, 2005). http://ssrn.com/abstract=557121.

Roth, Kenneth. "Despots Masquerading as Democrats." *Journal of Human Rights Practice* 1, no. 1 (March 1, 2009): 140–155.

Sanford, Victoria. *Buried Secrets: Truth and Human Rights in Guatemala*. New York: Palgrave Macmillan, 2003.

Santa-Cruz, Arturo. "Constitutional Structures, Sovereignty, and the Emergence of Norms: The Case of International Election Monitoring." *International Organization* 59, no. 03 (2005): 663–693.

——. "Monitoring Elections, Redefining Sovereignty: The 2000 Peruvian Electoral Process as an International Event." *Journal of Latin American Studies* 37, no. 04 (2005): 739–767.

Schaffer, Frederic C., ed. *Elections for Sale: The Causes And Consequences of Vote Buying.* Boulder, CO: Lynne Rienner Publishers, 2007.

Schargrodsky, Ernesto, and Sebastian Galiani. "Property Rights for the Poor: Effects of Land Titling." *SSRN eLibrary* (January 28, 2010). http://ssrn.com/abstract= 1544578.

Schedler, Andreas, ed. *Electoral Authoritarianism: The Dynamics of Unfree Competition.* Boulder, CO: Lynne Rienner Publishers, 2006.

Schedler, Andreas. "The Menu of Manipulation." *Journal of Democracy* 13, no. 2 (2002): 36–50.

——. "The Nested Game of Democratization by Elections." *International Political Science Review* 23, no. 1 (January 1, 2002): 103–122.

Schedler, Andreas, and Frederic C. Schaffer. "What Is Vote Buying?" In *Elections for Sale: The Causes and Consequences of Vote Buying*, edited by Frederic C. Schaffer. Boulder, CO: Lynne Rienner Publishers, 2007.

Schelling, Thomas C. *The Strategy of Conflict.* Cambridge, MA: Harvard University Press, 1960.

Schraeder, Peter J. "The State of the Art in International Democracy Promotion: Results of a Joint European-North American Research Network." *Democratization* 10, no. 2 (2003): 21–44.

Schultz, Kenneth A. *Democracy and Coercive Diplomacy.* Cambridge: Cambridge University Press, 2001.

——. "Domestic Opposition and Signaling in International Crises." *American Political Science Review* 92, no. 4 (December 1998): 829–844.

Sen, Amartya Kumar. "Democracy as a Universal Value." *Journal of Democracy* 10, no. 3 (1999): 3–17.

Simmons, Beth A., Frank Dobbin, and Geoffrey Garrett. *The Global Diffusion of Markets and Democracy.* Cambridge: Cambridge University Press, 2008.

——. "Introduction: The International Diffusion of Liberalism." *International Organization* 60, no. 04 (2006): 781–810.

Simmons, Beth A., and Zachary Elkins. "The Globalization of Liberalization: Policy Diffusion in the International Political Economy." *American Political Science Review* 98, no. 1 (February 2004): 171–189.

Simpser, Alberto. "Making Votes Not Count: Strategic Incentives for Electoral Corruption." PhD Dissertation, Stanford University, 2005.

——. "Unintended Consequences of Election Monitoring." In *Election Fraud: Detecting and Deterring Electoral Manipulation*, edited by R. Michael Alvarez, Thad E. Hall, and Susan D. Hyde, 255. Washington DC: Brookings Institution Press, 2008.

Simpser, Alberto, and Daniela Donno. "Can International Election Monitoring Harm Governance?" Manuscript, University of Chicago, 2010.

Sives, Amanda. "A Review of Commonwealth Election Observation." *Commonwealth & Comparative Politics* 39, no. 3 (2001): 132–149.

Slater, Jerome. *The OAS and United States Foreign Policy.* Columbus: Ohio State University Press, 1967.

Smith, Tony. *America's Mission: The United States and the Worldwide Struggle for Democracy in the Twentieth Century.* Princeton, NJ: Princeton University Press, 1994.

Snow, John. *On the Mode of Communication of Cholera.* 2nd edition. London: J. Churchill, 1855.

Spence, Michael. "Job Market Signaling." *Quarterly Journal of Economics* 87, no. 3 (August 1973): 355–374.

Stalin, Joseph, Franklin D. Roosevelt, and Winston S. Churchill. *Text of the Agreements Reached at the Yalta (Crimea) Conference between President Roosevelt, Prime Minister Churchill and Generalissmo Stalin, as released by the State Department.* Text, February 11, 1945. http://avalon.law.yale.edu/wwii/yalta.asp.

Starr, Harvey. "Democratic Dominoes: Diffusion Approaches to the Spread of Democracy in the International System." *Journal of Conflict Resolution* 35, no. 2 (1991): 356–381.

Sugden, Robert. "Spontaneous Order." *Journal of Economic Perspectives* 3, no. 4 (Autumn 1989): 85–97.

Tannenwald, Nina. "The Nuclear Taboo: The United States and the Normative Basis of Nuclear Non-Use." *International Organization* 53, no. 03 (1999): 433–468.

Taylor, Lewis. "Patterns of Electoral Corruption in Peru: The April 2000 General Election." *Crime, Law and Social Change* 34, no. 4 (December 1, 2000): 391–415.

Thomas, Daniel C. *The Helsinki Effect: International Norms, Human Rights, and the Demise of Communism.* Princeton, NJ: Princeton University Press, 2001.

Tomz, Michael. *Reputation and International Cooperation: Sovereign Debt across Three Centuries.* Princeton, NJ: Princeton University Press, 2007.

Tomz, Michael, Jason Wittenberg, and Gary King. "Clarify: Software for Interpreting and Presenting Statistical Results." *Journal of Statistical Software* 8, no. 1 (2003). Available at http://www.jstatsoft.org/v08/i01.

Trounstine, Jessica. "Challenging the Machine-Dichotomy: Two Threats to Urban Democracy." In *The City in American Political Development*, edited by Richardson Dilworth, 77–97. New York: Routledge, 2009.

United Nations, *Declaration of Principles for International Election Observation and Code of Conduct for International Election Observers.* New York: United Nations, 2005.

Vachudova, Milada Anna. *Europe Undivided: Democracy, Leverage, and Integration after Communism.* New York: Oxford University Press, 2005.

Vreeland, James Raymond. "Political Institutions and Human Rights: Why Dictatorships Enter into the United Nations Convention Against Torture." *International Organization* 62, no. 01 (2008): 65–101.

Walt, Stephen M. *The Origins of Alliances.* Ithaca, NY: Cornell University Press, 1987.

Wambaugh, Sarah. *A Monograph on Plebiscites, with a Collection of Official Documents.* New York: Oxford University Press, 1920.

——. *Plebiscites Since the World War, with a Collection of Official Documents.* Washington DC: Carnegie Endowment for International Peace, 1933.

Wantchekon, Leonard. "Clientelism and Voting Behavior: Evidence from a Field Experiment in Benin." *World Politics* 55, no. 3 (2003): 399–422.

Weingast, Barry R. "The Political Foundations of Democracy and the Rule of Law." *American Political Science Review* 91, no. 2 (June 1997): 245–263.

Welt, Cory, and Ian Bremmer. "Armenia's New Autocrats." *Journal of Democracy* 8, no. 3 (1997): 77–91.

Whitehead, Laurence, ed. *The International Dimensions of Democratization: Europe and the Americas.* New York: Oxford University Press, 1996.

World Bank. *World Development Indicators.* Washington, DC: World Bank Group, 2007.

Young, Oran. "Regime Dynamics: The Rise and Fall of International Regimes." In *International Regimes*, edited by Stephen D. Krasner, 93–114, 1983.

Youngs, Richard. *The European Union and the Promotion of Democracy*. Oxford: Oxford University Press, 2001.

Zacher, Mark W. "The Territorial Integrity Norm: International Boundaries and the Use of Force." *International Organization* 55, no. 02 (2003): 215–250.

INDEX

Abbink, Jon, 164
Abstention buying, strategic manipulation
    and, 180–81, 184
Abu Seda, Hafez, 86
Advocacy-based theories of norm creation,
    15–18, 203–4
Afghanistan, 76
Africa
    criticism of monitoring in, 164
    democracy-contingent benefits and, 68,
        101–2
    strategic manipulation in, 175, 182
    trends in election monitoring, 67
    See also specific countries
African Union, 89, 105. *See also* Organiza-
    tion of African Unity (OAU)
Akerlof, George, 9, 10, 11
Algeria, 84–85, 195
Aliev, Ilham, 179–80
Alliance for Progress, 97
Angola, 164
Annan, Kofi, 86
Arab League, 89, 170
Argentina, 97
Aristide, Jean-Bertrand, 116–17
Armenia, 111, 113, 128, 129, 132–42, 195
    checking "as if" randomization, 138–40
    data and results, 140
    effect of monitors on vote share, 141–42
    natural experiment research design, 135–38
Asia, trends in election monitoring, 67. *See
    also specific countries*
Asian Network for Free Elections
    (ANFREL), 34
Australia, 41, 74

Austria, 86, 87
Autocratic regimes
    decision to invite observers, 103
    election monitoring in, 195–96
    norm diffusion and, 41
    See also specific countries
Axelrod, Robert, 10–11
Azerbaijan, 179–80

Bahrain, 122, 123
Balaguer, Joaquín, 59
Barnett, Michael, 24
Batista, Fulgencio, 1, 57, 95–96
Belarus, 47, 111, 176, 178, 185, 192, 195
Belgium, 41, 74, 86, 194
Benefit-seeking signals. *See* Signaling norms
Benin, 123
Betancourt, Rómulo, 96
Bhutto, Benazir, 177
Bilateral investment treaties (BITs), as
    signal-based norm, 197–99
Bjornland, Eric, 40
Blair, Tony, 104
Bolivia, 58, 99
Bouteflika, Abdelaziz, 85
Boutros-Ghali, Boutros, 100
Boycott of elections, by opposition parties,
    182–83
Bratton, Michael, 175
British Parliamentary Human Rights
    Group, 64, 99
Burnham, Forbes, 99
Bush, George H. W., 103
Bush, George W., 7, 103–4, 105, 201
Büthe, Tim, 197